THE ROYAL AIR FORCE
The Past 30 Years

THE ROYAL AIR FORCE
The Past 30 Years

A.G. TREVENEN JAMES

Macdonald and Jane's · London

For all past members of the Royal Air Force, men and women, who in their lives, or by their deaths, have laid the firm and glorious traditions of the youngest of the three Services; for those who by their present service are maintaining these traditions, and for the next generation who have yet to experience the satisfaction of such service.
Also for my wife and daughter who, in war and peace, through many lands and various vicissitudes, followed the drum and revelled in the life.

First published in 1976 by
Macdonald and Jane's Publishers Limited
Paulton House
8 Shepherdess Walk
London N1 7LW

Printed in Great Britain by
REDWOOD BURN LIMITED
Trowbridge & Esher

ISBN 0356 08425 6

Contents

Foreword

by Marshal of the Royal Air Force
the Lord Elworthy GCB, CBE, DSO, MVO, DFC, AFC, MA

GOVERNOR'S OFFICE
WINDSOR CASTLE

I am pleased to have been invited to write a brief foreword to this book. The author faced a considerable challenge in aiming to cover, in fifteen chapters, half the life of the Royal Air Force.

For those who are still, or who have at any time or in any way been associated with the Royal Air Force, this book is one that will be read with interest, pleasure and a touch of pride. Equally, I feel sure, that for a wider readership of men and women, young and old, who are concerned for the future of our Country and our society, there is much in this book which will help to confirm or to restore their faith in the best of modern youth which is well represented in the three Services.

The book is valuable because it comes at a time when great changes are occuring in the balance of economic and military power in the world. It shows the contribution made by the Royal Air Force to the North Atlantic Treaty Organisation which has been the main instrument in the prevention of war between East and West. It also shows what the Service has done in various parts of the world where Great Britain had particular responsibilities, in containing violence and protecting life. It deserves to be read by those who are interested in flying as a vocation, in aircraft as instruments of power, in the men who fly them and in that great company of men and women on the ground, without whose devotion to their many and varied tasks, no aircraft would fly.

June, 1976.

Elworthy

Acknowledgements

This book is in no sense an *official* history, and although it has been read by successive heads of the Air Historical Branch of the Ministry of Defence and several senior officers who have served in important posts during the years concerned, I alone am responsible for the accuracy of the facts and for any particular interpretation I have placed upon them. Space prohibits my naming all those who have helped and with whom I have flown and talked in visits to RAF Commands and Stations at home and overseas.

I am, however, grateful in particular for the help and encouragement I have received from Air Chief-Marshal the Hon. Sir Ralph Cochrane, from the late Air Marshal Sir Hector McGregor and Air Vice-Marshals Sir Colin Scragg and Peter Chamberlain, who have read and commented constructively on all or most of the manuscript. For the practical help and advice needed to complete the last three chapters I am indebted to Air Commodore J. R. Forsythe and Group Captains R. E. Vaughan-Fowler and D. W. Baker of the Directorate of Public Relations (RAF) and their staffs, to Air Vice-Marshal D.L. Attlee, when Director of Recruiting (RAF) and his staff, and to other members both Service and civilian of the Ministry of Defence (Air) whom I have consulted on specialist matters.

I wish also to express my gratitude to Mr L.A. Jackets, Head of the Air Historical Branch of the Ministry of Defence until 1970, to his successor Mr E.B. Haslam, Mrs M.B. Simons, Mr. F.S. White and Mr D.C. Bateman on their staffs and to Mr Tom Wellard of MoD (OS12). All their ready help and friendship have made my task less difficult and more enjoyable. Finally, I must thank all those too numerous to name individually who, in their many and various ways — the flights, the visits, the briefings and the prompt and accurate typing — have contributed immeasurably to the interest and accuracy of the book.

I am especially grateful for permission to quote from the following publications: *Flight International*, published by IPC Business Press Ltd; *Air Clues*, published by Ministry of Defence, Director of Flying Training (RAF); *The Journal of the Royal United Services Institute for Defence Studies*; *Captains and Kings*, by Alan Bramson and Neville Birch, published by Pitman and Sons, 1972; *Defence. Britain's Policy in the '70s*, An Economist 'Brief Book' by Gordon Lee. 1971; *The Military Balance 1973/74*, published by the International Institute for Strategic Studies.

1973; *The Profession of Arms*, the 1962 Lees Knowles lectures given at Trinity College Cambridge, by Lt. General Sir John Winthrop Hackett KCB. CBE. DSO. MC. and republished in full by The Times Publishing Co Ltd; *History of the Second World War. The Strategic Air Offensive 1939-1945 Vol. III* 'Victory', by Sir Charles Webster and Noble Frankland 1961, HMSO. Other publications which have provided valuable background reading are listed in the Bibliography.

April, 1976.   A.G.T.J.

A Beginning of Peace

'Rather a cessation of war than a beginning of peace'   TACITUS

I write this introduction travelling towards the early morning sun at a ground speed of just under 600 mph, some 33,000 feet over the Mediterranean, in a VC.10 of 10 Squadron Royal Air Force. Their motto *Rem Acu Tangere* (To Hit the Mark) is as appropriate in their peacetime strategic transport role as it was in their wartime bomber role. When you head out over the Arabian Sea towards a landing strip on a small coral island nearly 2,000 miles away it is important to hit the mark. After about four hours flying since a dawn take-off from RAF Brize Norton in Oxfordshire, our route today has brought us directly over Knossus in Crete, Europe's largest city fifteen centuries before the birth of Christ. Had the Carthaginian general Hannibal been able to make a similar aerial voyage in his time (instead of using elephants) and had the air been clear enough and his eyesight good enough, he could have gazed down upon perhaps six of the seven wonders of the ancient world from our present vantage point. The pyramids of Egypt and the Pharos of Alexandria to the south; north-east the temple of Diana on the Greek island of Samos; the tomb of King Mausalus on the Turkish mainland opposite the island of Kos; on the island of Rhodes the huge bronze statue of the Sun God Helios bestriding the mouth of the harbour of Rhodes; while glancing over his shoulder north-west, he might have seen the morning sun light up the temple of Zeus at Olympia in the Peloponnesus, which housed the ivory and gold statue of the supreme God of the Greeks.

This is indeed a far cry from the war years when I last flew with 10 Squadron in Halifax night bombers over Germany, flying at best at 24,000 ft and 170 mph[1], with the rain oozing through the cockpit canopy and dripping onto one's knees.

But much has already been written of the Royal Air Force in war and little of the remarkable developments and achievements of the last thirty years of peace: yet more than half the RAF's life has now been lived since the end of Hitler's war in 1945. The object of this book is, therefore, to record some of the more important aspects of the RAF's post-war activities, before they are forgotten and overtaken by the pressures of the years to come. In writing this peacetime story of the youngest of the armed

---

[1]"Indicated air speed" or about 240 mph TAS adjusted for altitude.

11

Services, one was constantly reminded of the increasing inter-dependence of all three Services, and if the reader carries away the impression that the RAF is more closely linked with its older brothers than they are with each other, the explanation is perhaps that the element in which airmen operate covers both land and sea. In this sense, the wheel has turned full circle.

From its origins in the individual air services of the Royal Navy and Army in the First World War, the primary role of the RAF in the 1970s has become once again that of providing air support, in the fullest meaning of this phrase, from overall command of the air to close support of ships at sea and men in the frontline; from long range strategic and maritime reconnaissance to the cutting of an enemy's communications deep inside his own country; from air trooping and casualty evacuation to land and sea rescue and other humanitarian missions.

No attempt is made within the confines of a single volume to produce a story that is complete. Nor is it simply a chronology of events (which would make dull reading). My object has been to record only what has seemed to me most likely to interest the widest possible readership, both within and without the Services, and in particular those who are still searching for background to the facts with which to view and comprehend the important issues of the day. War and peace is one of these. The way in which a particular profession, the profession of arms, and a particular Service, the Royal Air Force, has contributed to the resolution of this issue since 1945 is a subject worthy of study, for how can any of us arrive at sensible views unless we study the facts, and probe beneath the surface to examine their often complex and contentious background?

As the Editor of the Journal of the Royal United Services Institute for Defence Studies pointed out in the autumn of 1970:

"The hard fact is that the way to peace lies through a recognition of the reality of violence and of its control through methods which are better understood by the Armed Forces of Great Britain than those of any other country. If this sounds a presumptuous claim, let foreigners be the judge. Over half the membership of the United Nations sends students to our military establishments. Our troops are invited to train in nearly 50 countries. They are respected primarily because they have mastered an art which most countries would be glad to learn: the art of saving lives. From Borneo via Cyprus to Ulster, they have saved ten lives for every one they have taken. This is something which commands respect from the world outside these shores."

RAF helicopters alone, in their first ten years of service, saved more than 1,000 lives. Many amongst the younger generation who are looking for constructive ways of serving humanity would do well to think on these things.

When the Nazi regime surrendered unconditionally in May 1945 the strength of the Royal Air Force consisted of 9,000 operational aircraft and more than a million men and women, including 195,000 aircrew. During the war aircrew had flown in a wide variety of aircraft to carry out all of the traditional roles: reconnaissance over land and sea; air defence and close support of armies in the field. But the primary role had been that envisaged by General Trenchard when the Royal Naval Air Sevice and Royal Flying Corps combined to form an independent Air Force in 1918: strategic bombing. Altogether, Bomber Command aircraft had delivered a million tons of bombs in nearly 400,000 sorties. The cost matched the achievement, for Bomber Command aircrew had suffered 67% of the total RAF wartime casualties. Even so, as the official history of the bomber offensive emphasises: "both cumulatively in largely indirect ways and eventually in a more immediate and direct manner strategic bombing and, also in other roles, strategic bombers made a contribution to victory which was decisive. Those who claim that the Bomber Command contribution to the war was less than this are factually in error."[2]

After victory in Europe, the RAF prepared for large-scale reinforcement of Allied air forces in the Far East. But on August 6, 1945, President Truman announced to the people of the United States and to the World: "Sixteen hours ago an American aeroplane dropped one bomb on Hiroshima, an important Japanese Army Base. That bomb had more power than 20,000 tons of TNT. It is an atomic bomb. The force from which the sun draws its power has been loosened against those who brought war to the Far East." On August 9 a similar bomb was dropped at Nagasaki and the Japanese formally sued for peace on the terms of unconditional surrender which had been offered by the Allies, but refused before either atomic bomb had been dropped.

It is difficult to make precise comparisons between the power of conventional high explosive (TNT) bombs and nuclear weapons because in the former (amongst other complicating factors) some 50% of the weight is taken up by the case. During the Second World War Ƒof the Bomber Command dropped about one million tons of bombs on Germany. It would be broadly true to say, therefore, that fifty of the Hiroshima 20 kiloton bombs would be at least equal in destructive power to the total of bombs dropped on Germany by Bomber Command during the war. By 1952, the Americans had exploded a thermo-nuclear or hydrogen bomb several hundred times more powerful than the Hiroshima bomb and by 1961 the Russians had detonated a device yielding some fifty megatons, equal to fifty million tons of TNT. One aircraft today, therefore, could deliver in a single attack destructive power fifty times greater than that of all the bombs dropped by RAF Bomber Command on Germany in six years of war! Only if we appreciate this staggering fact can we begin to understand the meaning of air power in the world of today and tomorrow, and only in this light can we properly assess the power of the Royal Air Force — infinitely greater in the 1970s than ever before in its history — with more than 1,900 aircraft in flying units, a significant proportion of

[2]"History of the Second World War. The Strategic Air offensive 1939-1945 Vol III 'Victory'" By Sir Charles Webster and Noble Frankland 1961. HMSO.

which are capable of carrying nuclear weapons if the need should ever arise.

The existence of such weapons inevitably has been the most important single factor influencing the capability, tactics, strategy and philosophy of the post-war RAF. The argument about whether their very existence has prevented another World War will continue, but what no one can dispute is the fact that, in 1939, only twenty-one years after the end of the "war to end wars", World War had again broken out. Today, more than thirty years have passed since the end of Hitler's war. Prior to 1939, the RAF Staff College taught the classic Clausewitz doctrine defining war as: "the continuation of Government policy by other means". The Government Statement relating to Defence published in February 1947, however, stated that: "The supreme object of British policy must be to prevent war", and this new and constructive doctrine has been taught in all British Service Colleges ever since.

Another fact which has become more startlingly clear with each succeeding international crisis is the severe limits of the nuclear deterrent policy. It did not prevent the Russian blockade of Berlin in 1948, nor the war in Korea from 1950 to 1953 involving a sixteen-nation United Nations force. It did not deter Iraq from threatening Kuwait in 1961, nor the three year confrontation between Indonesia and Malaysia in which 50,000 men from all three British Services were involved from 1963 to 1966. It did not prevent the loss of millions of lives in south-east Asia — Vietnamese both North and South, French, Cambodian, Australian and American — in a long drawn out guerrilla war in the last eight years of which more bombs were dropped on North Vietnam than were drpped on Germany during the war in Europe. Finally, it did not prevent the fourth and most dangerous Arab-Israeli war of 1973, although it was undoubtedly a factor encouraging the two major powers to set up, with help from the United Nations, the Geneva peace conference. Thus the nuclear deterrent has not prevented British Forces from becoming involved in more than ninety emergencies large and small around the world, since the end of the Second World War.

That the nuclear deterrent does nevertheless deter in certain situations was demonstrated for all the world to see at the height of the Cuban crisis in 1962, when both the USAF Strategic Air Command and RAF Bomber Command were ordered to a high state of readiness. There can be little doubt that the threat presented by the two Air Forces together was a decisive factor in Prime Minister Khrushchev's decision to withdraw Russian inter-continental ballistic missiles and their Russian crews from Cuba. But what the years of so-called peace have taught us is that nuclear power is only good to balance nuclear power. The nuclear power of the Western Alliance can do no more than balance that of the Soviet Union. The United Nations dared not use nuclear weapons in Korea nor the Americans in Vietnam. The Russians achieved their aims in Hungary and in Czechoslovakia without their use. We are left, therefore, with the situation that, under the umbrella of the nuclear balance maintained between the NATO and Warsaw Pact Alliances, the less technologically advanced nations in Asia, Africa, the Middle East and South America, struggling to develop politically, nationalistically and economically, and to secure the simple basic needs of life, engage in every form of warfare known to man. These range from forms of terrorism such as postal bombs, hijacking, kidnapping, political murder and sabotage, through subversion and psychological warfare to infiltration by parachute, as occurred during confrontation with Indonesia, to large-scale guerrilla operations and terrorism of the sort that the British had to contend with in Palestine from 1945 to 1947, in Malaya from 1948 to 1960, in Cyprus from 1956 to 1958, in Aden from from 1957 to 1967, in Northern Ireland from August 1969 to the present time, and the Americans in Vietnam. To these there is no easy answer, either from the ground or from the air.

Waging peace, therefore, during the past thirty violent years has been no job for the lily-livered, nor for the man who is resistant to change. Apart from its violence, this period has been outstanding for the sheer pace of technological progress. In no field of endeavour has this fact been more apparent than in aerospace, in which man has advanced from speed and altitude records of just over 600 miles per hour and 56,000 feet in 1946 to more than 4,500 miles per hour in the earth's atmosphere in 1967, and walking on the moon in 1969. In no vocation have the effects of technological developments been more dramatic than in the profession of arms, and inevitably most of all in the Royal Air Force. Development of the jet engine, of guided weapons, computerised aids to pilotage and navigation, television, radar, satellite communications and reconnaissance, infra-red photography, data processing and nuclear power, to name only some of the more important, all have contributed to a rate of change which has no parallel in any other profession in any period of history spanning less than a man's normal working life.

A further fundamental factor influencing the shape and size of the RAF since the war has been the steeply rising costs of military aircraft and their complex electronic equipment. Two examples will serve to make the point. When the Shackleton maritime reconnaissance aircraft first entered service in 1950, it cost about £157,000. Twenty years later its replacement, the Nimrod, cost about £2½ million, sixteen times as much. (With the cost increases of recent years and including more highly developed electronics, it is now on sale to overseas customers at around £6M). Similarly, in 1945, the Meteor fighter cost about £29,000: the Phantom fighter in 1970 cost about £1½ million, nearly fifty times as much.

Much of the increased cost of the RAF's offensive aircraft of the 1970s can be accounted for by the complex avionics which enable them to approach targets at high speed and very low level, and therefore survive in a hostile defensive environment in which their predecessors of twenty-five years ago would not have survived. In this sense one could argue that today's offensive aircraft are infinitely more cost effective than those of the

15

1950s and, because it is as true today as it was then to say that offence is the best means of defence, the greater effectiveness of contemporary RAF aircraft more than offsets their greatly increased cost.

To limit the cost effectiveness argument purely to the much increased accuracy of airborne weapons against ground targets it is worth quoting a specific example. Mr Packard, the American Deputy Secretary of Defence, giving evidence before the House Appropriations Committee in March 1971, explained that terminal guidance was the key to the accuracy of tactical weapons. "This example," he said, "relates to the ability to destroy targets with the most effective weapons we have in our inventory compared to free-fall bombs which in the past have been the standard weapon of tactical aircraft. The example is based on an analysis of F-4 aircraft delivering their weapons at an altitude above 2,000 feet[3], but the results are reasonably independent of the aircraft used. The analysis demonstrates that the military capability of the overall system is improved by a factor of nearly 50 to 1 in terms of sorties required, and by a factor of 25 to 1 in terms of cost by the selection of the most effective weapon in the inventory for the specific target contrasted with using the least expensive weapon in the inventory — free fall bombs — for all the targets."

In Vietnam, the USAF flew some 600 sorties (and lost thirty aircraft) in unsuccessful attempts to destroy a particular bridge with free-fall bombs. The same bridge was later put out of action in a single attack by three Phantoms employing two guided bombs. The RAF's Harrier is infinitely more cost effective in yet another sense. Its ability to operate away from conventional runways means that its dispersed sites cannot be seen from the air, and it is, therefore, much less vulnerable to attack from the air, at least by conventional weapons.

To provide for the proper use and care of expensive aircraft and much other increasingly costly equipment, computer-aided systems of supply and servicing have been introduced. To ensure that increasingly costly training is not wasted upon men and women unlikely to achieve the high professional standards required, new selection and aptitude testing procedures have been developed. To ensure also that a fighting machine which, in recent years, has been costing an average of £850 million a year to maintain and operate, is managed in a cost effective way, new management techniques and new organisations have become necessary. Finally, there have been essential developments in the recruiting and training, career structures and management of personnel, for in the words of Lord Tedder, when Chief of Air Staff in 1949: "The human factor is still the governing one and human efficiency the key to technical and operational efficiency."

Computers are no better than the men who programme them and in the final analysis it is upon human intelligence, foresight and efficiency that the RAF must continue to depend during the next decade and beyond, in

---

[3]The RAF considers that, in the European theatre, contemporary RAF aircraft will only survive over hostile territory at very low level. They are, therefore, actively studying the use of appropriate guided weapons in low-level attacks.

identifying and assessing the tasks that the Service is likely to be called upon to perform, and in planning and selecting the aircraft and weapons necessary for doing them, in estimating the numbers and calibre of men and women required in specialist officer branches and in skilled and less-skilled trades and, finally, in deciding upon the Command organisation essential for efficient control.

A Time of Change

'All Things Change and We Change with Them' MATHIAS BOURBON

The first thing that had to change when the war was over was the attitude of RAF aircrew to safety. In January 1946 the then Chief of the Air Staff, Marshal of the RAF Sir Arthur Tedder, explained the requirement thus:

"Through six years of war the Royal Air Force has gained a reputation second to none. Men of great courage, memorable deeds and aircraft of the first quality are linked with the title RAF. Now, as we enter the years of peace, we must see — everyone of us — that the Royal Air Force keeps the high place it has earned.

"Now the war is over we shall have fewer aircraft and most certainly none to waste. Production will be switched to peacetime products and, of the aircraft we produce, civil aviation must have its share. As demobilisation speeds up there will be fewer skilled tradesmen to maintain aircraft and repair them. All this means we must get the last ounce out of what we have. The accident rate must be drastically cut; we cannot afford accidents."

With the return of peace there was to be no more 'pressing on regardless' with one engine out of action and the radio unserviceable. The days of taking extreme risks and of hazarding lives to achieve vital wartime purposes were over. Bomber crews were now flying transport aircraft and bombers themselves were carrying passengers, with their bomb bays filled with suitcases and kit bags.

The progress of demobilisation and the movement of replacements in Europe, the Middle East and Far East required air transport to supplement shipping, particularly for speedy repatriation of ill and undernourished prisoners of war. The lifting of a wartime security ban meant that accidents to RAF transport aircraft received wide publicity in Press and Parliament. So critical did some sections of the Press become that Air Marshal the Hon. Sir Ralph Cochrane, at that time Commander-in-Chief of RAF Transport Command, decided to hold a Press conference at his Headquarters in Bushey Park. With the aid of pillar graphs and route maps displayed on the walls of the Officers Mess, he showed how the Command was engaged on a great task of air transportation, covering every corner of the globe. The wall charts proved beyond dispute that the accident record in relation to the amount of flying carried out could be favourably compared with the best pre-war civil airlines.

One diagram compared RAF Transport Command's record in 1945 with that for all British airlines in the five years before the war. Even when the immense trooping figures for October to December 1945 were added (when bomber aircraft and crews reinforced the Command's transport fleet), the fatality rate was only about half of the civil airlines' pre-war rate, yet the amount of passenger flying in Transport Command in one post-war year was about four times that achieved by all British airlines in five pre-war years.

Towards the middle of 1945, however, the Group Captain at the head of Transport Command's Training Branch had become increasingly concerned about the unacceptably high accident rate among Ferry Units throughout the world, all of which at that time came under HQ Transport Command. On his staff he had a very experienced Qualified Flying Instructor — at that time Wing Commander Training. The Wing Commander visited every RAF Ferry Unit from India to Southern China, from Algiers to the Persian Gulf and throughout the United Kingdom. From what he saw and heard at these units it was obvious that a fundamental reorganisation of the Command's training was essential, and that there was an urgent need for the introduction of a continuation training syllabus incorporating specified exercises, particularly covering action in event of engine failure, night and instrument flying.

He found it was not uncommon, for example, for an RAF Ferry pilot to fly a four-engined Liberator, from his base at RAF Cairo West to Teheran, pick up a twin-engined Dakota and fly it to Karachi; then transfer to a four-engined York and fly it to Delhi where he might pick up a single-engined Harvard (regardless of whether he had flown such an aircraft before) and fly that to Rawalpindi. One Polish pilot with wanderlust was known to have been away from his base for three months, flying any aeroplane he could lay his hands on, anywhere it was required to go!

On the Wing Commander's return to the UK it was decided to introduce a two-hour monthly training syllabus on each type of aircraft — single-engined, twin-engined and multi-engined — that a pilot was qualified to fly. A pilot, navigator and engineer were attached to the Command training staff from 511 Squadron (Avro Yorks). This team worked hard and enthusiastically to devise sixteen different ground examinations.

At the same time, three flying tests were drawn up covering general flying, although concentrating on emergencies, instrument and night flying. Early in 1946, armed with his 'categorisation tests' the Wing Commander revisited the Ferry Units world-wide to discuss the proposed tests with all concerned.

The way the scheme worked out in practice was that each member of a transport squadron or ferry unit took the tests appropriate to his aircrew specialisation (pilot, navigator, engineer, wireless operator etc.) after completing the laid down monthly continuation training. He was then awarded a category indicating precisely the standard of proficiency achieved. The category of each crew member dictated whether the crew as a whole could be used for carrying VIPs, ordinary passengers or freight only. Transport Command's continuation training and categorisation schemes became the envy of civil aviation and a new era in RAF aircrew standards of proficiency, safety and professionalism had dawned.

In 1946 HQ Transport Command tried to persuade the Civil Aviation authorities to collaborate in a joint aircrew categorisation or qualification system so that, on leaving the Service, RAF transport pilots could graduate automatically into civil aviation with their RAF experience and qualifications appropriately recognised. The civil authorities considered the proposal but claimed it was essential for civil aviation to be entirely separate from RAF standards. This decision was to lead to an unfortunate situation a quarter of a century later.

Following Transport Command's example, all RAF Flying Commands introduced similar aircrew categorisation schemes. With the advent of peace, increased emphasis was already being placed on training in all-weather flying in the air as well as in flight simulators. The introduction in 1947 of instrument ratings for all RAF pilots, without which they were not permitted to fly in bad weather, provided the necessary stimulus to this essential aspect of flying training, and was a direct copy of the Transport Command scheme.

In this first post-war year, RAF Transport Command was still responsible for world-wide strategic routes and transport aircraft supplemented by bombers were airlifting on the Eastern route alone some 9,000 passengers a month in each direction. But as increasing numbers of RAF men and women were demobilised, the air trooping programme had to be correspondingly reduced.

It was on the higher performance aircraft, the Spitfire and in particular the Meteor, that the accident rate was highest. In October 1946 Air Chief Marshal Sir John Slessor, as Air Member for Personnel, wrote:

"There is no single cause which, if removed, would end all aircraft accidents. But there *is* one aspect of Royal Air Force life which, more than everything else, has a vitally important bearing upon accidents generally. I refer to discipline. Unsatisfactory aircrew or groundcrew discipline is either a sole cause or a permanent contributory cause of the majority of accidents."

Encouraging results in reducing accidents were, however, already being achieved by Accident Prevention Committees at RAF flying stations. These committees were meeting once a month under the chairmanship of the Station Commanders and included Squadron and Flight Commanders, the Chief Technical Officer, Air Traffic Control and Motor Transport Officers, the Clerk of Works and the station Accident Prevention Officer. Subjects for discussion ranged from accidents which

21

had occurred during the month to suggestions for new or modified safety precautions.

The Air Ministry Accident Preventions staff had introduced an intelligent young blonde named Prudence to confound the irresponsible stupidity of the popular Pilot Officer Prune, a famous character in the wartime flight safety magazine 'Tee Emm'. Prune symbolized as a pilot the truth of 'Murphy's Law', which stated that if something *can* be done the wrong way it *will* be. He was the pilot who forgot to lower his aircraft's undercarriage before landing, or who set his compass needle 180° the wrong way round so that, intending to fly north, he flew south.

Ten thousand lives were lost in the RAF in 1944 alone as a result of aircraft accidents. There were 20,000 crashes, involving the loss of £167,000,000. Pilot Officer Prune had, therefore, an important life saving role to play in war. With the advent of peace, however, it was better that Prudence should demonstrate the right way to avoid accidents, in place of Prune whose cartoons by W. Hooper had so vividly depicted the mistakes that lead to them. Prudence graced posters in aircrew rest-rooms such as "A Lot Depends on a Strap — her Modesty — Your Life!"; and she flew East to make an accident prevention film called "Flying With Prudence".

Nevertheless, in 1946 statistics showed that in 66% of accidents to RAF aircraft, some error on the part of the pilot was involved. This raised again the question of how best to select young men for flying training. During the war attempts had been made to pre-determine by tests whether a man was likely to make the grade as a pilot, and if so, for what type of flying he might be best suited. For this purpose, an RAF medical officer had devised a test for muscular co-ordination. Validation of this test had been carried out in wartime flying training schools and showed a significant relationship between success in the test and ability to learn to fly. Such a test, however, could only give a small part of the answer, for temperamental suitability for military flying was a major factor in the assessment of overall suitability. A wealth of valuable information on this subject had been accumulated during the war and was now available at the School of Aviation Medicine at Farnborough. From 1946 onward, therefore, all RAF medical officers on entry were given the benefit of the knowledge and experience that the war years had provided. Some doctors were being selected each year for flying training and a subsequent period of service in a squadron so that as 'flying doctors' they would have a better understanding of the psychology of flying men and could give advice on fatigue and such other factors which lead to flying accidents.

At the same time, psychologists on the Air Ministry staff were asked to produce specifications for a standardised interview technique, and in May 1946, a single Aircrew Candidates Selection Board was set up at RAF Hornchurch. A year later the Board amalgamated with the Aptitude Testing Centre and its associated Medical Board from RAF Bridgnorth to form the new Combined Selection Centre at RAF North Weald.

By 1947 Air Ministry plans for the future were well advanced. In spite of the turbulence of the immediate post-war period and the weight of RAF commitments throughout the world, provision has been made for re-arming with the most modern types of jet-propelled fighter aircraft — Meteors and Vampires — the replacement of the Dakota transport aircraft and for the development of a modern aircraft specially designed for the carriage of airborne forces. Plans also included a replacement for obsolete training aircraft; this was recognised as a requirement of fundamental importance to the efficiency of flying training at the beginning of the jet age. Rapid progress was also being made with the 'humanisation' of Service life. All unnecessary restrictions on freedom off duty were being removed. It had become an accepted fact that such steps were not only reconcilable with a high state of discipline, but helped to achieve it.

The RAF at this time became increasingly concerned to ensure that it was casting its net as widely as possible to attract to a professional career, both on the ground and in the air, a due proportion of the best of the country's youth. The introduction of a more scientific and objective selection system was an important step in this direction.

While the RAF was re-adjusting remarkably quickly to peace at home, the situation was far less satisfactory in the Far East, where the RAF was deeply involved in helping to cope with the results of Japanese occupation of allied territories over the vast area of South-East Asia. By the beginning of 1946, RAF Seletar on Singapore Island had a strength of more than 3,000 men in uniform, 1,600 civilians and 400 Japanese. Sunderland flying boats of 205 and 230 Squadrons which were based there were flying round the clock carrying food and medical supplies to the sick and starving throughout the whole of the Far East as well as evacuating prisoners of war. Throughout that year Singapore-based Mosquitoes of 84, 89 and 110 Squadrons and Thunderbolts of 60 and 80 Squadrons were engaged in supporting allied ground forces against Indonesian insurgents armed with Japanese weapons, and endeavouring to maintain order and liberate prisoners of war in the Dutch East Indies. By April 1946, RAF airfields at Changi and Tengah had taken the place of Seletar as the main centres for land-based aircraft on Singapore Island, Seletar remaining the main RAF maintenance base in the Far East and providing a home for the flying boats.

Towards the end of 1946, pirate and robber activities on islands and marshes off the Malay coast had become so serious that a Brigade of the 7th Indian Division was sent into the islands to flush out the culprits. The RAF provided air reconnaissance and close support. Most of the pirates got away, but the operation at least acted as a deterrent to further similar activities.

Meanwhile, discontent was growing amongst RAF Servicemen in Karachi, Delhi and Singapore at overcrowded conditions, inadequate leave facilities, poor rations and disappointment at the slow rate of repatriation. In Karachi, Air Marshal 'Ugly' Barratt, Inspector General of the RAF, was howled down when addressing a large assembly of men at

RAF Drigh Road. By 0800 hours on January 26, 1946, the men at RAF Seletar had downed tools. Later that day, Air Marshal Sir Keith Park, the Allied Air Commander-in-Chief, arrived to address them. The majority appeared to be glad to return to work. The next day, however, the strike broke out again. The Station Commander arranged with unit commanders to address their men independently. Measures being taken to remove grievances were explained in detail. The men were also told that the British Government was taking an extremely serious view of their action, and that unless they returned to work by 2 o'clock that afternoon, the so-called strike would be regarded as mutiny. They did not need telling that there was only one way of dealing with mutiny: the trouble was over, both in Singapore and India.

Within two months of these unhappy incidents in the Far East, more than 100 aircraft of the Royal Air Force and Royal Indian Air Force took part in a 'Victory Week' display at Willingdon airport, Delhi. It was attended by the Viceroy, Lord Wavell, the Commander-in-Chief, Sir Claude Auchinleck and the Air Officer Commanding-in-Chief, Air Marshal Sir Roderick Carr. It was the greatest air display ever staged in India and was watched by a crowd of more than 100,000 people. The following year, 81(PR) Squadron, flying Spitfires, completed the first ever photographic survey of the whole of Sarawak and North Borneo.

Sunderland flying boats, approaching a decade of RAF service, were still flying throughout the Far East during these first two post-war years and 88 Squadron based at Hong Kong was busy carrying mail and supplies for allied forces of occupation in Japan, including RAF squadrons based there. One unusual load consisted of an aircraft full of curry for Indian troops. Another was a load of Japanese war criminals (guarded by Ghurkas with naked kukris) being brought for trial.

Most of the islands in the Canton River estuary, of which Hong Kong is one, have jagged mountain peaks rising to 2,000 feet or so, and during the monsoon season these are often cloud covered. But using their ASV (anti-surface vessel) radar and helped by a Blind Approach Beacon System (BABS), pilots could usually fly through the Eastern gap into Kowloon Bay below a cloud base of 500 feet. Iwakini, their island destination off Japan (whose nearest town was the ill-fated Hiroshima, never-to-be forgotten first target for an atomic bomb), was surrounded by mountains up to 6,000 feet. Icing and heavy snow storms were serious hazards in winter, and ironically the only possible alternative if weather at Iwakini was impossible for flying boats to alight was the sea-plane base at Nagasaki (target for the second and hopefully the last atomic weapon used in war). Despite the weather difficulties (even flying boats under repair had to get airborne to preserve them from typhoon damage), 88 Squadron never missed a mail delivery. At RAF Seletar in Singapore, two further flying boat squadrons were still operational, 205 and 209, but the last flying boat had been built in 1945 and although new designs were on the drawing boards at Shorts and

Saunders Roe, no new orders were being placed in these early post-war years.

During the same two years the RAF Mediterranean and Middle East Command, whose Headquarters initially in Cairo and in 1947 transferred in part to Ismailia on the Suez Canal and in part to Abu Sueir (with an Advanced HQ maintained for a time at Caserta in Italy), was occupied with an enormous clearing up task in Italy, in policing and garrisoning from Gibraltar to Aden and in setting up and manning the staging-post airfields necessary for Transport Command's huge trooping commitment. Geographically greatly extended, its subordinate formations included Air Headquarters Levant, Iraq and Persia, Italy, Malta and East Africa, together with Headquarters British Forces Aden, RAF Station Khartoum, and 205, 216 and 219 Groups.

By the beginning of 1947, conditions in Greece had permitted the RAF to withdraw its operational squadrons and set up a mission to advise the Greek Government on the re-establishment of an air force. In Italy, large stocks of explosives had to be cleared, some of which were handed over to the Italians, together with aircraft, after reconstruction of the Italian Air Force. Meanwhile, increasingly serious outbreaks of lawlessness and violence were occurring in Palestine. The first Arab-Israeli war had started, with the British in their traditional position, caught between two fires. British pledges to the Jews and Arabs could not be carried out in full because they were mutually irreconcilable. The British Government had proposed partition as the only solution having any hope of success, but within two years of the end of the war, the decision had been taken to withdraw from Palestine altogether. Throughout these two years, the RAF in Palestine was heavily committed to co-operating with the Army and the civil power trying to maintain order, prevent illegal immigration and finally to evacuate British civilians.

It was not only the situation in Palestine that caused statesmen and military planners to look elsewhere for more secure and politically stable areas for Britain's post-war defence bases. Active consideration was being given to transferring bases from the Eastern Mediterranean to Kenya and Tanganyika in East Africa. The peoples of Egypt, Iraq and Transjordan were developing nationalistic sentiments which rendered the presence of foreign armed forces increasingly unpopular. Communications with all these countries were inadequate for rapid reinforcement, and the recent war had shown how dangerous a sea the Mediterranean could be with a strong hostile power dominating its northern shores. And even though the Suez Canal were kept open, the Red Sea might become unsafe for the passage of men and material to and from bases in the Middle East, if Iraq and parts of the Arabian peninsula were occupied by an enemy possessing powerful air forces.

With the independence and partition of India in 1947, bases on the western shores of the Indian Ocean were considered all the more necessary for the security of British communications with Australia and New

Zealand, Singapore, Malaya and Hong Kong, and with countless island colonies in Eastern waters.

In Europe, RAF tactical air forces provided the British Air Forces of Occupation in Germany and Austria. There was also a British Air Command in Berlin. Initially the RAF's primary concern was disarming the Luftwaffe, but each month Bomber Command sent over training raids of about 100 aircraft and the squadrons in Germany practised intercepting them. Also during 1946, specially modified Lancasters of XV Squadron carried out trials with the latest types of British deep-penetration bombs, mainly 12,000- and 22,000-pounders, against the U-boat pens at Farge, near Bremen, and other heavily protected targets.

In the United Kingdom, in 1946, we find Bomber, Coastal, Fighter, and Transport Commands, with a pretty mixed bunch of aircraft. The heavy bombers included old warriors such as the Avro Lancaster and the American Liberator, together with the newly arrived Lincoln. Amongst light bombers, night intruders and nightfighters, both the de Havilland Mosquito and the Bristol Beaufighter still had some years of useful service ahead of them. The Douglas Dakota still bore the brunt of the air transport task throughout the world, but there was also the Avro York in Transport Command (a transport development of the Lancaster bomber) and Halifaxes transferred from Bomber Command, while Sunderland flying boats were used on many occasions to supplement the transport fleet. Two pre-war aircraft, the de Havilland Tiger Moth and the Avro Anson, were still going strong, while fighter squadrons were equipped mainly with Spitfires, Mustangs and Tempests, and the first two jet aircraft to enter squadron service — Meteors and Vampires.

By April 1947, just under a million men and women had been released from the RAF and WAAF since VE day. Another sixty thousand or so were due out by the end of 1947. Only 2,250 officers who had held permanent commissions in the RAF before the war were still serving and in consequence the quality of pre-war short service officers and of those who had entered during the war and who were now being selected and offered permanent commissions, would set the standard of efficiency in, and determine the character of, the Royal Air Force for many years to come. Applications for permanent commissions were far more numerous than the peacetime requirement, thus the quality of officers chosen was high. By the end of the year, the regular officer cadre of a peacetime RAF had been successfully re-formed. The situation was far less satisfactory in the noncommissioned ranks. Although recruiting of men from civil life with no previous Service experience had been good (considering how much greater was the requirement of the force compared with pre-war) there was an urgent need for more trained and esperienced men to re-engage for regular service, and more than 100,000 new men were required by the end of 1946 in more than 100 different trades. Early in that year, new rates of pay were introduced for officers and other ranks, while the 1946 White Paper provided for four main officer branches: General Duties

(Flying), Technical, Equipment and Secretarial. Regarding women, the Air Council was at this time planning on converting the Women's Auxiliary Air Force into a permanent part of the RAF. Those still serving were being encouraged to extend their service and some already released to return.

Before the first two years of peace were over, several further decisions of importance to the immediate and long-term future of the RAF had been taken. The Central Flying School (for training flying instructors) was re-formed at RAF Little Rissington under the command of Group Captain E. A. C. Britton. A new post with the title of Air Member for Technical Services was created on the Air Council and filled by Air Marshal Sir Roderick Hill. The Auxiliary Air Force was granted the prefix 'Royal' and was to be re-formed with thirteen dayfighter, three nightfighter and four light bomber squadrons, and a new type of unit to man the Operations Rooms and Reporting Stations which would have been required at that time to control the fighter and anti-aircraft operations in war. University Air Squadrons had been formed at eleven universities in the United Kingdom, and an Air Training Corps — with a ceiling of 75,000 cadets — was to be established to encourage air-mindedness and provide creative activities for youth. RAF Reserve Command was formed to supervise the training of such reserve organisations in particular. It was also decided that the Royal Air Force Regiment, formed to meet the wartime need for specialised airfield defence, was to continue as an integral part of the RAF. It would contain rifle, armoured and light anti-aircraft squadrons, and other units would be trained as airborne and parachute troops.

The RAF's most newsworthy achievement in 1946 was probably the setting up of a new world speed record of 616.81 miles per hour by Group Captain E. M. Donaldson, who was at the time commanding the RAF High Speed Flight. The Gloster Meteors used in the record attempt were standard RAF Mk 4 fighters, except that the gun mountings had been blocked up and special duralumin cockpit covers fitted. Experience of great value for the future was obtained by all concerned with the High Speed Flight. With air speeds of more than 600 miles per hour the problems of shock stalls increased as the speed of sound was approached. The speed of sound had been established at about 760 miles per hour at sea level, but this varied with temperature. On advice from the Meteorological Office, therefore, a three kilometre stretch of the south coast near Littlehampton — where temperatures were constant for reasonable periods — was selected for the attempt on the record. Timing camera boxes were wired to the National Physical Laboratory at Teddington to ensure accurate recording of the speeds attained. The record-breaking aircraft is now to be seen in the RAF Museum at Hendon.

In the same year standard Gloster Meteor 3s, without any modification to engines, had returned from highly successful tropical trials in Khartoum. Jet engines in hot and dusty conditions appeared to present fewer problems than their propeller-driven predecessors. The following

27

year, a second post-war world record was set up when Squadron Leader Martin flew a Mosquito 6,700 miles from England to Cape Town in 21 hours 31 minutes.

Africa was also in the news because of an air survey carried out by the RAF throughout 1946/7, which involved photographing 145,000 square miles of Nigeria, the Gold Coast, Gambia and Sierra Leone; while back at home, in October 1946, the first post-war course of cadets for permanent commissions as pilots and navigators entered the RAF College, Cranwell.

Finally, to honour the past, a Battle of Britain Memorial Chapel was dedicated in Westminster Abbey in the Presence of King George VI, and to help insure the future, agreement was reached for regular exchange postings between officers of the United States Air Force and Royal Air Force — allies in peace as well as war.

The Victories of Peace

'Peace hath her victories no less renowned than war'   *MILTON*

In the years 1948 and 1949, decisions were taken by the British Government which were to have a profound long-term effect upon the Royal Air Force. On the transfer of power in India, and the creation of the two new Dominions of India and Pakistan, it was agreed that all United Kingdom forces would be withdrawn. Certain British army units stayed on, however, for twelve months or so to give what assistance they could during the initial stages of the reorganisation of India's armed forces, and a number of RAF officers were seconded to help in building up the Indian and Pakistan Air Forces. In the same year, Burma left the Commonwealth and the British withdrawal from Palestine radically altered the disposition of her forces in the Middle East.

The signature of the North Atlantic Treaty in April, 1949, in the words of Lord Ismay, NATO's first Secretary General, "marked the beginning of a revolutionary and constructive experiment in international relations." In signing the Treaty, twelve independent sovereign states — later to be joined by three others — undertook pledges which called for immediate and continuous collective action, primarily in the military field.

June 1948 saw the beginning of RAF operations against terrorists in Malaya in support of the security forces. Code-named 'Operation Firedog' this campaign was to continue for twelve years.

Back in Europe, on June 28, the RAF joined with the United States Air Force in operation 'Plainfare', better known as the Berlin Airlift. Since January 1948, the Russians had gradually been tightening their grip on all surface movement into and out of the Western Sectors of Berlin, which were administered by America, Britain and France respectively. By June 24, the blockade on the ground was complete with movement only possible by air. Contingency plans were available to supply by air the British occupying forces in Berlin, but there were also more than two million West Berliners to be fed. On June 30, Headquarters 46 Group of RAF Transport Command issued an operations order which stated:

1. Following the breakdown of the surface communications between the British Zone of Germany and the British Sector in Berlin, the latter will be supplied completely by air.

2. The airlift into Berlin is to be built up as rapidly as possible to 400 tons per day and maintained at that level until July 3, 1948. Therefrom it is to be increased to 750 tons per day by July 7, 1948.

Initially the main requirement was for food, and the speed of the operation was dependent upon the rate at which the two airfields in the British and American sectors, Gatow and Tempelhof, could be developed to accept more traffic. This meant that aircraft also had to carry to Berlin an assortment of bulky, heavy machinery and building raw materials.

Eight airfields and one flying-boat base were chosen as the western support for the air bridge of which six, including the flying-boat base, were in the British zone. In the north were Schleswigland, Lubeck and Fuhlsbuttel (the airport of Hamburg); the flying-boats were based at Finkenwerde, near Hamburg on the Elbe. To the south, in the Hanover area, were the ex-Luftwaffe airfields of Wunstorf, Celle and Fassburg. Frankfurt and Wiesbaden, in the American zone, were used exclusively by the Americans.

A great deal of repair and development work had to be done on most of the airfields by RAF Airfield Construction Wings and Royal Engineers, but by the end of 1948 they were all fully operational. To make best use of the only two airfields initially available at the Berlin end it was essential to land and dispatch aircraft at the shortest possible intervals. The aim at Gatow, with its one concrete runway (and a parallel reserve runway of pierced steel planking), was to land one aircraft and dispatch another every three minutes, by day and night. In bad weather the three minute interval was stretched to five. Such high intensity of air traffic could be maintained only with full use of available radio and radar navigation aids, including Eureka beacons, Ground Controlled Approach radar, and of a runway approach lighting system invented by the remarkable Mr Calvert of the Royal Aircraft Establishment at Farnborough. This new system was first used operationally at Gatow and consisted of a series of cross-bar sodium approach lights placed at right angles to a central bar of lights aligned with the centre-line of the runway. In bad visibility it not only helped a pilot to line up for his final approch to the runway, but the cross bars also helped him keep the aircraft's wings level on the approach and during the final seconds before touch-down. After its successful debut during the Berlin airlift the Calvert lighting system was installed at London Airport and it has since become the standard system for all RAF and most civilian and military airfields throughout the world.

Initially, Headquarters British Air Forces of Occupation was responsible for twenty-four-hour control of the operation, but as soon as practicable a Transport Group Headquarters was set up in which British and American controllers and staffs, working in shifts, co-ordinated the hour-by-hour progress of the airlift.

The RAF started operations with the twin-engined Dakota, capable of airlifting some 3½ tons, and then brought in four-engined Yorks and Hastings, each carrying payloads of about 9 tons. In addition, Sunderland flying boats operated from the River Elbe, near Finkenwerde, to the Havel Lake in the British sector of Berlin until they had to be withdrawn when the water started to freeze.

The RAF was reinforced by aircraft and crews of British civil companies (most of the civilian crews having been trained in the RAF during the war). Many of the civil aircraft, fitted with special tanks, carried liquid fuel in bulk to Berlin. International co-operation was the keynote of the airlift and aircrew from America, Britain, Australia, South Africa and New Zealand were to be found in half a dozen different types of aircraft converging upon the airfield at Gatow every day. With the approach of Winter 1948, the dangers of a crowded twenty mile wide air corridor in bad weather and on dark nights were quickly appreciated. Closer control of the allied operation became essential and this was achieved by combining British and American forces in a single organisation called the Combined Airlift Task Force. An American General was in command with an RAF Air Commodore as his Deputy, each being responsible to the Commander of their respective Air Force of Occupation in Germany. An important aspect of this closer control was a one-way traffic system with British aircraft eastbound mainly on the northern corridor, American on the southern and almost all returning on the central corridor (except for a few British using the north-west corridor) at pre-arranged heights according to speeds.

By May 12, 1949, the Berlin blockade had been officially raised. RAF aircraft engaged in the airlift at this time consisted of some forty Yorks, forty Dakotas and fourteen Hastings, the last being the planned replacement for the York, specially designed for paratroop and supply dropping; RAF aircrew had flown over 18 million miles in nearly 50,000 flights carrying over 300,000 tons and nearly 70,000 passengers in both directions. The largest air supply operation ever attempted was officially at an end, although the airlift continued until October to build up stocks in Berlin. But it was not only aircrew who worked hard throughout this operation. The high intensity of aircraft movements and the safety of aircrew in the air had depended — as always — upon the high morale and conscientious labours of RAF men on the ground. One example will suffice to make the point. It concerns a certain corporal Fitter II named Ryman at RAF Wunstorf. He was responsible for an engine change on an urgently needed York. In spite of the need for speed in changing the engine, he made time (meaning 'overtime' without overtime pay!) to check on associated airframe components. Detecting a slight lifting of the point on the engine bearer sub-frame, he looked closer and found that a tubular member adjoining a welded joint was cracked. Had this crack gone unnoticed, a complete fracture could have occurred in flight and a valuable aircraft and the even more valuable lives of all of its crew could have been lost. Should he read this 'account' will he accept it on behalf of all his many thousand colleagues, as a tribute from the author who is alive to tell this tale because of all the careful, painstaking men on the ground like Cpl Ryman.

The Berlin airlift was thus a remarkable story of sustained and successful

31

endeavour, not without casualties, considerable strain, overwork and discomfort for aircrew and ground staffs. In all material things, the Western Powers could claim that the airlift had beaten the blockade. But as the official account points out, in one respect the operation was probably unique:

"The famous sieges of history, from ancient Troy to modern Paris have conformed to a rough pattern. The besiegers drew up in strength around the city and attempted to obtain physical possession of it by force of arms and the long slow method of starvation. But the blockade of Berlin was a siege directed not only at the citizens' stomachs, but also at their minds. It was a curious battle of willpower, a struggle not only for physical possession of the city, but for its souls as well."

The achievement of the RAF, in association with the USAF and civil charter firms, was to win respect for the Western democracies, and to revive in millions of doubting minds a belief in the strength of freedom. It was a milestone in history, and after it was over, East-West relations were never quite the same again.

Meanwhile in the Far East there was trouble brewing. It stemmed from the fact that during the Japanese occupation the Malayan Communist Party supporting the Allies had been armed, equipped and trained in guerrilla warfare by the British. When the return of arms was ordered after the war a branch of the MCP, dominated by dissident Chinese, retained their weapons. In the Spring of 1948 Malaya was hit by a communist insurrection.

It appeared that the aim of the Malayan Communist Party was to drive all Europeans, Government officials and police from isolated parts of the interior. During April and May, violent incidents were reported from many parts of the country, and on June 16, three European rubber planters were murdered. On June 17 a state of emergency was declared and 'Operation Firedog' had started. During this and following months Mosquitos and Ansons of 81 Squadron, flying boats of 209 Squadron and Beaufighters of 45 Squadron strafed and bombed terrorist hideouts, in addition to many reconnaissance sorties flown by Spitfires in a campaign that was to continue for twelve long years until 1960.

Air Command Far East operations during 1948 and 1949 were not, however, confined to Malaya. Although Burma had been granted independence in January 1949, its future was uncertain. At 1 a.m. on February 22, a message was received at Headquarters Air Command Far East in Singapore that the political situation in Burma had deteriorated and urgent evacuation of British civilians was necessary. Within three hours a flying-boat of 209 Squadron was airborne en route to the Burma oil fields, where it alighted in heavy tropical rain on the Irawadi River near Chauk. At dawn the next morning, forty-one civilians — mainly women and children — were flown out, and by this time a second Sunderland was ready at Rangoon for action if it became necessary to evacuate the remaining men.

Plate 1 A well decorated VIP Dakota with the RAF in Germany 1946/47. Decorations include the 'Five Stars' of a General, the symbol of the Control Commission, the 8th Army Insignia and the Badge of RAF Transport Command.

Plate 2 Avro York transport aircraft (developed from the Avro Lancaster bomber) of the RAF, queuing to unload at RAF Gatow during the Berlin airlift (June 1948–May 1949).

Plate 3 An RAF Sunderland flying boat unloading supplies during the Berlin airlift on the Havel Lake in the British sector of Berlin.

Plate 4 Boeing B-29 Washington strategic bombers of RAF Bomber Command over the North Sea in 1951.

On April 29, news reached Headquarters Air Command Far East that HMS *Amethyst* had been fired upon, suffered damage and casualties and had run aground whilst steaming past communist Chinese batteries on the banks of the Yangtse River, where a battle was raging between communist and nationalist troops. No 88 flying-boat Squadron, based at RAF Kai Tak opposite Hong Kong Island, was ordered to send an aircraft to drop supplies and if possible alight and take off casualties. At first light next day a Sunderland piloted by Flight Lieutenant Letford, DSO, DFC, and with a RAF doctor and the Commanding Officer from RAF Seletar on board, took off. Nearing its destination, a wireless message was received from the cruiser HMS *London*, ordering the aircraft to divert to Shanghai on account of heavy gunfire around *Amethyst*.

At Shanghai the crew learned that although the frigate had been refloated, her hull was holed, charts destroyed, Captain and First Lieutenant severely wounded and doctor killed. Attempts by HMS *London* and HMS *Blake* to reach the *Amethyst* had failed. The Royal Air Force was asked for help. Flight Lieutenant Letford took off from Shanghai, flew direct to the ship and on sighting her, carried out two low fly-pasts. Meeting no gunfire, he decided to alight. One of the *Amethyst's* officers rowed over to the flying-boat in a sampan by which time shells were falling all round. The flying-boat's co-pilot, Flight Lieutenant Fearnley, scrambled into the sampan with medical supplies, and the naval officer transferred to the flying-boat. Before the RAF doctor could get aboard, the sampan's Chinese crew had rowed off with Flight Lieutenant Fearnley alone. With fire getting heavier and nearer, there was no alternative for the flying-boat's Captain but an immediate take-off.

That night HMS *Amethyst* took shelter in a creek and evacuated her wounded. The remaining three naval officers together with Flight Lieutenant Fearnley, fifty-two ratings and eight Chinese, remained on board and were soon joined by Lieutenant Commander Kerans, Assistant Naval Attaché at Nanking, who then assumed command. Next day, Letford was asked by the Navy to alight again alongside HMS *Amethyst* to transfer eight officers and ratings and a naval chaplain to conduct burial services aboard. After coming down on the river to transfer the reinforcements and supplies, the flying-boat received several hits and had her aerial shot away and attempts to transfer men and supplies had to be abandoned. After take-off unidentified aircraft were sighted astern by Letford's rear gunner, so he wisely took refuge in low cloud and flew in cloud all the way back to Shanghai. The following day Letford was asked again to reconnoitre the situation. Low cloud forced him to fly at 800 feet, and accurate fire from the ground holed the navigator's computer, a main petrol tank and the hull in several places. Rapidly losing fuel and with consequent danger of fire, Letford was forced to return to Shanghai. A few days later, the frigate made a successful dash down river to safety. When she eventually returned to Plymouth, the Naval General Service Medal was awarded to those concerned including all members of the flying-boat crew.

On May 14, 1949, news was received by the RAF at Kai Tak that 88 Squadron flying boats would be needed to help evacuate British nationals from Shanghai where communist forces were closing in. At 4 a.m. on the following day the Squadron Commander, Squadron Leader D. M. Gall, took off, arriving in Shanghai some five hours later. He picked up twenty-six people and had them safely back in Hong Kong by mid-afternoon. On May 16, Flight Lieutenant Letford picked up another thirty-eight British refugees and later the same day a third aircraft from 88 Squadron collected a further thirty-five. On the third day, Pilot II Bartrum collected the last twenty-two refugees, the evacuation was complete and Shangai fell to communist forces a few days' later.

In the Middle East, amongst the RAF's main taks in 1948 were the provision of air support for the evacuation of Palestine, for three brief operations in the rugged hinterland of the Aden Protectorate and for police and military forces in Eritrea. In the Aden Protectorate air action had demonstrated quickly and economically that peaceful caravans must be allowed to cross the desert unhindered and unharmed and that the rule of law must be respected. Similar action on a smaller scale had been taken against the Shifta bandits in Eritrea. In Palestine, on May 23, 1948, four or five Egyptian Spitfires attacked the RAF airfield at Ramat David, south-east of Haifa, in three separate attacks. The first was unopposed, but during the two subsequent raids, RAF fighters were scrambled and claim to have shot down some of the attacking aircraft. On the ground, four British airmen were killed and three severely injured.

While overseas Commands were engaged in this wide variety of operations, and notwithstanding the intensive effort being devoted to the Berlin Airlift, training in the United Kingdom and Europe was continuing. During 1948, all Commands at home, together with Royal Auxiliary Air Force squadrons and British Air Forces of Occupation, had taken part in operation 'Dagger' to exercise the early warning and fighter control systems. Bomber Command exercises had included periodical detachments of squadrons to the Mediterranean and, in exercise 'Red Lion', the transplanting of 97 (Straits Settlement) Lincoln Squadron to Singapore where, as a self-contained reinforcing squadron, they came under the operational control of Air Command Far East during their month's stay.

The same year, a new pilot training scheme came into operation at RAF Feltwell. This new scheme incorporated three main departures from earlier practice: first, the 'all-through' training programme; second the all-weather policy; and third the provision of two new types of training aircraft designed for basic and advanced training respectively. The advantage of the 'all-through' scheme was that the pupil pilot remained in the same unit with the same flying instructor until receiving his wings. The course lasted eighteen month and consisted of five months intensive ground training followed by three phases of flying training: initial, advanced and applied. The de Havilland Tiger Moth, for so long the backbone of the RAF's initial flying training schools, was soon to give way to the Chipmunk: the Percival Prentice was taking the place of American Harvards for basic flying training and the Boulton Paul Balliol was planned as the new type for advanced flying training. With 200 hours flying in his log book and wings on his chest, the pilot then went on to an operational training unit to fly the type of aircraft he would meet in his first squadron.

Perhaps an even more important development of this period, however, was that of Planned Servicing. The essence of Planned Servicing is Planned Inspection involving the careful pre-study of every item of an inspection schedule and of the optimum number of men that can be employed together on a given job. By arranging the inspectional processes in a logical sequence, and by timing the individual jobs as co-ordinated elements, congestion and interference in such places as aircraft cockpits is avoided and work can be progressed and controlled by the NCO in charge. Servicing schedules were introduced which detailed the tools, spares, equipment, men and time required. Each man was issued with a work card telling him precisely what he had to do, the time and tools required for the job, and the assistance he could expect from other tradesmen.

The economies achieved by the scheme were spectacular. For example, a major inspection on a Sunderland flying-boat prior to the introduction of planned servicing used to take twenty-eight days to complete, with the expenditure of some 4,000 man-hours. With planned servicing, the inspection could be completed in five days and only 2,300 man-hours.

Efficient use of man-power in the RAF was becoming increasingly important. By April 1, 1949, RAF strength was down to 232,000, but it was not so much from lack of numbers as from lack of experience and skill that the RAF was suffering. As *Flight* commented at the time: "National Service is of no use whatsoever in the RAF — it is a hindrance rather than a help. The period of service is too short."

In May 1948, while RAF Commanders at all levels were preoccupied in coping with their urgent everyday problems in many parts of the world, the Prime Minister, Mr Attlee, spent a day at RAF Old Sarum at the Chief of Air Staff's annual exercise. Named 'Pandora' the object of the exercise that year was to study the effect of scientific developments on future air warfare. The advent of weapons of mass destruction, it was concluded, profoundly influenced both the preparation for and the conduct of war. Their existence increased the possibility of surprise attacks, since decisive results could be obtained by their use alone.

No review of the years 1948 and 1949 would be complete without at least passing mention of several other RAF milestones. By the beginning of 1948 seven new Royal Auxiliary Air Force Regiment squadrons had been formed. In April 1948, an Anglo-French Military Air Transport Agreement was signed, regularising flights by military aircraft of Britain and France over both countries and providing for servicing such aircraft at RAF and French Air Force bases. In May 1948, the Royal Commission had made an unprecedented award of £100,000 to Air Commodore Frank

Whittle for his pioneer work on the jet engine. Then in July of the same year, six RAF Vampires of 54 Squadron made the first Atlantic crossing by jet aircraft via Stornoway, Iceland and Greenland to Labrador. Also during 1948, seven Lancasters of the Empire Air Navigation School completed a training and research flight into the Arctic Circle. The purposes of the flight were to establish an effective arctic navigation drill using standard Service equipment; to collect information on weather and signals; to investigate any arctic phenomena which might manifest themselves; and to acquire experience with long-range radio aids and pressure-pattern flying.

In February 1949, the Women's Auxiliary Air Force was re-named Women's Royal Air Force. This was more than simply a change of name. It was a final recognition of the truth of John Drinkwater's words: "There are women whose talent it is to serve." Having proved their worth in two wars, women would henceforward serve on a permanent basis, fully integrated into the Royal Air Force, with equal opportunities of advancement in the Service as men. In June, the Empire Air Navigation School, Air Armament School and Flying School combined to form the RAF Flying College at Manby in Lincolnshire, and in October, following agreement between Britain, America and the Bahamas, a guided-missile range was established at Cape Canaveral, under the control of the United States Air Force Long Range Proving Ground Division.

For the first time in the history of the RAF, a King's Colour was presented to the RAF College Cranwell by His Majesty King George VI on July 6, 1948, in the course of his first post-war visit to the College. In a white frame in the centre of the colour was the College badge, and the figure of Daedalus who made the earliest recorded attempt at flight.

On March 4, 1948, concern was expressed in the House of Commons at Bomber Command's lack of strike power. Group Captain Max Aitken doubted whether we could put more than 100 bombers into an operation. The re-equipment of heavy bomber squadrons with Avro Lincolns (and twin-engined Brigands for the light bomber squadrons) was far from re-assuring when it was known that they were generally inferior in performance to America's war-time B-29. Although the prospect of jet bombers was in sight it gave the House little confidence that the quality of the strike force could be improved in less than three years. In reply to these criticisms, Mr Arthur Henderson, Secretary of State for Air, pointed out that we were engaged in building a third Royal Air Force. The first was demobilized in 1919, the second from 1946 to 1947. We were now looking forward to manned bombers and fighters operating in the stratosphere, employing highly sophisticated navigation and bombing techniques and equipment. It was unwise, he emphsised, to go into expensive large-scale production of interim aircraft types which would soon be out of date.

But more serious for the RAF than even lack of new aircraft was the problem of manning in its broader sense. Lord Tedder made this the subject of his Chief of Staff's Exercise Ariel in May, 1949. "In consequence of full employment", he said in his introduction, "men of the calibre required by the RAF are equally in demand in industry and the professions. The manning problem is not just a temporary phase, the aftermath of war, but a new long term problem.

"No longer is the Serviceman a separate individual, simply airman, soldier or sailor; he is one unit of national manpower who for a period is doing his service for the country in uniform. It is in the interest both of the Nation and the Air Force that his working capacity is fully utilised throughout his life.

"Possible solutions to the problems involved can only be found with the willing co-operation of the civil community, the main branches of which will be represented during the second part of the Conference. The Service session of the Conference will therefore concentrate its thought upon how best to use and train men within the RAF and its Reserves."

In bringing the Conference to a close three days later, the Chief of the Air Staff said: "The Nation must see to it that the Services get their proper economical share of the right quality of the nation's manpower. Equally, of course, it is the Services' responsibility to see to it that we use properly the human material that we receive. It is a two-way responsibility: the community to the Services and the Services to the community. And we feel that those responsibilities cannot really effectively be discharged unless we in the Service have a much better appreciation of the manning and training problems of industry, education and the professions. On the other side, the community at large must have a closer contact with us and a better appreciation of our particular Service problems and needs."

A major obstacle to efficient use of men in the RAF in the years immediatey following the war was the imbalance between different trade groups, and the overall imbalance between 'teeth and tail'. The former was the recurring problem of popular and unpopular trades: the latter was a problem peculiar to the post-war period with its rapid reduction in the strength of front-line aircraft and the inevitable time-lag in bringing about a corresponding reduction in the administrative 'tail'. The problem of unpopular trades could only be tackled by attempting to make them more popular by raising their status; the problem of a top-heavy administration could best be tackled by the continuous process of reviewing the manpower approved for headquarters and subordinate units, and by increasing standards of administrative efficiency under the economic pressures that become greater as the memories of major wars receded.

At the same time as the RAF was rapidly reducing its size, its role was assuming ever greater importance; in 1948, on the other side of the Atlantic, Air Vice-Marshal T. M. Williams, Commandant of the RAF Staff College, emphasised this fact in addressing the American Air War College. He pointed out to his audience that the British Government had placed research and development as top priority in Service matters and the RAF first in the United Kingdom's line of defence. "We take pride of place over the Navy and Army," he said, "for the first time in our history."

But during the years 1948/49, one fact stands out head and shoulders above all others in the critical impact it had upon the defence policy of Western powers in general and of British armed forces and the Royal Air Force in particular. During the summer of 1949, scientific intelligence supported by other intelligence sources provided conclusive evidence that the Russians had exploded an atomic device. This event was all the more traumatic because American studies such as the Finletter Report 'Survival in the Air Age' and the Chief Scientific Adviser to the Air Ministry had all claimed the Russians could not catch up with British and American nuclear weapon development before 1952/53 at earliest.

The USSR had retained more than four million men under arms during the first four post-war years, while within one year of the war's end the total of British, Canadian and American forces in Europe had been reduced from over four-and-a-half million to under 900,000. The Western Allies had, therefore, counted absolutely upon their sole possession of atomic weapons to counter-balance the Russians overwhelming superiority in military manpower.

Furthermore, to counterbalance Soviet post-war expansion (started during the war with the annexation of the Baltic States and parts of Finland, Poland, Rumania and Czechoslovakia) which had resulted in Albania, Bulgaria, all Czechoslovakia and Poland, East Germany, Hungary and Rumania falling completely under Soviet domination, on March 17, 1948, Belgium, France, Holland, Luxembourg and the United Kingdom, signed the Brussels Treaty pledging mutual assistance. Defence responsibilities were assigned to the Western Union Defence Organisation (WUDO). Field Marshal the Viscount Montgomery of Alamein was appointed Chairman of a Commanders-in-Chief Committee with Headquarters at Fontainebleau, France. Air Chief Marshal Sir James Robb of Great Britain, General de-Lattre de Tassigny and Vice Admiral Janjard both of France were named as Commanders-in-Chief of Air, Land and Naval Forces, respectively, and during 1949, British fighters and ground radar equipment were being supplied to France, Belgium and Holland.

The combined resources of these five nations alone were, however, inadequate in the face of the increasing threat from Russia: thus on April 4, 1949, Denmark, Iceland, Italy, Norway, Portugal and the United States joined them in signing the North Atlantic Treaty of mutual defence. (Greece and Turkey joined the North Atlantic Treaty Organisation — NATO — in 1952 and the Federal Republic of Germany in 1955).

From the autumn of 1949 RAF thinking and planning began to change rapidly. The Air Ministry started to write operational requirements for surface-to-air beam-riding defensive missiles, air-to-air beam-riders, air-to-ground bombs guided by TV and other means: the pace and scale of effort put into technological developments hotted up in an almost belated attempt to keep pace with Russia's remarkable technological progress (assisted particularly in the field of nuclear weapons by successful espionage). The West had been caught napping and it had suddenly become apparent that Russia was not, in spite of official complacency, so far behind the USA in the development of nuclear warheads and of systems for their deliery by aircraft and long range missiles.

Crisis in the East

'If you wish for peace, prepare for war' PROVERB

Following close upon the heels of the Russian nuclear explosion in 1949 the event of greatest significance for the Royal Air Force during the next two years was the war in Korea. On June 25, 1950, North Korean forces crossed the 38th Parallel and invaded South Korea. In response to a Security Council recommendation that the United Nations should furnish assistance to repel the attack, sixteen nations, including the United States of America and the United Kingdom, came to the aid of the Republic of Korea. A unified command under the leadership of the United States was established on July 8.

The United States quickly moved forces into South Korea from Japan where 88 Squadron RAF, equipped with Sunderland flying-boats and detached from its base at Hong Kong, was exercising with British and American fleets. The squadron at once became involved and was soon joined by RAF flying-boats of 205 and 209 Squadrons from Singapore, fresh from recent operations in Malaya.

The Sunderlands were located at the ex-Japanese naval air base of Iwakuni in Japan, about 100 miles from the southern coast of Korea. Their main tasks were coastal reconnaissance and air-sea rescue. Just before Christmas, 1950, for instance, a flying-boat captained by Flight Lieutenant Hunter made two landings in the open sea to rescue twenty-three crew of a motorship which had struck a mine. The climatic contrast from the heat of Singapore to the snow storms and gales of winter which were met with on fifteen-hour patrols around the coast of Korea could not prevent the morale of aircrew reaching a high level as a result of engaging in active operations.

Meanwhile, the ebb and flow of war in Korea, combined with the greatly increased threat from Russia in Europe, were having a dramatic effect on the minds of honourably, but sometimes dangerously, peace-loving and pacifist Labour politicians in power at home. After some critical weeks during which the United Nations forces had been compressed by numerically superior communist forces into a comparatively small bridgehead around the southern part of Pusan, they had advanced almost to the Manchurian frontier. Then, in November, hordes of Chinese 'volunteers' poured over the Yalu river and by sheer weight of numbers forced the United Nations forces to withdraw to a line south of Seoul, the capital city of South Korea.

On January 29, 1951, the British Prime Minister, Clement Attlee, made a statement in the House. It was intended, he said, to expedite the British rearmament programme and to call up reservists for training. World war was not, he emphasised, inevitable, but peace could only be ensured if the defences of the free world were made sufficiently strong to deter aggression. "It is for this purpose, and for this purpose only," he said, "that the Government now think it right to take still further measures to increase the state of preparedness of the Armed Forces."

When the Korean campaign started in 1950, the RAF immediately made arrangements to increase ten-fold its annual intake of pilot trainees (from 300 to 3,000) and in addition 500 ex-RAF navigators were asked to volunteer for further service. Then, during 1951, the RAF recalled for fifteen day's training some 10,000 officers and men who were required to man the control and reporting organisation in an emergency. Similarly, officers and men of the Royal Auxiliary Air Force fighter squadrons were called up for three month's continuous training, to bring them more nearly to the operational standard of regular squadrons. In addition to the Royal Auxiliary Air Force, about 1,000 aircrew reservists of the Regular and Volunteer Reserves were recalled for three month's refresher training, and reserve flying instructors were recalled for up to eighteen months, to help with the greatly increased pilot training task.

Throughout 1951 the practice adopted by the Royal Air Force at the start of the fighting in Korea, of retaining regulars beyond the normal expiry of their service, was continued. The general purpose of all these measures was to enable additional squadrons to be formed more quickly, to improve overall efficiency and readiness of air defences, and to provide for additional training requirements.

In the field of re-equipment, the aim was to double the rate of production of combat aircraft and to introduce new types more quickly. In particular, production of the twin-jet Canberra light-bomber was increased and the first orders were placed for a four-jet bomber.

The Government White Paper on defence published in January 1951 recognised the effect of the increased production programme on the economy of the United Kingdom. This growing burden, it stated, came at a time when a further large increase in exports was already needed to meet rapidly rising bills for imports. In meeting the situation, the Government stated they had one clear aim before them; namely to refrain from mortgaging the future by running into debt abroad or reducing the investment on which the country's industrial efficiency depended. It was a task of great difficulty because the industries which had to carry most of the increased defence orders, the engineering and metal-using industries, were the very ones on which reliance had been placed to make the biggest contribution to exports and industrial equipment. It was emphasised that a sound and robust economy was an essential condition for the preservation

41

of free institutions and an essential support for military strength. In preparing the Defence programme, therefore, the Government had weighed carefully the probable effect on the social and economic standards of life in the country. Although, therefore, in terms of rising prices and shortages of consumer goods the burden was heavy, it was considered to be not more than the country could bear.

On September 26, 1951, the biggest air battle of the Korean campaign was fought over the Yalu river, between 77 Allied jet fighters (including Meteors flown by RAAF pilots) and about 120 Russian fighters. In Tokyo, Air Marshal Jones, the Australian Chief of Air Staff admitted that both the Russian MiG-15 and the American F-86 Sabre were faster than the Meteor Mk 8. Before the end of the year volunteers were called for from amongst RAF fighter pilots for attachment to USAF and RAAF squadrons in Korea, to gain modern operational experience. The response far exceeded the requirement.

The American Air Force had asked earlier for the loan of an RAF pilot experienced in night operations designed to cut the enemy's communications and interfere with his movement. Thus Wing Commander Wykeham-Barnes had been attached to the Headquarters of the Commanding General of the Fifth Air Force to plan this type of operation, also taking part in several. In summing up his experience in Korea, Wykeham-Barnes emphasized three main limitations on the effective use of air power in this 'limited' war. Firstly, the enemy, as the aggressor, had the initiative; secondly, the terrain being almost 100% mountainous was particularly ill-suited to tactical air operations in close support of troops on the ground, without sophisticated communications; thirdly (and this was the most serious limitation), since all enemy air bases were situated beyond the frontiers of Manchuria, the United Nations air forces were, for political reasons, denied the opportunity of destroying the enemy air forces on the ground.

In September 1950, RAF Transport Command flew British troops to Japan to reinforce British forces already in Korea. Two months later, Vampires were flown from 8,500 miles away in the United Kingdom to Singapore to re-equip Far East Air Force fighter squadrons, so creating a record for the longest peacetime delivery flight by any air force.

The RAF's main pre-occupation in the Far East during 1950 and 1951, however, was Operation 'Firedog' in Malaya. During the first year of this emergency, some 350 air strikes had been made against terrorist forces. RAF aircraft types involved included Tempests, Spitfires, Beaufighters, Lincolns, Sunderlands and Harvards, reinforced by Royal Navy Seafires and Fireflies. Dense jungle had made it difficult to assess the results of such strikes, and because of long delays between the time of strikes and the arrival of friendly ground forces in the target areas, the RAF had initially been largely dependent upon reports from surrendered bandits to discover the effects of their attacks.

The primitive and temporary nature of jungle dwellings in bandit camps

42

meant that material damage was often slight and easily repaired. More important were the effects upon morale of cannon fire, rocket and bomb attacks against which bandits were helpless to do anything but attempt to hide and shelter. The discovery by our ground forces of abandoned camps with documents, clothing, arms and meals in course of preparation nevertheless provided ample witness to the effectiveness of air attacks and the surprise achieved by them. Air attacks, therefore, not only destroyed the morale of bandits, causing many to surrender, but also impressed peaceful local inhabitants with the strength of forces available to maintain law and order, even in a land of jungle and mountains in which surface communications were difficult or non-existent.

As well as air strikes against terrorists the RAF also carried out continuous and large-scale supply dropping operations — mainly with Dakotas — for British troops and police patrols in the depths of the jungle, casualty evacuation by helicopters and the always important photography of large areas of which the only available maps were frequently inaccurate.

Unrest in the early 1950s was not confined to the Far East, however. In Egypt, RAF and Army bases were by now confined to the Canal zone. The radar that should have been looking for threats from further afield was in fact turned inwards against the threat from the Egyptian Air Force itself. With the local population becoming increasingly unfriendly and engaging in isolated shooting incidents and acts of sabotage, the RAF was learning rapidly how easily offensive potential can be dissipated on self protection, when airfields are located in territory, some of whose inhabitants are friendly, some indifferent and others hostile, with no certain means of distinguishing one from the other until a shot rings out from the roadside, or a hand grenade explodes in the market place.

November 1951, therefore, found Transport Command operating a shuttle service to the Canal zone via Mersa Matruh in Libya. Three thousand officers and men of the 19th Infantry Brigade, comprising units of the Highland Light Infantry, the East Surreys and the Devons, plus Royal Engineer, Royal Artillery and Royal Army Service Corps detachments and a Brigade Headquarters, were flown out in 42-seat Hastings. When the increasing threat to life and property rendered repatriation of RAF families advisable, Transport Command brought home some 586 families from the Canal Zone in 62 round trips.

Transport Command had also been required to carry out an African air lift the previous year when Lancasters of 82 (Photographic Survey) Squadron had completed photographing thousands of square miles of Nigeria, the Gold Coast and Sierra Leone, on behalf of the Colonial Office. There was further photographic work to be done in East Africa, and a flight of six Hastings carrying a normal army replacement draft flew from Wiltshire via Malta, Castel Benito and Kano to Takoradi. From there they transported 18,000 pounds of equipment and eighty-five men to 82 Squadron's new base in Bairobi, flying via Kano and Khartoum.

In Aden, on the other hand, life was comparatively tranquil. The RAF

Marine Craft Unit, for example, was going about its normal business of air-sea rescue, target towing for firing practice by squadrons from RAF Khormaksar and coast artillery batteries, and maintenance and supervision of a flying-boat alighting area. The first RAF marine craft unit had been established in Aden in 1927, but it was not until 1949, after they had gained a high reputation for wartime air-sea rescue work, that RAF marine craft crews were established as a separate branch of the Service and granted the honour of calling their high-speed launches 'His Majesty's Air Force Vessels'.

In Iraq also, relations with the Government and local armed forces were still on a friendly basis, and a squadron of the Royal Iraq Air Force — equipped with Hawker Fury fighters — completed a month's operational training with the RAF at Habbaniya.

In Europe, by far the most important event during this two year period was the development of the NATO military Command Organisation. General Eisenhower assumed his powers as Supreme Allied Commander, Europe, on April 2, 1951, and during the year, Supreme Headquarters Allied Powers Europe (SHAPE) in Paris had been built up into a fully organised military headquarters, with subordinate commands for Northern, Western and Southern Europe. RAF officers filled appointments in all these headquarters. A British Air Officer, the Air Officer Commander-in-Chief, Coastal Command, was appointed also as Allied Air Commander-in-Chief in the Eastern Atlantic.

In September 1951, the British Air Forces of Occupation in Germany were placed at the disposal of the NATO Supreme Commander. A substantial expansion was started and at the same time all units were reorganised on a fully mobile basis and the wartime title of 2nd Tactical Air Force was restored. In the same month, the British Army of the Rhine and the 2nd Tactical Air Force operated alongside Belgian, Dutch, Norwegian, Danish and American formations in a large scale tactical exercise called 'Counter Thrust'. The aims were to exercise an Army Corps in mobile operations on wide fronts, against superior enemy land and air forces, and to practise the technique of Army/Air co-operation and in particular the correct use of air reconnaissance, employing Meteor 9s for fighter-reconnaissance and Meteor 10s for high altitude photographic reconnaissance.

The increasing co-operation between European air forces had been marked in 1950 by the formation of a Western Union Examining Squadron. Based initially in Britain, its first Commanding Officer was an RAF Squadron leader, its officers were experienced flying instructors from Great Britain, Belgium, France and Holland, and each country in turn provided the Squadron Commander. Its function was to inspect, analyse and as far as possible standardise, to a uniformly high standard, the flying training methods of all four countries in the Western Union.

Because the operational efficiency of a flying Service has always depended upon its technical efficiency, the introduction of the RAF's new

Trade Structure in January 1951 was an event of profound importance. A new trade structure had become necessary for several reasons. Firstly, aircraft and ancillary equipment were becoming increasingly complex: it was neither practical nor economical any longer for one man to be trained to look after all aspects of mechanical, or all aspects of electrical maintenance: aircraft maintenance now called for a team of men and women each doing a specialised task, backed up by versatile and highly skilled individuals. Secondly, the unsettled state of the world meant that the RAF was of a greater size and employing more men and women than ever before in peacetime: in a time of full employment, it depended upon large numbers of National Service men to maintain its strength, and they had to be found employment appropriate to the limited training they received and the short period for which they were available for productive service. Finally, to build up the essential nucleus of highly skilled regular manpower, it had become necessary to increase the length of their service which, in the past, had always been limited in order to provide adequate opportunities for advancement for the younger regular recruit.

Prior to 1951, one hundred or so RAF trades had been classified into four pay groups: A, B, C and D, with Group A carrying the highest rates. Unless, however, the recruit already had the civilian skills that would permit his entry direct to a higher group he had to start at the bottom of the ladder and, after gaining skill and experience, remuster to another group, in which, because his skill was relatively less, he would again start at the bottom. In the new trade structure, however, twenty-two trade groups were established, each corresponding to some major function in the RAF. The list was as follows: aircraft engineering, radio engineering, armament engineering, electrical and instrument engineering, general engineering, motor transport, marine craft airfield construction, air traffic control and firefighting, general service, ground signalling, radar operating, safety and service, photographic, medical, dental, accounting and secretarial, supply, catering, police, music and RAF Regiment.

Each Trade Group (except Regiment) comprised a variety of jobs ranging from completely unskilled, through semi-skilled, to skilled and advanced trades; and each covered the whole range of pay. With the new structure, the recruit could choose the group in which his interest lay, or for which he appeared best fitted. Normally, he would remain in the same group for the whole of his Service career, progressing without having to overcome the hurdles of conversion and remustering.

The new structure is best explained with the aid of a diagram for a typical Trade Group (see Appendix IX). Entering normally as an Aircraftman Second Class, the recruit was remustered after recruit training as a Trade Assistant. Basic training was either 'on the job' or on a short course of basic trade training. With greater specialisation, basic training could be shorter, turning out semi-skilled men who gained promotion to skilled ranks from on the job experience. Under the old system, initial courses were sometimes too long and covered too wide a field, often more than a man could reasonably absorb on a single course. Resources were wasted in high training overheads, and wastage in training was high.

Under the new arrangements, if a fully skilled airman in about the fifth year of service decided to extend his service to ten or twelve years, or re-engage for pension, he was offered an advanced training course. Part 1 of the course consisted of training in leadership, ground combat duties, and trade subjects to the standard required of a junior NCO. Part 2 was devoted to trade training to advanced standards to turn him into an expert in his trade, or 'technician'. If the individual man turned out to be a good 'all rounder', leader as well as technician, he could progress up the 'Command Career', through the traditional non-commissioned ranks of Corporal, Sergeant and Flight Sergeant to Warrant Officer. If he was strong as a technician, but not as a leader, he could progress up the Technician ladder to new Technician ranks.

In the sphere of aircrew training, by the beginning of the 1950s, simulation of aircrew training on the ground — 'synthetic training' — was playing an increasingly important part at all flying training schools and in continuation training on squadrons. The D 4 link trainer was in general use for instrument flying training. The Crew Procedure trainer was in use for complete bomber crews — except gunners — to simulate on the ground long distance flights over enemy territory. With definite targets to bomb, the crew were fully briefed and afterwards retired to their cubicles — five in all — to complete the exercise. During the 'operation' various landmarks and targets were projected on the epidiascope screen for identification and logging. For realism, engine noise was simulated and bursts of anti-aircraft fire and search-light beams appeared on the screen.

Another simulator was in use to assist in training all-weather and night-fighter crews. It exercised both pilot and navigator in the use of Air Interception radar. The saving in training costs by the introduction of synthetic training on the ground was increasing all the time. A wartime estimate had indicated that use of some 2,000 aircrew trainers on the ground had been equivalent to the employment of a force of 4,000 aircraft flying a total of 2 million hours with a petrol consumption of 250 million gallons!

In the General Election campaign leading up to polling day in February 1950, neither the Labour Government nor the Conservative Opposition had much to say on the subject of the Royal Air Force. Some opposition spokesmen emphasised the importance of the Royal Auxiliary Air Force and stated that a Conservative Government would make it a matter of first priority to induce more men and women to join. Opposition spokesmen also considered that the nation was not getting value for money spent on the RAF, largely because the National Service period of call up was too short both for the training of pilots and for the training of high-grade technicians. To secure more regulars, the Conservatives considered that pay and living conditions for all ranks must compare favourably with those offered in civil life. The Labour Government, however, limited themselves to saying that they wanted to see the RAF given the best aircraft and kept at a high level of efficiency.

On March 8, 1950, the last of the Lancasters left Bomber Command. Seldom had there been an aircraft employed in so many different roles: from massive saturation raids to precision attacks such as that which sank the *Tirpitz*, and low level raids such as that which burst the Mohne Dam. It had supplied the underground armies of Europe, provided close support for allied ground forces, hunted down submarines and, in the final months of the war, fed starving Holland. Originally designed to carry a maximum size bomb of the 4,000lb type, the Lancaster was eventually developed to carry the 22,000lb 'Grand Slam'.

What then of other less famous aircraft entering service or still in service in 1950 and 1951? The Percival Prentice was already well established as the RAF's standard basic trainer and Harvards were still in use for advanced training. In addition, deliveries of the de Havilland Chipmunk trainer to units of the RAFVR had started early in 1950. Its introduction was greeted with enthusiasm by Reserve pilots. The allocation to the RAF by the USAF of seventy Boeing B-29 bombers, on the other hand, had been greeted with rather less enthusiasm by engineer staffs in Bomber Command. Known by the RAF as the 'Washington'. the B-29 was a large and complicated aircraft by comparison with the Lincoln and Lancaster, and every detail of equipment, in addition to the airframe, engines and services, were new to RAF groundcrews. Aircrew, however welcomed the capability of the Washington to strike more heavily at longer range. They also welcomed their first pressurised bomber with up to a 10,000-foot increase in operating altitude. It would be a good lead-in to the British four-engined jet bombers now under construction. Moreover, the generous provision of these aircraft by America under the Atlantic Pact mutual arms aid agreement signed in Washington on January 27, 1950, removed the problem of payment — in dollars!

The total bomb-load of the Washington was 20,000 lb. Its maximum speed was 350 miles per hour at 24,500 feet and it had a range of up to 2,850 miles. The insulation of pressure cabins also afforded protection against cold (and engine noise) thus introducing a new standard of comfort for pilot, co-pilot, navigator, bomb-aimer, flight engineer and radio operator. The four air gunners' fire-control section was also pressurised, as was the adjacent crews' rest area.

By November 1951, the pilots and navigators of 101 Bomber Squadron had converted to the twin-jet Canberra, which had nearly doubled its predecessor's performance in terms both of speed and service ceiling, but as the Canberra B.1 was designed for a crew of three — pilot, navigator/plotter and navigator/bomb aimer — the squadron had had to say goodbye to all its signallers, flight engineers and air gunners. The functions of the two navigators were to some extent interchangeable but the primary duty of the navigator/plotter was to navigate the aircraft from base to the target area, where the navigator/bomb-aimer would move up to the bomb sight in the nose and identify the target with the help of radar.

Various Marks of Meteor and Vampire aircraft were now equipping most of the regular fighter squadrons, while Spitfires were still doing good service in Auxiliary fighter squadrons. There were two-seat trainer and night fighter variants of the DH Vampire, as well as ground attack versions. The Gloster aircraft company had also produced a tactical ground-attack version of the Meteor Mk 8.

In September 1951, no less an authority than the air correspondent of the New York Herald Tribune, reported that, at the Society of British Aircraft Constructors display at Farnborough: "The cold facts are that England demonstrated the finest jet fighter and jet bomber operating in the world today." He was referring to the Hawker P.1067, powered by a Rolls-Royce Avon engine and demonstrated with shattering effect by Squadron Leader Neville Duke, Chief Test Pilot, Hawker Aircraft Limited, and to the four-jet engined Valiant bomber. On its introduction to RAF squadron service, the P.1067 was re-designated the Hawker Hunter; the Vickers Valiant was the first of the V-bombers to enter squadron service, in 1952.

In Coastal Command, the Avro Shackleton General Reconnaissance aircraft with a crew of ten (and powered by four Rolls-Royce Griffon engines and de Havilland contra-rotating airscrews) started to replace the Lancasters in 1950. In 1951, Coastal Command was further reinforced with Lockheed P-2V Neptunes which, at that time, held the world long-distance record of 11,236 miles.

Amongst other events of 1950-51 which must be touched upon in passing, there was the re-organisation of the Air Ministry Air Staff under the new Chief of Air Staff, Air Chief Marshal Sir John Slessor, into two main groups under a Vice-Chief of Air Staff and a Deputy Chief of Air Staff. The Vice-Chief, Air Chief Marshal the Hon. Sir Ralph Cochrane, was to be mainly concerned with questions affecting the strength and fighting efficiency of the RAF, while the DCAS, Air Marshal Sir Arthur Sanders, would be chiefly occupied with inter-Service and international policy and planning, including co-operation with NATO and Commonwealth air forces. In this way it was hoped to deal efficiently with the extra workload arising from RAF involvement with other NATO and Western Union air forces.

In April 1950, the Royal Observer Corps had celebrated its 25th anniversary, and His Majesty the King had consented to become its Air Commander-in-Chief. On May 26, 1951, the first Royal Colour ever to be presented to the Royal Air Force was presented by Princess Elizabeth on behalf of the King, at a parade in Hyde Park. In the course of her speech the Princess said: "Your duties at all times call for high qualities of endurance and skill, to which must be added the dash and zest of youth. The courage and determination which have marked your achievement in war have been matched, in their quiet heroism, by many years of daring and enterprise that your service has been called upon to perform in peace."

Three days later, in the early hours of the morning, a Wellington aircraft crashed and burst into flames about three miles from RAF Station, Hullavington. Leading Aircraftman Jarrett was in charge of the crash crew that night and was first on the scene of the accident. Showing complete disregard for his own safety, he extricated one member of the crew from the burning aircraft entirely unassisted. Returning again to the aircraft, he attempted the rescue of a second member. His gallantry, devotion to duty and exceptional courage earned him the award of the George Medal.

On Saturday, September 16, 1951, the eleventh Anniversary of the Battle of Britain was marked by the opening of sixty-six RAF stations throughout the United Kingdom to the general public. On the Sunday, there was a thanksgiving service in Westminster Abbey. The Prime Minister and Mrs Attlee and many members of the Air Council, Army Council and Anti-Aircraft Command were present. Following the procession of church dignataries, the RAF Ensign was carried in, a shaft of sunlight spotlighting the colour party as they passed through the Screen into the Sanctuary. Here, as the Ensign was draped over the High Altar — a patch of blue in a surround of gold — the strident notes of a trumpet fanfare rang out. The anthem was adapted from the words of John Milton:

Nothing is here for tears, nothing to wail,
Nothing but well and fair,
And what may quiet us in a death so noble ......
Thither shall all the valiant youth resort,
And from his memory inflame their breasts,
To matchless valour and adventures high.

Counting the Cost

'He that counts all costs will never put plough in the earth' PROVERB

The accelerated defence measures put in hand by a Labour Government as a result of both cold war pressures in Europe and a shooting war in Korea, meant that, when a Conservative Government returned to power in the Autumn of 1951 (with Winston Churchill as Prime Minister and Secretary of State for Defence) they found themselves faced by a likely expenditure of £4,700 million on a greatly expanded rearmament programme covering a three-year period.

Lord De L'Isle and Dudley, VC, was the new Secretary of State for Air, and as far as the Royal Air Force was concerned the object was to increase the front line in all theatres and in particular to expand the forces placed under the Supreme Allied Commander, Europe; to provide more modern aircraft; and to overhaul the defence radar network of the United Kingdom.

The threat was considered to fall broadly into two parts, though these overlapped. First there were the United Kingdom's traditional and long-standing overseas obligations linked with the post-war requirement of resisting communist overt and covert political and military pressures; and secondly there were the preparations that had to be made, together with allies and Commonwealth partners, against the risk that communist policy, whether by accident or design, might result in a major shooting war. In the first part fell all the forces which the United Kingdom maintained overseas and in particular the British contribution to the United Nations Forces in Korea and the campaign against organised banditry in Malaya.

It was the threat of major war, however, that had stimulated the RAF's expansion and re-equipment, and the building up of reserves of men and material for all three Services. These preparations had put the British Services into a better position to fight if world war came; but they also acted as a powerful deterrent both to open war and, by strengthening the confidence of the free world, to an extension of the Cold War whether by the technique of vicarious aggression, as in Korea, or by subversion from within, as in Malaya.

"Only if we are strong", the 1953 Statement on Defence said, "can we achieve our supreme object of preventing a Third World War. If the risk of war has receded in past months, this is the direct result of the growing power of the Western nations; but there is still much to do before the strength is sufficient, and the effort must continue."

In mid-July 1952, the Chief of the Air Staff, Marshal of the RAF Sir John Slessor, was making a timely pronouncement to coincide with a great NATO gathering in Brussels, culminating in a spectacular air display. "The RAF", he said, "has three main functions in the North Atlantic Treaty Organisation: it has to make its contribution to the integrated Allied Air Force under the Supreme Allied Commander Europe (SACEUR); to play its part in the protection of the Allied sea lanes of communication under the Supreme Allied Commander Atlantic (SACLANT) and to defend the United Kingdom, which is not only the British homeland but a vitally important Allied base in war.

"The primary object and interest of the Free World is to prevent a hot war. As part of that we have to win the cold war, to stabilise the anti-communist front in the countries this side of the Iron Curtain in Europe and Asia, to build up confidence among the free peoples, to thwart the familiar tactics of infiltration, encroachment and subversive action and, ultimately, we hope, to extend the frontiers of the free world.

"The supreme deterrent to active aggression, and the instrument under whose cover we are building up our strength and holding the line in the cold war, is atomic air power. The RAF can never hope to equal the United States' strength in that sphere. But the medium range bomber force is even now playing its small part and will do so to an increasing extent as the new four-engined jet bombers — the best in the world — come into the line."

As further proof of the important part then played by the RAF within Allied Air Forces Central Europe, Air Chief Marshal Sir Basil Embry took over this NATO Command from General Lauris Norstad USAF at Fontainebleau on July 16, 1953. Within his Command were two Allied Tactical Air Forces formed the previous year, the 2nd and 4th ATAF. The former, commanded by Air Marshal Sir Robert Foster, comprised the British 2nd Tactical Air Force, together with Dutch and Belgian squadrons.

It had been planned that defence production would rise at the peak of the expansion programme to more than four times the pre-Korean level, but the economic position had seriously deteriorated and it became necessary to adjust the defence programme so that it would take more than three years to achieve. The aircraft programme in particular, which included several new production lines for jet engines, required the building up of a large labour force. Before the programme started about 150,000 people were employed in the aircraft industry, but by March 1953 this number had increased to some 200,000.

By this time good progress was being made in the development of the new breed of four-jet engined medium bombers, soon to comprise the RAF V-bomber force. The Vickers Valiant BK1 (with four Rolls-Royce Avon 204 single-shaft turbojets) was due in squadron service by 1955; the Avro Vulcan, which would be the first operational delta wing bomber had been ordered in quantity, and a prototype of the Handley Page Victor was already flying. In view of this good progress in the heavier bomber field, some cut-back was possible in the Canberra light bomber re-equipment programme.

In the fighter world, the Gloster Javelin two-seat all-weather fighter, also of delta wing design and powered by two Bristol Siddeley Sapphire 203/204 single-shaft turbo jets, was undergoing pre-acceptance tests. Among other intercepter fighters, the Vickers Supermarine Swift single-seat day fighter had been joined by the single-seat Hawker Hunter. Meanwhile, the delivery of American F-86 (Sabre) jet fighters, adaptable for the ground-attack as well as the interceptor role, continued throughout 1953. Canada was producing and paying for the airframes, and the engines and equipment were supplied by the United States under the Mutual Security Programme.

During 1952 substantial progress had been made with the Rolls-Royce Conway by-pass engine which provided increased power by 'by-passing' additional air through the compressors direct into the jet efflux.

In the 2nd Tactical Air Force in Germany, the higher performance Venom fighter-bomber (Mark 1) was replacing the Vampire, while in Coastal Command, the twin turbo-propeller-engined Lockheed Neptune anti-submarine and maritime reconnaissance aircraft had joined forces with the Shackleton Marks 1 and 2. Operational flying of the Neptune required a crew of nine consisting of two pilots, a navigator-plotter and navigator-radar, flight engineer, signallers and gunners. Its armament included bombs, depth charges, rockets, two 20mm gun turrets and one 5 inch turret. In 1952, it was the only Coastal Command aircraft fitted with the airborne searchlight, originally developed by the Command. This, combined with improved radar, was a considerable advance on the war-time Coastal Command equipment. In the same year, the first British designed helicopter to enter RAF service, the Westland Sycamore, was delivered to Coastal Command at RAF St Mawgan in Cornwall.

Building up strength was not only a question of new equipment; there was also the problem of adequate manpower. Regular recruiting on long-term non-commissioned engagements in 1952 had been disappointing. The three-year short term engagement introduced by the RAF in 1950, however, had produced good results. It involved three years with the Colours followed by a period of reserve service. But short-term engagements were only genuinely fruitful if a reasonable proportion of initially short-term recruits extended their service and re-engaged, and insufficient men showed signs of doing this. It was nevertheless fair to say that the attractions of the new trade structure and the pay increases of September 1950 had resulted in many more joining the RAF in the period 1951 to 1953 than in the three preceding years.

Following the Chief of the Air Staff's Conference 'Ariel' in 1948 to examine the problems of RAF manpower in the post-war world, it had become more widely appreciated that the attitude of the community

52

towards service in the Forces and towards the employment of their members when they returned to civilian life, was a most important factor affecting recruiting. The Air Member for Personnel had, therefore, been made a member of the Advisory Council on the relationship between employment in the Services and civilian life to help ensure that the attitude was favourable. Although members of the RAF must be young and fit enough for flying and fighting and moving around the world, the Air Force was now offering the prospect of a career to age fifty-five for all non-commissioned men who had satisfactorily completed their initial four years service. Similarly, for officers there was a wide and increasing range of staff and administrative duties for which their experience would be valuable after it ceased to be practical to employ them on full flying duties.

One of the most important innovations in the career field in 1952 was the introduction of 'Branch' commissions. This was an ambiguous title given to a scheme whereby Warrant Officers and Chief Technicians of the main Ground Branches could be selected for permanent commissions as 'Branch' officers. The idea was that they would specialise in work appropriate to their previous trade qualifications and for which their long practical experience 'on the shop floor' would be invaluable. By 1970, there were in the Engineer Branch alone over 900 'Branch' officers who had learnt the job the hard way and who, with years of practical experience behind them, could give a tip or two to young engineer graduates fresh from university. Ultimately, nearly one third of the strength of the Engineer Branch came from this source, and the RAF could not have done without them!

Before the end of 1953, a new flying training pattern had been introduced. The object, as described by Air Vice-Marshal T. N. McEvoy, at this time Assistant Chief of Air Staff (Training), was to have a sequence of training like a flight of stairs that has as few steps as possible — every step of equal height. One of the reasons for change was the increasing number of jet-propelled aircraft now in RAF service. It had become undesirable for pupils to fly piston-engined training aircraft for so long that they formed 'piston' habits to which they might revert in emergency when flying jets. Jets, it had been found, were not necessarily more difficult to fly, in fact generally they were easier, but they were different and called for different techniques.

The new training aircraft now becoming available were the piston-engined Provost and two jet-engined aircraft — the Vampire T.11 and the Canberra T.4. The Provost had been built to an Air Ministry specification as a replacement for the Prentice for basic flying training. It had initially been intended that the Boulton Paul Balliol should replace the Harvard for the applied stage of flying training. Production of the Balliol had, however, been long delayed. Before its delivery began, the dual control Vampire was produced and it became clear from trials of the Provost and the Vampire that between them they shared so many of the Balliol's advantages that the latter would be unnecessary as an

53

intermediate step. More important still, elimination of the Balliol would enable the pupil pilot to get onto jets earlier by closing the gap.

From 1953 onwards, therefore, basic flying training was carried out on the Provost, Advanced flying training on the Vampire T.11 and from the Advanced Flying Training Schools, pilots destined for jet squadrons went direct to Operational Conversion Units on Hunters, Swifts, Javelins and Canberras, thus cutting out a third stage of training that had been done on Meteors. It was still necessary to have a piston-engined Advanced Flying School (equipped with the twin Bristol Hercules-engined Vickers Varsity) for pilots destined for squadrons equipped with piston-engined aircraft such as the Shackleton and Hastings.

As a striking example of the constant need for thinking and planning ahead in a fast developing technological Service, at the same time as one new flying training pattern was being introduced, the next step was already being seriously considered. Thought was already being given in 1953 to doing away altogether with initial training on piston-engined aircraft, in an increasingly jet equipped Air Force.

Another noteworthy feature of RAF flying training at this particular post-war period was the help received from the Royal Canadian Air Force. During 1952 there were nearly 800 RAF pilots and navigators undergoing flying training in Canada. During the war, under the British Commonwealth air training scheme, Canada had trained about 131,000 aircrew and now, as a result of the RAF's expansion at the time of the Korean war, she had again become a vast aircrew nursery with training schools in Ontario, Manitoba, Alberta and British Columbia. One problem resulted from training in the usually excellent visibility of Canada, with the Rockies often visible from up to 100 miles away; on return to the smoke and mists of the British Isles and the multiplicity of landmarks in a densely populated island, acclimatisation courses proved necessary to help Canadian trained pilots and navigators to adjust to the different weather in general and to the poor visibility in particular.

Moving on from training to some of the operational activities of this period we find a forced landing on the Greenland ice-cap, 8,000 ft above sea level some 700 miles from the North Pole; more pilots being posted for duty with American and Australian squadrons in Korea; RAF participation (on October 3, 1951) in the first British atom bomb test in the Monte Bello Islands in the Indian ocean; while in Malaya operations against terrorists continued.

The four-engined Hastings of Transport Command that forced landed on the Greenland ice-cap was engaged in dropping supplies to the British North Greenland expedition. In addition to the seven-man RAF crew, there were four British Army men and a USAF officer on board. Fortunately they landed on the ice only a mile from the expedition's winter quarters. The expedition team quickly moved its camp over to the aircraft whose fuselage was not badly damaged, and the twelve stranded Hastings men had the advantage of moral support and practical survival advice from men experienced in arctic living conditions. It was decided to break with normal arctic and survival principles and live *inside* the aircraft. Despite intense cold and freezing wind they survived, aided by supplies air-dropped to them and by insulating the inside of the aircraft with layers of parachute; after a few days they were flown out by USAF rescue aircraft.

The object of sending more RAF pilots to Korea was to create a nucleus of RAF fighter pilots with first-hand combat experience against Russian jet fighter aircraft in use by communist forces. Volunteers were called for and selected from Fighter Command and 2nd Tactical Air Force in Germany. Those from Fighter Command converted to F-86 Sabres in the United States before joining USAF fighter squadrons. Some from 2nd Tactical Air Force went direct to 77 (Meteor 8) Squadron RAAF, now allocated to the ground-attack role, and others went to USAF F-84 Thunderjet squadrons, also in the ground-attack role.

One of the RAF fighter pilots in Korea at the time was Squadron Leader Graham Hulse, DFC. Attached to the USAF 4th Fighter Interceptor Wing he was interviewed by a reporter from *Flight* magazine in early 1953. At that time there stood to his credit one-and-a-half MiGs destroyed and one damaged. The destroyed aircraft had been one of a pair spotted by Hulse when he was flying, as escort for a photographic reconnaissance aircraft, at 30,000 feet. "They were just across the Yalu at about 5,000 feet", he said, "so I dived after them and shot one down." The MiG had attempted to out-climb him, but the Sabre's impetus after the dive had enabled him to stay within range and fire three bursts of machine gun fire into its fuselage and wings. The canopy had flown off and the pilot ejected at 8,000 feet, leaving the MiG to crash on a sand bank just off the Korean coast. The half MiG claimed by Hulse was finished off by him after it had first been damaged by the American leader of a Sabre flight. The one he claimed as only damaged he intercepted at 40,000 feet. "I nipped in behind him at mach 0.96 and hit him three times before he got out of range." Later in the same month, Hulse shared with another American colleague credit for downing yet another enemy aircraft.

The joint RAF/Army Air Observation Post and Light Liaison Flights (Nos 1093 and 1913) were also earning a splendid reputation in Korea for their service to the Commonwealth Division and to the American Army, in difficult and dangerous circumstances. Their aircraft — Austers plus one Cessna L-19 borrowed from the Americans for VIP flying — were flown by Army pilots and serviced by a mixture of Army and RAF men. These Flights were doing much of the work that pre-war would have been done by RAF Army Co-operation squadrons in Hawker Audax or Westland Lysander aircraft: short-range visual reconnaissance, communication flying and helping artillery fire onto targets of opportunity. Over enemy territory, Austers usually flew above the range of small arms fire, but very much within the range of 20 and 37mm fire, so pilots acquired the habit of flying with one ear outside their radio head-sets to be able to hear when they were under fire and take evasive action.

On July 27, 1953, an armistice was signed in Korea between the United Nations Commander and the Commanders of the North Korean and Chinese People's Volunteer forces. Thus the biggest local war since the end of the Second World War had ended in an uneasy peace.

In Malaya the long drawn out conflict with communist dominated terrorists continued to occupy most of the effort of the Far East Air Force. In October 1953, the largest leaflet dropping operation since VJ-day had taken place. RAF and RAAF Lincolns assisted by DH Hornets had dropped 20 million leaflets in 200 target areas in the Federation. They were addressed mainly to communist junior leaders who, it was believed, had been responsible for surrenders since bandits began to give themselves up in groups rather than singly. Simultaneously, the 500 dollar reward paid to civilians who safely handed over surrendered terrorists was extended to junior communist commanders who did the same.

Fighter operations in Malaya during 1953 were made more comfortable for Vampire pilots as a result of the replacement during the previous year of the Vampire 5 by the Mark 9 fitted with a refrigerator unit to alleviate cockpit over-heating in tropical temperatures. The replacement had involved an 8,618 mile ferry operation from England to Singapore, staging through sixteen airfields:— Dijon, Istres (Marseilles), Tunis, Castel Benito (Tripoli), El Adem (Libya), Fayid (Egypt), Habbaniya (Iraq), Sharjah (Trucial Oman), Mauripur (Karachi), Jodhpur, Palam (Delhi), Dum Dum (Calcutta), Mingaladon (Rangoon), Bangkok, Butterworth (Malaya) and so finally to Seletar (Singapore). (By 1970, the majority of these airfields were no longer available, for political reasons, for RAF reinforcement of the Far East. Fortunately, in the intervening years, Air Staff plans had allowed for this situation arising by provision of tanker aircraft, and re-fuelling in flight had become standard reinforcement procedure for all fighter squadrons.)

Shortly before the end of 1952, the six-year photographic task of 82 Squadron in Africa was finished. This brought to an end one of the biggest air mapping programmes ever attempted in peacetime. Avro Lancasters had been converted for photography and two Dakotas had been used for passenger and freight carrying and supply dropping to parties manning remote radar-beacon sites required for accurate navigation. From the photographic survey topographical maps were made for colonial development schemes such as planning a rail link between East and Central Africa, irrigation projects in Basutoland, hydro-electric schemes in Rhodesia and West Africa, and for plotting international boundaries and planning agricultural and mineral developments in other parts of the continent.

With one highly constructive task in Africa thus successfully completed, the RAF was next faced with another more frustrating. Seven Lincolns of 49 Squadron, commanded by Squadron Leader A. Newitt, were employed in Kenya in an attempt to flush out members of Mau Mau gangs taking refuge in the Aberdare forests. With lack of clearly identifiable land marks

56

in vast areas of jungle, targets proved difficult to find and means used to establish the precise whereabouts of Mau Mau headquarters often alerted the gangs in time for them to move off before being attacked. More successful in some respects were the RAF Harvards detached from training schools in Rhodesia and operating from an improvised airstrip 8,000 feet up in the Kenya mountains. Each aircraft was fitted with a machine gun and racks for eight 19lb bombs, and helped by reconnaissance reports from Piper Cubs working closely with local security forces they were able to react to 'hot' information far more quickly than the bombers. But perhaps the bomber operations also had their long term psychological effect, for years after, when Kenya had gained independence, a young Kenyan boy wrote to the Air Ministry saying he had been much impressed by RAF bombing in the jungle which had succeeded in killing several of his relatives who had been with Mau Mau and he had, therefore, developed a burning desire to join the RAF and learn to fly!

In the United Kingdom, the first two RAF bomber squadrons to be equipped with jet-engined aircraft — English Electric Canberra B.2s — were 617 ('Dambusters') and 101 Squadrons based at Binbrook in Lincolnshire. Introduction of the Canberra into RAF service marked the start of a Bomber Command expansion which was not merely a re-equipment programme. Selected crews from Lincoln and Washington (B-29) squadrons were converted onto Canberras to form new squadrons, while the piston-engined bombers remained in service until replaced by Valiants. Probably the most important characteristic of the Canberra when first in service was its ability to cruise fast at heights from 45,000 to 50,000 feet. At these heights the Canberra retained an exceptional standard of manoeuvrability by virtue of its low wing loading, whereas most contemporary fighters would have suffered from compressibility stall.

In February 1952, there came the end of an era when a composite detachment of 350 officers and men, drawn from all RAF Commands at home, the RAF Regiment and the Royal Auxiliary Air Force, led the funeral procession of His Late Majesty King George VI from Westminster Hall to Paddington Station. The contingent was headed by the RAF Central Band. Marshals of the RAF Lord Newall, Viscount Portal of Hungerford, Lord Tedder and Lord Douglas of Kirtleside were present, and the Air Council was represented by Air Chief Marshals Sir William F. Dickson and Sir Arthur P. M. Sanders.

In the field of recruitment, there were two small but particularly important innovations during these two years. First, in 1952, a scheme was introduced to enable boys of sixteen to undergo medical and aptitude tests, to ascertain in good time whether they were likely to be acceptable for aircrew training when old enough and educationally qualified. Known as pre-assessment tests, they provided the means by which a boy could ensure that he was not misdirecting his efforts in aiming at a flying career. Second, in 1953, the Secretary of State for Air announced in the House of Lords the introduction of an RAF Scholarship Scheme. Any boy interested in a cadetship at Cranwell, leading to a career in the RAF flying branch, could apply for one of sixty scholarship awards. If selected, the RAF would contribute towards tuition fees at his own school during the two years required to complete an A-level GCE course and so qualify educationally for a Cranwell Cadetship.

The other main events of interest in the years 1952 and 1953 were the formation of the first RAF helicopter squadron, No 194, primarily for casualty evacuation duties in Malaya; the London-New Zealand air race from October 8 to 10, 1953, won by a RAF Canberra flown by Flight Lieutenant R. L. E. Burton with Flight Lieutenant D. H. Gannon as navigator, who covered 12,270 miles in 23 hours 50 minutes 42 seconds; and the Coronation Review of the RAF by the Queen at Odiham on July 15, 1953, when the fly past, under the control of Air Vice-Marshal the Earl of Bandon, included 640 aircraft, of which 440 were jet propelled.

The two events which cast the longest shadows over the future were RAF participation in the first British A-bomb test in the Monte Bello Islands in the Indian Ocean off West Australia in October 1952; and detonation by the Americans of a thermonuclear weapon, the first hydrogen bomb, at Eniwetok Atoll in the Pacific in November 1952. Following these traumatic events, a speech in October 1953 by Lord Tedder on preventing war was all the more significant. "Despite all the hopes which buoyed people up during the trials and horors of the late war," he said, "the world has been forced to the bitter conclusion that the law of the jungle still prevails; that security without strength is a mirage and that, in fact, weakness invites and indeed provokes aggression.

"National strength is not solely in military affairs; it is a complex of moral, political, economic and military factors, and weakness in any one might be fatal in the whole. It can not be said too often, or emphasised too strongly, that the military strength which the free world has felt it necessary to build up has one prime objective — to prevent another war. It is questionable whether the two world wars, or indeed the Korean war, would ever have happened had it not been for both political and military weakness which misled the aggressor into thinking he could get away with it. Our object is to secure peace not by winning, but by *preventing* another war.

"During the last conflict it was the war in the air," Lord Tedder emphasised, "unforeseen by many and still not understood by some — which was largely responsible for altering the shape of the war, it became one of areas and it might well be that if there were a war in the future it would be one of continents." Lord Tedder went on to identify the possible aggressor as Soviet Russia and emphasised that the history of Napoleon and Hitler should be sufficient to illustrate the folly of attempting land invasion of those vast areas. "Only from the air is Russia open to attack. There is still a tendency in this country to regard the war at sea, on land and in the air as separate problems. People forget or ignore the force which in the last war proved to be the one common factor, and did, in fact, unify operations in the three dimensions — the bomber force.

"It is forgotten or not known that the bombers played a vital part in limiting the production of submarines, that the waters around Denmark were littered with German shipping sunk by bombers' mines. The end of the *Tirpitz* is forgotten. It is forgotten it was the bombers which were mainly responsible for strangling Rommel's supplies; that the bombers knocked the Luftwaffe out of Sicily and made the entry into Southern Europe possible; that the bombers strangled the communications in Northern Europe, hamstrung the German transport and grounded the Luftwaffe through lack of fuel, making 'Operation Overlord' possible. It is forgotten or not realised that, after the first round of the Battle of Britain had been so gallantly fought by day and night fighters, it was the bombers that pushed the air war away from British skies to be fought out and won over Berlin. It is forgotten that the bombers had delayed the V1 and V2 attacks for vital months and reduced them to an unpleasant nuisance. The bombers were the only antidote to the V2."

Lord Tedder said he emphasised all this about the bomber — the offensive component of defence — because he felt it was absolutely essential to remember that purely passive defence with no offensive element was in fact, no defence at all. In 1944 the Germans were producing more defensive fighters per month than the total British and American production, but they were, in fact, losing the air war and consequently the whole war.

Lord Tedder then spoke of new developments in aircraft and weapons, but concluded that all the indications were that in the immediate future it would be more true than ever that the bomber, and therefore the bomb, would get through. This introduced the subject of the atomic weapon.

"There are very sincere people", he said, "who would ban its manufacture or use." He believed the armoured knights of old wanted to ban the use of gun powder. He could understand the Russians proposing that the atomic weapon should be banned, since it was the *only* effective counterweight which the Western powers could wield as a deterrent. "There are few people in this country," he continued, "who have more than the vaguest idea as to the fearful potentialities of the atomic weapons now in sight. The development of the atomic weapon has brought the world face to face at last with the ultimate realities of war. I am convinced that this country has a vital part to play in the scientific, technical and political field of the atomic world. If we play our part we can show an example of courage and determination, patience and faith, which will help to inspire the world and give *time* for the fundamental human rights of free speech and thought to spread over the whole world — time for truth to prevail. On this issue I agree with Cromwell: 'Let us trust in God and keep our powder dry'."

On October 18, 1953, there gathered on Coopers Hill, overlooking the mist-veiled meadows of Runnymede, some 25,000 relatives and friends of the 20,500 airmen who gave their lives in the 1939-45 war and had no known grave, for the unveiling by the Queen of their memorial. "It is very fitting," said Her Majesty, "that those who rest in nameless graves should be remembered in this place, for it was in these fields of Runnymede seven centuries ago that our forefathers first planted a seed of liberty, which helped to spread across the earth the conviction that man should be free and not enslaved. With prophetic foresight," the Queen concluded, "Pope wrote of this hill on which we now stand: 'On Coopers Hill eternal wreaths shall grow, while last the mountain, or while the Thames shall flow'." It is a splendid site for such a memorial, and for those who have the time and the memory, it is possible to stand there awhile and to this day still hear all the great company of aircraft in which so many of their crews, to use Stephen Spender's words, 'travelled a short while towards the sun and left the vivid air signed with their honour.'

A Message of Hope

'Hope it is which makes the shipwrecked sailor strike out with his arms in the midst of the sea, even though on all sides he can see no land'   OVID

Overshadowing all else in 1954 was the emergence of the thermonuclear bomb. It was in this year that official information was first released by the United States Government on the experimental explosion of a weapon at Eniwetok (in November 1952) several hundred times more powerful than the atomic bombs dropped on Hiroshima and Nagasaki in 1945. On March 1, 1954, an even more powerful thermonuclear weapon was exploded in the Marshall Islands. It was stated at the time that there were no technical or scientific limitations on the production of nuclear weapons still more devastating.

The United States Government announced that they were proceeding with full-scale production of thermonuclear weapons. The Soviet Government was clearly following the same policy, though it was not known at that time how soon they might have such weapons ready for operational use. The United Kingdom also had the ability to produce such weapons and after fully considering all the implications the Government decided it was their duty to proceed with their development and production. "To fail to maintain our defence effort up to the limit of our strength," Sir Winston Churchill said, "would be to paralyse every beneficial tendency towards peace, both in Europe and Asia."

Delivery of atomic weapons to the Royal Air Force had already begun, and in January 1955, the first RAF aircraft capable of carrying them, the Vickers Valiant, was introduced into service with 138 Squadron at RAF Gaydon. If such weapons were ever used in war, it was recognised that they would cause destruction, both human and material, on an unprescedented scale. It would result in a struggle for survival the catastrophic results of which were impossible to foresee with any degree of accuracy. The Government considered it essential that such facts should be known not only to citizens of the United Kingdom, but to all the world. All should realise the magnitude of the disaster nuclear war would bring. Such understanding would, it was hoped, bring home to people and Governments everywhere the consequences of war and generate a compelling will for peace strong enough to influence the most dictatorial rulers. This was considered to be the first implication of the nuclear weapon. It was one not of despair but of hope.

In 1955, the free world had a marked superiority both in the nuclear weapon itself and in the means for delivering it. In the view of the Government, so powerful a deterrent had significantly reduced the risk of major war, but the bulk of the deterrent force at this time was provided by the United States Air Force Strategic Air Command. It was therefore agreed that the United Kingdom must contribute more to the deterrent, and thus to its own defence, by building up a stock of nuclear weapons of all types and by increasing the capability of the RAF to deliver them. If, despite the deterrent, it should ever come to global war, it was recognised that in the critical initial stage the primary role would fall to the RAF. With this fact in mind, the allocation of funds to the Air Ministry was increased, both to build up the strategic bomber force and to provide a modernised United Kingdom defence system including an improved control and reporting capability, all-weather radar equipped fighters and air-to-air and ground-to-air guided weapons. In pursuance of this policy, the first British swept-wing fighter, the Swift, entered service with 56 Squadron in February 1954, and the Hunter entered service with 43 Squadron at Leuchars in July of that year. By the end of 1954 delivery of F-86 Sabres was virtually complete and the air-to-air guided weapon with which it was planned to equip new fighters was expected to increase their lethality by as much as four times.

The United Kingdom air defence exercise 'Dividend' in 1954 had shown beyond any possible doubt that UK air defence and NATO air defence were henceforth indivisible. The NATO early warning system in Europe had made it possible to scramble UK fighters in time to intercept 'enemy' bombers up to 100 miles from the English coast. From 1955 onwards, therefore, the air defence of the NATO area was closely co-ordinated between the Southern Region which included Turkey, Greece and Italy, the Central Region which included Germany, Holland, Belgium, Luxembourg and France, the Northern Region which included Norway and Denmark and the United Kingdom.

Regarding the threat on the ground, it was known in 1955 that the Soviet Union and her Eastern European satellites had some six million men under arms backed by enormous reserves. On the German front the Soviet Army could be increased to well over 100 divisions within thirty days. Over the whole field of deployment East and West the Soviet and satellite land forces could be raised to the level of 400 divisions. Even allowing for the essential West German contribution the free world could not put into the frontline anything comparable in conventional forces. The threat of nuclear weapons was, therefore, the only means by which this massive preponderance could be countered. If full use could not be made of the nuclear weapon as a last resort, Europe could not be protected from invasion and occupation. NATO plans at that time therefore assumed the use of nuclear weapons against major aggression. Hesitation to use all the means of defence at NATO's disposal would not, it was considered, reduce the risk. All history proved the contrary.

In support of NATO's front in Europe, therefore, it was decided to increase the fighting capacity of the RAF's 2nd Tactical Air Force in Germany. In exercise 'Battle Royal' in the Autumn of 1954, 2nd TAF was given the opportunity of testing its operational efficiency in realistic conditions and its reconnaissance capability in particular. RAF Meteor Mark 9 fighter reconnaissance and Mark 10 photographic reconnaissance aircraft, with Canberra PR9s for high altitude photography over longer ranges, operated at full stretch alongside Dutch and Belgian Thunderjets. "We must know", the Commander-in-Chief said "where the enemy is before we can hit him." Although reasonably successful in finding and reporting targets, 2nd TAFs reconnaissance capability was still severely limited in bad weather, and it was clear from this exercise that more and better radar aids would be required to overcome this dangerous disability.

During 1954 and 1955 the wind of change was blowing with increasing strength outside Europe, yet the United Kingdom was still responsible for maintaining law and order in many parts of the world. To assist in this, the RAF was required to maintain forces of high quality in the Middle and Far East. The Air Forces in the Middle East were re-organised in July 1955 into two Groups; the Northern Group was under Air Headquarters Levant, in Nicosia, to control units in Iraq, Jordan, Libya and Cyprus. (A state of emergency was declared in Cyprus in November 1955; Archbishop Makarios was deported and British forces found themselves in their traditional situation, trying to keep the peace between the Greek and Turkish communities, and drawing most of the terrorist fire upon themselves). The Southern Group was under Headquarters British Forces in Aden, responsible for units in the Aden Protectorate, along the South Arabian coast, in the Persian Gulf area and also in Kenya.

In the Kenya emergency some 20,000 Mau Mau had been killed or captured by the end of 1954, but it was thought that at least a further 7,000 were still at liberty. Liquidation of these tenacious 'hard core' terrorists, most of whom had formed small nomadic bands within 100 miles of Nairobi, appeared likely to be the only way of preventing the Mau Mau disease from lingering and perhaps spreading indefinitely. The work of air and land forces against these bands was co-ordinated under a Joint Operations Centre in Nairobi. The RAF, operating alongside light aircraft of the Police Reserve Air Wing, was carrying out strikes, fighter sweeps and supply drops daily in the Aberdare mountains, to the north-west of Nairobi, and over the thickly wooded foothills of Mount Kenya to the north-east.

RAF aircraft were operating from Nairobi with six Lincolns of 214 Squadron on detachment from their home base in the United Kingdom; four Vampires and two photographic reconnaissance Meteors from squadrons in Aden; and with twelve Harvards of 1340 Flight. The Harvards were armed with 19lb fragmentation bombs and 450 rounds of 0.303 ammunition fired from a single gun under the starboard wing. Lightly armed as they were there was much evidence of accurate and successful attacks against Mau Mau gangs carried out by these ageing, well worn, but most respected training aircraft. An Auster and later a Pembroke also operated from Nairobi with sky-shouting apparatus for propaganda in the Kikuyu language.

In another anti-terrorist campaign in far-away Malaya an aircraft new to the RAF, the Scottish Aviation Prestwick Pioneer, was making a name for itself. This was the more remarkable because it had undergone no Service trials before entering service with the RAF in the Far East. Its great virtue was its extremely short take-off and landing run (the 550 horsepower take-off power and high-lift wing enabled it to clear 50 ft, under temperate conditions, in only 180 yards). The heat and hazards of the Malayan jungle could hardly be described as temperate, but operating from Kuala Lumpur, the Pioneers were successfully employed in flying relief garrisons to remote Malayan jungle forts.

In these same operations in the summer of 1954, Valettas of 52 Squadron of the Far East Transport Wing, reinforced by a Transport Command Hastings, established a record for the amount of supplies dropped by parachute in twenty-four hours to security ground forces operating in many parts of the Federation. The twenty-one dropping zones included jungle forts and Special Air Service unit camps, and the 200 'parapacks' dropped included equipment for constructing airstrips, fresh food supplies, fuel and ammunition for police posts, Ghurka, Malay and British units and for the King's African Rifles.

In July 1954, while the RAF overseas was engaged in this wide variety of operations, RAF Fighter Command in the United Kingdom was carrying out by far the biggest air defence exercise since the war. Code-named 'Dividend', its object was to practise defence against nuclear attack. Some 6,000 bomber sorties were flown against targets in the United Kingdom by aircraft from Bomber Command, USAF bombers from Europe, the Fleet Air Arm and Flying Training Command. The NATO control and reporting system was closely co-ordinated with the United Kingdom system throughout the exercise, as it would be in war. On the defence side, some 80,000 men and women were engaged, including Regular and Auxiliary fighter squadrons, control and reporting units, Royal Observer Corps and anti-aircraft units.

In summing up his initial reactions to the exercise, Air Marshal Sir Dermot Boyle, Air Officer Commander-in-Chief Fighter Command, stressed the fact that, in spite of the bad weather, the United Kingdom air defences had shown themselves effective. Interceptions had taken place at 40,000 to 50,000 ft, 100 miles out to sea. Four Hunters operating from the Central Fighter Establishment had been particularly successful. New and improved radar techniques and procedures had worked well and the Continental early warning system had proved effective. As a final assessment he said that we were: "rather ahead of threats as they exist at present."

Nevertheless it was recognised that the threat of nuclear attack would

Plate 5 One of the last photographic reconnaissance Spitfire PR MK 19s operating in Malaya (1954) during the emergency, with its successor the Gloster Meteor PR10.

Plate 6 The RAF's farewell parade for the last serving Lancaster at RAF St. Mawgan (October 15, 1956) where 'D-Delta' had been flying in a maritime training role. The Station Commander, Group Captain Bevan-John, OBE, is addressing the parade.

Plate 7 Her Majesty Queen Elizabeth II and HRH The Duke of Edinburgh at the re-consecration of the RAF Church of St. Clement Danes, October 19, 1958.

Plate 8 On May 15, 1959, the last operational Sunderland flying boat in RAF service makes a final flight over Singapore harbour.

Plate 9 On December 15, 1954, a Mosquito of 81 (PR) Squadron carried out its last operational sortie (in the Malayan anti-bandit campaign) before this superb aircraft was withdrawn from service.

Plate 10 15 Hunter F MK 6s of 92 Squadron 'The Blue Diamonds', the RAF's premier aerobatic team in 1962.

continue to present grave problems to the United Kingdom air defence forces, and although the expansion of Fighter Command was now complete, the development of new fighter aircraft had been passing through a difficult stage and the Supermarine Swift had proved far from satisfactory in service. Development of new weapons also required new facilities that were not available within the United Kingdom. Fortunately, the Long Range Weapon Establishment and the Woomera Range, set up in Australia under the Joint United Kingdom/Australian Guided Weapon Project, were playing a rapidly increasing part in the later stages of development and testing of both air-to-air and surface-to-air guided weapons.

Later in the year, however, the Minister of Defence, Mr Harold Macmillan, referred in the House to the Government's decisions concerning anti-aircraft gun defences in the United Kingdom. "The development of nuclear weapons and of long range aircraft of high speed and capable of operating at great altitude has radically reduced the effectiveness of anti-aircraft gun defences." It would be necessary, he thought, to retain a number of heavy and light ack ack regiments to defend field forces and certain vital targets, but this would not justify the retention of Anti-Aircraft Command.

Regarding the Royal Auxiliary Air Force: "The Government," he said, "has given a great deal of consideration to the problems of organisation, equipment and training of the squadrons of the Royal Auxiliary Air Force, problems which have become intensified by the introduction of the swept-wing fighter and the growing complexity of the air-defence system." After paying a tribute to the high traditions and "glorious record" of the Royal Auxiliary Air Force, the Minister continued: "It will not be possible for the Auxiliary squadrons, if they are re-equipped with the swept-wing aircraft, to train to a standard high enough to enable them to take their place in the frontline, as squadrons, immediately on the outbreak of war, and that is what all fighter squadrons must be required to do in present conditions, because they are needed at the very first moment. So an effective fighter squadron of modern aircraft must really be a whole-time duty.

"The Government has, therefore, decided to alter the organisation of the Royal Auxiliary Air Force in such a way as to enable those auxiliary pilots who can give the time to it to train on swept-wing aircraft. We have decided not to re-equip the squadrons with these machines, but to train the men. By this means the Auxiliary squadrons will provide reserves behind the Regular squadrons in war. Each squadron will be linked with a Regular squadron and Auxiliary pilots will fly the aircraft of the Regular squadrons. This will be instead of equipping the Auxiliary squadrons with machines of their own, with all the difficulties of maintenance. The pilots will fly the new modern machines, but those which are held and maintained in the Regular squadrons.

"The Auxiliary squadrons will retain their town headquarters and their present airfields, and each squadron will retain a training flight composed of Meteors or Vampires. The Auxiliary pilots will fly as necessary to Regular airfields to carry out their training on swept-wing aircraft. Auxiliary ground personnel will continue to be employed at their home airfields, and plans are being considered to train them so that they will be able, in the event of war, to service the latest types of fighter aircraft. These changes will be introduced progressively as the Regular squadrons are re-equipped with modern swept-wing fighters. Affiliation will not begin until Regular squadrons have worked up to full efficiency on their new aircraft."

Several other contentious RAF policy matters were being aired during the winter of 1954. The hoary old question of the control of RAF Coastal Command by the Air Ministry was once again under discussion. Another issue was the future of anti-aircraft artillery. With the abandonment of heavy ack ack guns RAF control of the ground-to-air missiles which were to succeed them was being questioned in some quarters. The Army's air mobility was another field in which important changes and developments were expected, and here again questions of control and operation of light aircraft and helicopters were involved. One sensible compromise had already been arrived at with the decision to form a joint RAF/Army helicopter school for training Army helicopter pilots. This decision had been taken none too soon because, for various reasons, principally a lack of suitable aircraft and the lack of finance, the United Kingdom and the RAF had so far paid no more than lip service to the possibilities of military transport and air/sea/land rescue services offered by the helicopter.

In a slightly different field, the training and provision of test pilots, and the point at which the RAF or Navy should start to take a practical interest in the development flying of the aircraft they had ordered, was giving cause for some hard thinking. According to a leading article in *Flight* in December 1954: "There seems to be a definite pattern running through these matters which directly reflects the growing significance of the Royal Air Force — already the most important of the three Services — and at the same time implies a dwindling usefulness and scope of the traditional weapons and activities of the other two."

One of the RAF's own famous 'weapons' that had been retired during the year was the Vickers Supermarine Spitfire. The last operational Spitfire squadron, a photographic reconnaissance squadron of the Far East Air Force based in Malaya with a detached flight in Hong Kong, had been re-equipped with Meteor PR.10s. The only remaining Spitfires, fewer than fifty of them, were those used by the Civil Anti-Aircraft Co-operation Units, which also made the daily meteorological climb from RAF Woodvale in Lancashire, and a few on miscellaneous duties at home and abroad. The last few months' work of Far East Spitfires constituted a worthy record, for between them they flew some 800 photographic reconnaissance sorties in the Malaya anti-bandit campaign.

Meanwhile, with new jet aircraft such as the Canberra, the RAF was setting new world records. Flown by Wing Commander A.H. Humphrey with Squadron Leaders Powell and Bower as navigators, a Canberra set a new record between London and Cape Town on December 17, 1954. The distance of 6,009 statute miles between the two cities was covered at an average speed of 486.6 mph. In the same year, Bomber Command Canberras carried out a good-will tour of Southern Europe and Mediterranean countries. In a rather different field and at a rather different speed, Flight Lieutenant Colin Mitchell broke the one-man bob-sleigh record on the Cresta Run in February 1954 with an average speed of 43.5 mph and in the same year, the RAF also won the race for the four-man bob-sleighs.

With increasing numbers of jet aircraft in service with the Royal Air Force, more interest was being shown by Parliament in RAF training methods and costs and in jet accidents. As far as methods were concerned, the pilot training scheme in which pupil pilots completed jet flying training before gaining their wings was — in the summer of 1954 — operating satisfactorily at No 5 Flying Training School at Oakington. One of the results of this new system was that unsuitable trainees could be more quickly discovered than previously, with consequent saving in time and money. The cost aspect of training was becoming increasingly important, for as Mr George Ward, Under Secretary of State for Air, explained in the House, it was now costing £25,000 to put a single pilot into a bomber squadron. Mr Ward defended the piston-engined Provost/Vampire jet training sequence in the House, and added that the introduction as an experiment of a jet aircraft in place of the piston-engined Provost for *basic* pilot training was being considered. He went on to emphasise that the fatality rate in jet accidents during 1953 had been roughly one-half of the lowest fatal-accident rate for the Spitfire when in comparable service. "This statement made an extremely favourable impression on the House", reported *Flight* magazine, "and the loud cheering that followed was clearly intended as a tribute to the high standard of flying instruction and airmanship in the Royal Air Force."

In August 1955, the 'all-jet' training programme referred to by the US of S the previous year was started on an experimental basis at No 2 Flying Training School, Hullavington, with Jet Provost aircraft. In October, the first pilot to fly solo on jet aircraft without any previous flying experience on piston-engined aircraft did so after 8 hours 20 minutes dual instruction. As further evidence of the fact that the jet age was now firmly established amongst RAF combat aircraft, the latest night fighter version of the Meteor — the NF.14 — entered service with 85 Squadron in the Autumn of 1954; at about the same time, 542 Squadron was completing intensive flying trials on the latest version of the Canberra — the photographic reconnaissance Mk 7. The same year, the Canberra 'Aries 4' from the RAF Flying College at Manby in Lincolnshire, made the first Arctic proving flight by a British jet aircraft, and later in the year the same aircraft made the first British jet flight over the North Geographic Pole. Much valuable experience was gained of the navigational techniques necessary for high flying jet aircraft in this remote area of the world.

Although the day of the jet aircraft had clearly arrived, some of the older war horses of the RAF were still doing valiant service in the middle 1950s. For instance, four maritime reconnaissance Shackleton aircraft of 206 Squadron Coastal Command carried out a 40,000 mile flight to the Far East in the latter part of 1954, participating in maritime exercises in the Indian Ocean, off Ceylon, and making good-will and training visits to Australia, New Zealand and Fiji. The visit of these aircraft to the Far East coincided with the signing, in September 1954, of a collective defence treaty for the South-East Asia area; thus with their signatures, the Governments of France, New Zealand, Pakistan, the Philippines, Siam, the United Kingdom and the United States, gave further evidence of the desire amongst people of good-will to unite for mutual protection.

But all the treaties and new aircraft and weapons in the world would be of little use unless the RAF could overcome its manpower problems. At the beginning of 1955 it was the shortage of skilled men and the deterrent to regular engagements in the RAF that was the cause of most concern. At this time, most Stations in the RAF were under-manned in the advanced trades and this had resulted in excessive pressure on those men who were available. Advanced tradesmen, who were far short of the agreed requirement, could not supervise properly because they had to do themselves much of the work that ought to have been done by men with rather less skill. Furthermore, the advanced tradesmen could not give sufficient time to the highly skilled work for which they alone were qualified, because of the excessive amount of supervision they had to give to the relatively inexperienced craftsmen who were in their charge. Most RAF Stations were getting their tasks completed by overworking their few advanced tradesmen and by improvisation. Yet many Stations had a greater *total* of men than the theoretical requirement, but this was often due to an attempt to compensate for the lack of the right type of advanced tradesmen either by having a surplus of mechanics or by mis-employing other types of advanced tradesmen. Either of these courses was wasteful.

A Parliamentary Committee on Estimates considered that a great saving in the demands for the highly skilled craftsmen would be achieved if instruments and sub-assemblies were returned to the manufacturers for repair and re-issue. Such a system, it was admitted, would necessitate the building up of a very large replacement stock. On this same theme, the Committee reported details of a contract granted to Flight Refuelling Limited, to operate a jet-flying training school at Tarrant Rushton. Service instructors gave tuition in aircraft serviced by civilians, and the Air Ministry estimated that the work the firm did with 145 civilians would probably have required about 350 Servicemen.

Under-manning in the higher technical grades, the report continued, was an expensive problem. Another, more widespread and much more expensive, was the small number of volunteers for long-term regular engagements, resulting in about 75% of the ground staff being on engagements of five years or less and over 50% on National Service or three-year engagements. One consequence, the report pointed out, was that whereas a course of training need only be give once if the trainee intended to serve for twenty years, it had to be given four times to men engaging for five years, and ten times to National Servicemen.

Principal deterrents to regular engagements at this time, the Committee considered, were bad accommodation, particularly married quarters, difficulties over children's education, and what was known as 'turbulence', or the unceasing movement of officers and men from Station to Station. In six months ended April 30, 1954, 13.4% of the trained regular ground airmen moved from one place to another; overseas postings accounting for another 10.7% and losses to civil life a further 19.8%. In fact, the report concluded, quite apart from the movements of trainees and National Servicemen, nearly half of the trained regular ground staff moved in the course of one year.

The arrival of increasing numbers of new jet-engined aircraft in squadrons rendered solution of manning problems increasingly urgent. By the middle of 1955, more than 375 British aircraft, consisting of Canberras, Valiants and Hunters, had been delivered to the RAF and paid for with the help of American 'offshore' purchase arrangements.

In November 1955, after thirty-eight years continuous service abroad, 216 Squadron flew its eight Valettas (military version of the Vickers Viking) from the Canal Zone via Malta to its new base at Lyneham in Wiltshire. It was not so much the home-coming but the reason for it that was exciting the air and ground crews of the squadron. Early in 1956 they were due to take over the first of the Comet 2s and so become the first jet-propelled transport squadron in the Royal Air Force.

In a rather different role, 22 Squadron of Coastal Command, one of the first of a chain of helicopter units being established by the Air Ministry for Search and Rescue duties throughout the British Isles, was fully operational with its Westland Whirlwind helicopters by the end of the Summer of 1955. Another RAF Whirlwind helicopter squadron that year completed its first five years of operational service in Malaya, where its ability to lift casualties quickly from the depths of the jungle was a great fillip to the morale of the soldiers concerned.

In November 1955 it was announced that Marshal of the RAF Sir William Dickson was to be appointed to the new post of Chairman of the Chiefs of Staff Committee. That an airman had been selected to be first holder of this office was generally recognised as a compliment and honour to the RAF. It was announced at the same time that Air Marshal Sir Dermot Boyle would succeed Sir William Dickson as Chief of the Air Staff. Sir Dermot Boyle's appointment was a milestone in the RAF's post-war history. He was the first cadet who had received pilot and officer training at the RAF College, Cranwell, to be appointed to this high office. Before he took up his appointment, he was invited for a private talk with Marshal of the Royal Air Force Lord Trenchard, as a result of whose vision and determination during the RAF's lean years in the 1920s, Cranwell and the Apprentice school at Halton had been formed, thirty-five years previously. Together these two schools provided the twin pillars upon which the RAF's enormous wartime expansion depended, and upon which its post-war traditions and professional excellence rested.

In concluding this chapter, two events must be mentioned whose significance for the future could not be fully appreciated at the time. In the Autumn of 1954 six Canberras of 57 Squadron from Cottesmore had visited Iraq, Jordan and Tripolitania in the course of a training and goodwill flight. This was to be the last occasion on which so complete a tour of Arab States would be politically feasible. The other event was the 21st Anniversary of Flight Refuelling Ltd. What had begun in 1935 as an almost casual experiment by Sir Alan Cobham — "the greatest of all Britain's long-distance airmen" — had in 1955 reached a point in its development where air forces of the world, including the RAF, had placed extensive orders for the 'drogue and probe' in-flight refuelling equipment. Later chapters will clearly show just how important this development was to be for the RAF when, in the years to come, one Middle East country after another closed its airspace to over-flights by RAF aircraft.

Your Hearts Together

'Keep your hearts together and your tents separate' ARAB PROVERB

On July 26, 1956, President Nasser announced the nationalisation of the Suez Canal Company. On August 11, in his appointment as Commander-in-Chief British Middle East Land Forces, General Sir Charles E. Keightley was informed that, in view of Egypt's action, the British and French Governments had decided to concentrate certain forces in the Eastern Mediterranean ready if armed intervention should become necessary to protect their interests. Certain naval, land and air forces were earmarked and alerted. A small Allied Headquarters was set up in London to prepare contingency plans.

It was soon recognised that one of the main limitations to prospective operations would be the shortage of airfields in Cyprus. Initially only one airfield, at Nicosia, was available but two further airfields, at Akrotiri and Tymbou, were quickly developed during September and October. During the last week in October intelligence sources were reporting from Tel Aviv and elsewhere strong indications of Israeli mobilisation, and on October 29, Israel attacked across the Sinai Peninsula.

On October 30, the British and French Governments issued an ultimatum to both Israel and Egypt to cease hostilities within 24 hours, to withdraw contestant troops ten miles from the Suez Canal and to allow occupation by Anglo-French forces of Port Said, Ismailia and Suez. At 0430 hours on October 31, General Keightley was informed that the Israeli Government had agreed to the ultimatum and that Egypt had refused; as Allied Commander, he was now required to interpose his forces between those of Israel and Egypt in order to bring about a cessation of hostilities and to occupy the three towns.

At the time, it was estimated that the Egyptian Air Force had 80 Russian MiG-15 fighters, 45 Russian Il-28 bombers, 25 British-built Meteors and 57 Vampires, together with about 200 transport and training aircraft. General Keightley appreciated that his first priority must be to eliminate the threat of Egyptian air action against landing craft conveying commando and armoured forces from Malta, and air transports flying paratroops from Cyprus. Action by Il-28 bombers against overcrowded airfields in Cyprus would have done damage out of all proportion to the effort involved.

71

Fortunately, as General Keightley later emphasised in his report: "The Royal Air Force was the most easily prepared [of the three Services] for action." The plan was, therefore, to attack the Egyptian Air Force with a combination of high level bombing using contact and delayed action bombs in order to damage runways and discourage aircraft from taking off; this to be followed by daylight ground attacks.

At 1615 hours GMT on October 31, 1956, RAF Valiants of 148 Squadron and Canberras of 10 and 12 Squadrons, based at Malta and under overall command of Air Marshal Barnett, began their attacks on the Egyptian airfields of Cairo West, Almaza, Bilbeis and Inches from an altitude of around 49,000 feet. Vickers Valiants, first of the RAF's V-bombers, had only entered RAF squadron service the previous year, and this was the first operation of war in which they had been engaged. These attacks were continued during the early part of the night with the aid of flares and encountered a certain amount of anti-aircraft fire but no night fighters.

By the end of the following day, after Bomber Command's work of the previous night had been followed up by strafing attacks on Egyptian airfields by RAF fighter-bombers based on Cyprus and Royal Navy carrier-borne aircraft, the Egyptian Air Force had been severely treated. Air reconnaissance showed that, except for some ten Il-28 bombers which had been flown out of the target areas, the majority of Egyptian Air Force combat aircraft had been destroyed or damaged on the ground. Only one RAF aircraft had been attacked in the air and suffered slight damage while others incurred minor damage from anti-aircraft fire. Also during the morning of November 1, Cairo radio was attacked and put out of action by low flying RAF Canberras with top cover provided by French fighters. Later the same day, air reconnaissance disclosed the first signs that the Egyptians were carrying out extensive blocking of the Canal. Ships were seen sunk across the entrance to Port Said.

By the end of November 2, it was evident that the task of neutralising the Egyptian Air Force was all but complete. A small number of Il-28 bombers still remained untouched at Luxor airfield and these were attacked during the night of November 2 and 3 and also on November 4, but during November 3 the bulk of the air effort was switched from airfields to other military targets — mainly to heavy movement in the Canal area.

Armed reconnaissance sorties found much military transport activity and considerable numbers of Russian tanks. These were heavily mixed with civilian vehicles of all descriptions and many military targets had to be discarded by pilots for this reason. "It is interesting", General Keightley reported, "to record the behaviour of all these vehicles on the arrival of our aircraft. In general military crews abandoned their vehicles, whereas the civilian traffic proceeded unperturbed. This speaks highly of the integrity of our pilots and the complete trust in our frequently broadcast intentions of attacking only military targets. Similar behaviour had been reported during our air attacks on airfields, when pilots stated that the only military activity seen was from anti-aircraft guns but that numbers of spectators watched their activities from the perimeter of the landing ground."

The airborne assault went in successfully on November 5. Although nine transport aircraft were hit all returned safely to base and anti-aircraft fire was dealt with by fighter aircraft operating on anti-flak patrols. The seaborne assault was equally successful on the following day, supported by Naval gunfire and an air strike. At 1700 hours on the seventh day of the Franco-British operations, orders were received from London that a United Nations force would take over from the British and French forces and a Cease-Fire was to take effect from 2359 hours on November 6.

Speaking at a meeting in Scotland a few weeks later, Mr Nigel Birch, the Secretary of State for Air, referring to the Suez operation said there had never been better co-operation between the Services. "Nowadays people often speak of the desirability of all three Services being merged into one. I do not myself believe this would be of benefit. I believe we should act in accordance with the Arab proverb: 'Keep your Hearts together and your tents separate'." The Air Minister added that the operations had shown how merciful the exercise of air power could be "provided your force is well trained and its technical equipment good enough. In the event, the great fleets of Russian aircraft were neutralised at the cost of only very few lives."

Although this phraseology savoured somewhat of political hyperbole, the RAF's own casualties were fortunately limited to three officers and one airman killed; no wounded; no missing. Two RAF aircraft were lost, one through enemy action and the other as a result of an accident. The RAF's first Chief of Air Staff, Marshal of the RAF Lord Trenchard, who died on February 10, 1956, had demonstrated in the 1920s, in Somaliland, Iraq, Waziristan and Aden, how economical and merciful the use of air power could be in undeveloped areas of the world where Britain was responsible for maintaining law and order.

One example of close co-operation between the RAF and the Royal Navy is worth recording. When on conclusion of the Suez operations the aircraft carrier HMS *Theseus* was on her way to Malta with Allied wounded on board, a Shackleton of Royal Air Force Coastal Command dropped emergency medical supplies. The drop took place in a storm and the Captain of the aircraft, Flight Lieutenant R. Buckwell, said afterwards: "Dropping instructions were passed to us by radio as we could not see the ship, due to a huge rain cloud in the area." The Shackleton made two runs alongside *Theseus* at 150 feet and released the supply containers over sea markers which had been laid by the carrier. Two naval helicopters already airborne picked up the canisters and had them on board within little more than one minute from the drop.

On November 4, with the eyes of the United Nations and much of the world on the war in the Middle East, Soviet forces had launched an attack on Budapest to crush the popular uprising in Hungary. The West was powerless to intervene, but when refugees poured across the Hungary-

Austria frontier the RAF carried 116 tons of bedding, food and medical supplies to the International Red Cross in Vienna in a three-day airlift. Some twenty aircraft were involved including Hastings and Valettas and movements staffs at RAF Wildenrath in Germany worked round the clock unloading lorries bringing supplies from Northern Army Group stores and re-loading them into RAF aircraft. By the third week in December, British independent airlines, following in the footsteps of the RAF, had contributed a major share to the evacuation of 12,000 Hungarian refugees from Austria to the United Kingdom.

Not enough is made perhaps of the opportunities for the younger generation to find constructive ways of serving humanity in the Services. Yet the quality of mercy would not be strained in talking of it rather more. In December 1956, for instance, a young RAF doctor, Flight Lieutenant J. Wilkinson, volunteered at ten minutes notice for an 850-mile flight from Singapore to Christmas Island, 200 miles south of Java, to provide aid for a dangerously ill woman. On arrival, the aircraft, piloted by Flying Officer Speer, made two dummy runs in visibility reduced by heavy monsoon rain, over flares marking the dropping zone. On the third run, Flying Officer Wilkinson parachuted from 800 ft and was followed by a pack of medical supplies and blood plasma.

Back in England, earlier the same year, an RAF Whirlwind helicopter had flown in gale force winds to rescue a man and woman from a disabled yacht off Hayling Island. The strop at the end of the helicopter's rescue line had fouled the rigging of the yacht and the winch had been torn out of the helicopter. A national service airman named Martin flew out as volunteer crewman with a second helicopter and, despite dangerous conditions, was lowered to the heaving deck of the yacht from where he supervised the rescue of the then unconscious man. He then stayed with the woman on the sinking yacht and, clinging to the rigging, prevented her from being washed overboard until the helicopter returned to rescue both of them. For conspicuous gallantry in disregarding his own safety in order to save two lives he was awarded the George Medal.

Before the end of 1956, the Comet 2 had entered service with 216 Squadron at RAF Lyneham, making it the first military jet-engined transport squadron in the world; the Vulcan delta-wing V-bomber had entered service with 230 Operational Conversion Unit at RAF Waddington, and the Gloster Javelin all-weather fighter had entered service with 46 Squadron at RAF Odiham.

In April 1957, Mr Duncan Sandys, then Minister of Defence, presented to Parliament a Defence White Paper which foreshadowed far-reaching changes in the RAF's strength and role. The present shape of Britain's Defence Forces, it pointed out, was largely settled by the re-armament programme launched in 1950 at the time of the Korean war. The ending of hostilities in Korea had radically altered the position. The immediate danger of major war had receded, but had been replaced by the prospect of a prolonged period of acute international tension. It had also become evident that a military effort on the scale planned in 1950, envisaging expenditure of £4,700 million over three years, was beyond the country's continuing capacity.

The White Paper went on to discuss specific aspects of vital concern to the RAF. It must be frankly recognised, it pointed out, that there was at that time no means of providing adequate protection for the people of the United Kingdom against the consequences of nuclear attack. Though, in the event of war, the fighter aircraft of the RAF should be able to take a heavy toll of enemy bombers, a proportion would inevitably get through. Even it if were only a dozen, they could with nuclear weapons inflict widespread devastation. This made it more clear than ever that the over-riding consideration in all military planning was to prevent war rather than to prepare for it. While admitting that, by comparison with the United States, Britain's nuclear deterrent power was modest, British atomic bombs were already in production and the RAF already held a substantial stock. Mention was also made of the development of a British megaton thermonuclear weapon which would shortly be tested and thereafter manufactured.

In November 1957, the first Handley Page Victor, third of the V-bombers, was delivered to 232 Operational Conversion Unit at RAF Gaydon. The medium bombers of the V-class were providing the means of delivering nuclear weapons and their performance in speed and altitude was recognised as being comparable to that of any bomber aircraft in service in any other country at that time. Agreement in principle had, however, already been reached with the United States Government for the supply of some intermediate-range ballistic missiles to supplement the V-bombers in this task.

Since peace depended so largely upon the deterrent effect of nuclear retaliation, it was regarded as essential that a would-be aggressor should not be allowed to think he could readily knock out the bomber bases in Britain before their aircraft could take off. The defence of the bomber airfields was, therefore, an essential part of the deterrent. The Sandys White Paper of 1957, however, stated that a fighter force smaller than at present (but adequate for this limited purpose) would be maintained, and would progressively be equipped with air-to-air guided missiles. Then came a more ominous statement: "Fighter aircraft will in due course be replaced by a ground-to-air guided missile system." Seventeen years of further fighter development have since indicated that this statement was somewhat premature! In a year in which the Government were planning to do away with National Service (after the end of 1960), publication of this view was hardly the best way to encourage voluntary recruitment of aircrew. To make matters worse the White Paper went on to say: "The aircraft of the Second Tactical Air Force in Germany will be reduced to about half their present number by the end of March 1958. This reduction will be offset by the fact that some of the squadrons will be provided with atomic bombs. A similar reduction will be made in the light bomber force in England, which is assigned to NATO".[1]

It was no new situation for armed forces to find their tools being removed more quickly than their responsibilities, and the same White Paper pointed out that: "Outside the area covered by the North Atlantic Treaty Alliance, Britain has military responsibilities in other parts of the world, in particular in the Middle East and South-East Asia. Apart from its own importance, the Middle East guards the right flank of NATO and is the gateway to the African continent. In the Arabian peninsula, Britain must at all times be ready to defend Aden Colony and Protectorate and the territories on the Persian Gulf, for whose defence she is responsible. For this task, land, air and sea forces have to be maintained in that area and in East Africa."

In addition, Britain had undertaken in the Baghdad Pact to co-operate with the other signatory States for security and defence, and for the prevention of communist encroachment and infiltration. In the event of emergency, British forces in the Middle East area would be made available to support the Alliance. These would include bomber squadrons based in Cyprus capable of delivering nuclear weapons. Practically the only relief in the RAF's worldwide commitments at this time resulted from termination of the treaty with Jordan, which enabled the RAF to withdraw from that country in 1957.

On Thursday, October 11, 1956, as though to show that in spite of a reduction in numbers the RAF's power was still increasing, the first British nuclear weapon to be dropped from an aircraft had been released by an RAF Valiant over Maralinga, South Australia, as part of 'Operation Buffalo'. A small bomb, as such weapons go, it was equivalent in explosive power to 10,000 tons of TNT. The height of the explosion was stated at the time to have played strange acoustic tricks. People at Kingoonya, 200 miles away, heard a "thunderous double explosion", but others living less than 100 miles from Maralinga heard nothing.

On May 15, 1957, the first British Hydrogen bomb was dropped at Christmas Island, a coral atoll in the Pacific, by a Valiant from 49 Squadron. The Pacific Island base had been prepared by the Army the previous year by the construction of twenty-five miles of road, and by RAF and Army airfield construction engineers of a 7,000-ft runway for bombers and an auxiliary airstrip. Thousands of tons of heavy equipment were taken to the island by sea, while mail and fresh food were flown in from Honolulu by RAF Hastings transport aircraft.

In the same year Aneurin Bevan, then the Shadow Foreign Minister in

---

[1]Correlli Barnett, the military historian, referred to this White Paper as: "Surely one of the most catastrophically cocksure and mistaken documents in British Defence history." In the interests of historical objectivity, however, it must be recorded that the Air Staff at this time was recommending a drastic reduction in fighter defence forces, including cancellation of a rocket powered interceptor fighter (a prototype of which was already flying). They were also recommending cancellation of a planned supersonic high level bomber in favour of a low level strike aircraft (TSR2), and the Blue Streak stand-off bomb for use in the V-force.

the Labour oppostion, made his courageous speech in the House of Commons concerning nuclear weapons. He could not accept a policy, he said, that would disarm Britain of the bomb and so oblige a Labour Foreign Minister to go naked into the conference chamber.

An Uncertain Sound

'If the trumpet give an uncertain sound who shall prepare himself to the battle' I CORINTHIANS.14.8.

The year 1958 was for the world the year of the Sputnik and for the Royal Air Force the year in which American Thor offensive intercontinental ballistic missiles were added to Bomber Command's armoury and British Bloodhound defensive ground-to-air guided missiles to Fighter Command's. The first event shook the confidence of the Western World in their supposed superiority over Russia in the field of rocket development; the last two shook the faith of some RAF flying men in the supposed superiority of manned aircraft over missiles.

It was in July that the first Bristol Ferranti Bloodhounds entered service at RAF North Coates. Powered by ram-jets, Bloodhound was the first intercepter missile using continuous-wave radar guidance to become operational in the free world.[1] It was not intended by the Air Staff, however, to take the place of manned fighters but to operate in conjunction with them. Similarly, in spite of the formation of the first Thor Intermediate Range Ballistic Missile Squadron, No 77 at RAF Feltwell in Bomber Command, in August 1958, most Bomber Command squadrons at this time were equipped with Valiant bombers, while Vulcans and Victors, with their better performance, were entering service in increasing numbers. "They can fly as high and as fast as any bombers in service in any other country," the 1958 Defence White Paper stated "and their navigation and bomb-aiming equipment is of the highest accuracy." In addition, good progress was being made with the development of self-propelled bombs — the so-called 'stand off' bomb — which could be released at a considerable distance from the target, thus making it unnecessary for the manned aircraft to fly into the more heavily defended target area.

As for Thor, the "wingless deterrent" as it had been called, by the middle of 1958 these weapons had emerged from being shadowy paper projects to become a series of "thunderous metal cylinders". Produced by the Douglas Aircraft Company of America, its overall length was 62 ft, it had a range of 1,500 miles and in the course of its flight would reach a peak speed about twelve times that of sound. Its two most obvious disadvantages, compared with the V-bombers, were its vulnerability to attack on the ground — it could not be dispersed from its permanent base in times of international

---

[1] Bloodhound Mk 1 introduced at the time used 'pulsed radar' for guidance. The 'Continuous Wave' (not strictly speaking radar) came later as the Mk II.

tension, and its lack of flexibility — it could not be transferred to an overseas theatre of operations.

A Thor squadron consisted of fifteen missiles and 600 officers and men. The fifteen launch pads were normally located in five groups of three, and each trio was in effect a self-contained unit. One complex of power generators, fuel tanks and power distribution trailers handled one group of three missiles, and the launch-control trailer, with its associated radar, processed three count-down stations, one per missile. For training RAF technicians to maintain this new weapon system, twenty separate training courses, varying from two to twelve weeks, had been held by the United States Air Force in different parts of America. When, early in January 1959, the first launch crews of 98 Squadron assembled at the Douglas Aircraft Company School at Tucson, Arizona, they little realised that some of their number would make history by being the first RAF crew to launch a Thor missile.

In the RAF, a launch crew consisted of a General Duties (Flying) Branch officer as Launch Control Officer, three aircrew NCOs as Launch Control Console operators and three technicians as Missile Maintenance Technicians. Upon graduation from the manufacturer's school in Arizona, the RAF crews moved to Vandenburg Air Force Base in California. Here their first Thor missile was delivered to them in the Receipt, Inspection and Maintenance hangar, and put through a full check of missile component systems by RAF technicians.

On transfer to the launching emplacement, every component of the system was re-checked. Meanwhile, the launch date had been set for April 14, 1959. On launch day minus seven, final launch preparations started. These included fitting the telemetry instruments for tracking and also for destruction in event of the missile diverging from its planned course. On launch day minus one, the system was handed over on schedule by the technical staff to the launch crews.

At Ready Time minus 48 hours the count-down procedures began. From then on weather forecasts were supplied at frequent intervals because it was necessary for safety reasons to be able to follow the path of the missile visually. At Ready Time minus 105 minutes the RAF launch crew assumed responsibility for the weapon system and the tempo of the count-down now increased significantly. Evacuation of all non-essential people to a safe area was started and all key men including the Range Safety Officer stated regular status reports to the Launch Control Officer. All activity progressed smoothly and on receipt of the telephoned launch order from headquarters Bomber Command through the Strategic Air Command network, the following announcement was made: "Attention all stations. This is the Launch Control Officer. On my 'mark' the terminal launch count-down will begin. Minus 5, minus 4, minus 3, minus 2, minus 1, 'MARK'."

On the executive word 'Mark' the phase sequence key was turned and the fully automatic progression of events began. The guidance system was aligned and checked, the shelter moved back to reveal the missile in its white gloss finish and RAF roundel and then the missile slowly rose to the vertical position. At this time the propellant should have started to flow at a very high rate into the missile, but an electronic fault developed and a hold had to be applied to clear this malfunction. Work started immediately, but meanwhile the weather deteriorated and the operation had to be postponed for 24 hours. As a result of inspection a defective component was located and changed, but a further malfunction occurred the next day and this, aggravated by marginal weather, caused a further postponement until the following day. Although not appreciated at the time, the operational training value of these postponements was high.

At approximately 0900 hours on April 16, a further count-down started. The weather was again border-line, although it was expected that the low cloud might break by the time the launch was made. After a further slight delay for range safety reasons, the terminal count-down started in a tense atmosphere. Except for a very slight delay in liquid oxygen loading, the count-down went perfectly through all phases. An amber light lit up indicating the engines were about to start and within five seconds they had developed the full 150,000lb of thrust, which lifted the sixty-five foot missile from its launch pad. Smoke and flame at the emplacement almost blotted out the view on television, but immediately reports started to come in from the visual observers that lift-off was normal and that the missile was climbing within programmed limits. The RAF had launched its first surface-to-surface ballistic missile.

There were in these years great arguments in military and aviation circles concerning the British Government's military missile policy A *Flight* editorial of 1958 suggested that: "Britain more than any other country, seems to have fallen into the trap of regarding military aircraft and missiles as direct competitors, fighting each other for the money available. Major General Ferguson, Director of Requirements of the USAF, put the case more logically: 'a balance of missiles and aircraft of varying performance is needed', he said, 'to produce the greatest threat to an aggressor and the one most difficult to defend against'."

"We say again", commented another *Flight* editorial, "that the famous, or infamous, White Paper by the British Ministry of Defence in April last year merely provided an essential jolt; it should not, and could not, have signified any sudden lack of interest in manned aircraft. Britain will have to have manned military aeroplanes for years to come: and somebody had better start ordering them."

Publication by the same magazine of the Vulcan Story well illustrated "the perceptive foresight and remarkable courage of the British Air Staff" who, shortly after the Second World War, had formulated a requirement for a bomber having twice the speed and operating altitude of the Lincoln, the then current RAF long-range bomber. The specification that A. V. Roe and Co drew up turned out in the end to be the most successful of the V-bombers, and the Vulcan was appreciably in advance of aircraft in the same role in other countries. In the field of fighter aircraft in May 1958, a further order of English Electric P.1Bs — later designated 'Lightning' — was announced in the House of Commons by the Minister of Supply, Mr Aubrey Jones. So the immediate future outlook for manned aircraft in the RAF was far less gloomy than the depression caused by the 1957 White Paper had led many people to think. But it was not sufficient simply to restore the confidence of the RAF in the future: it was necessary also for the RAF to regain the confidence of the British public, from whom its manpower — and money — must come. With this object in view, the Air Council convened a conference, on May 6, 1958, called 'Prospect 2'.

Some 350 representatives from industry, the professions, the other Services, trade unions, youth organisations and civic life, and including several MPs, were invited by the RAF to a one-day conference at the Royal Empire Society. The Chief of the Air Staff, Marshal of the RAF Sir Dermot Boyle explained its purpose: "Simply because there has been and still is great confusion in many people's minds about the role of the Royal Air Force both now and in the future. We feel that this confusion is bad for the country and for the Service and since we are quite clear in our minds what our responsibilities are and how we are going to meet them, we feel that nothing but good can come from telling you what we think and having the benefit of your comments and interest."

Sir Dermot emphasised that no attempt was being made to 'sell' the Air Force at the expense of either of the other Services; but since the RAF dealt in advanced techniques it was difficult for people to understand what it was about unless they were told. Reckoning itself a worthwhile nuisance and a good investment, the RAF intended to explain why: "We feel the more you know about us, the better."

In the course of discussion it was explained that the RAF believed in flexibly graduated deterrents, from conventional forces to meet minor aggressions, to tactical and strategic weapons for meeting greater aggression; and that its roles were to maintain the deterrent, to contribute to NATO, the Baghdad Pact and SEATO, and to provide forces for imperial policing.

Discussion covered the whole range of the RAF's work overseas including the 2nd Tactical Air Force in Germany, Middle East Air Force and Far East Air Force. The primary aim of the overseas Commands was stated to be that of providing support for alliances and for the fulfilment of obligations under treaties.

Future plans for new aircraft, recruiting and finance were covered under the head of 'Facing the Future', and the RAF Director General of Manning explained how it was proposed to have an all-regular Air Force with 120,000 airmen by the beginning of 1963 after the ending of National Service.

In bringing the conference to a close, the CAS made four main points: the RAF were ardent supporters of the deterrent; manned aircraft would be required for as far as could be seen because in war flexibility was needed and the nearer you could get a man to the target the longer you could use his brain; research was the life-blood of the RAF; and finally that the RAF was fully conscious of the responsibility that rested on its shoulders.

Although the introduction of offensive ballistic missiles and defensive guided missiles were the events which most exercised the minds of Air Force policy makers during these two years, several other achievements did more to gladden the hearts of flying men. In January 1958, for instance, many months of flying by RAF Valiants, Canberras and Meteors resulted in the completion of a 112,000 square miles photographic survey of Aden Colony and Protectorate for the Colonial Office and Directorate of Military Survey. In December 1958, the Secretary of State for Air (Mr George Ward) announced that: "It has been decided to develop a new strike/reconnaissance aircraft as a replacement for the Canberra. This will be capable of operating from small airfields with rudimentary surfaces and have a very high performance at all levels." This aircraft was later designated TSR.2.

Also in 1958, 216 Squadron RAF Transport Command completed three years flying on Comet 2s, the first jet transport aircraft to be operated by the RAF. Since 1956, the squadron aircrew had flown more than 26,000 Comet hours, visited fifty-two countries, and built up a fund of pure jet experience which, at that time, was probably unrivalled in the world. They had flown 200 million passenger miles, completed 130 scheduled return flights to the Near and Far East, operated a regular service to the Pacific, and completed 130 ocean crossings of the Atlantic and Pacific. In May 1959, Air Marshal Sir Denis Barnett, Air Officer Commanding-in-Chief Transport Command carried out an inspection — by Comet — of RAF air transport routes around the world in slightly under 80 hours flying time.

In America, RAF V-bomber crews gave an excellent account of themselves in the 1958 Strategic Air Command bombing and navigation competition. One British team came seventh in the overall competition, out of a total of forty-one participating Wings, and another team came twentieth overall. The following year, Vulcans of Bomber Command visited Nigeria to participate in regional self-government celebrations.

In Cyprus, in 1958, when Field Marshal Lord Harding had handed over the Governorship to Sir Arthur Foot, he had said that 284 (Sycamore helicopter) Squadron had: "contributed more to fighting terrorism on the island than any other single unit." During its two years service the squadron had pioneered two important techniques: the dropping of troops in mountainous terrain and night-flying, of which there was still comparatively little experience in the helicopter world. Since its formation the squadron had flown its Sycamores in more than 16,000 sorties. It had dropped well over 3,000 troops in terrorist-frequented country and trained 13,000 men in the art of scrambling down ropes from hovering helicopters. The number of casualties evacuated from hills and forests totalled more than 200, including troops seriously wounded in Eoka ambushes. Apart from many flights made on search and rescue, communications and reconnaissance operations, the squadron had helped to fight forest fires, and had dropped 113 tons of food, ammunition and stores to members of the security forces hunting terrorists in the mountains.

One of the squadron's most dramatic successes had been achieved in an operation near Makheras Monastery, a terrorist hideout 3,000 feet up in the Troodos mountains about twenty miles south-west of Nicosia. The operation, which could not have been undertaken without the aid of helicopters, had resulted in the death of Gregorious Afxenthiou, the Chief of Staff to Colonel George Grivas, the Eoka leader, and the capture of several other terrorists. Five helicopters had been employed to drop some forty troops who sealed off the area around the monastery while other forces moved in on the ground.

In the Far East, all normal flying for the RAF's remaining Sunderland flying boats ceased on May 15, 1959. The Chief of the Air Staff sent the following message to all Commands of the RAF and to Commonwealth Air Forces: "The cessation of operations by the two remaining Sunderlands of 205 Squadron on May 15 marks the end of another chapter in the history of the Royal Air Force. To all of us it is a sad occasion, as flying-boats have been in continuous employment since the birth of the Royal Air Force in 1918 and in the Royal Naval Air Service before that. It is, however, the task of the Royal Air Force to be ahead of requirements in all stages of evolution, and the flying-boat has unfortunately no part to play in our present concepts. To all ranks who have served in the Royal Air Force on 'boats' and to all those throughout the Commonwealth, Ministries and industry who have supported the Royal Air Force throughout the last forty-one years I send my warmest thanks and appreciation for a job well done."

In fact the death knell of the flying boat had been sounded nearly a decade earlier when a Wing Commander on the Air Plans staff of RAF Coastal Command HQ had been required to assess their future. He had prepared a paper for his Commander-in-Chief in which he pointed out that, in spite of their magnificent record of service in the Second World War, (and all their air-sea rescue and mercy missions since), the wartime construction of long-runway airfields throughout the world had completely supplanted marine bases on lakes, in lochs and in estuaries. The fact that had to be faced by the flying-boat enthusiasts was that, given the same engine power as a land-plane, the flying boat would always have a poorer performance because of weight and drag penalties that had to be paid to obtain a strong enough hull and wing-tip floats. Furthermore, whereas the land-plane pilot had only to compete with the vagaries of a single unstable element — the air, a flying-boat captain was also up against a second unstable element — water, and this introduced problems of corrosion and of the effect of tides and winds.

Thus on January 1, 1958, the first Avro Shackleton flight of the last (amalgamated) flying boat squadron (No 205/209) started to form at RAF Changi on Singapore island, under the command of Wing Commander McCready (who had also commanded the flying boats on the Berlin airlift).

By January 1, 1959, there were only three serviceable flying boats left in the squadron — Peter, Sugar and William. On May 15, Peter acted as escort to a naval vessel, with Air Marshal the Earl of Bandon, C-in-C Far East Air Force, on board. This was the last flight of a RAF Sunderland. On May 31, 1959, the squadron standard was trooped, followed by the beating of the retreat, with Air Marshal the Earl of Bandon taking the salute.

In the autumn of 1959, Mr Harold Macmillan became the first Prime Minister in office to visit the RAF College at Cranwell. In a speech to the cadets he said: "The air calls for great skills in this modern age, and a high degree of technical ability, but it still calls, and always will, for great individual courage. It is the possession of these qualities and the sense of achievement which comes from them, that provides this characteristic of your Service of calm confidence. It is very important for our country that all young men should realise the challenge and the opportunity which service in the Royal Air Force offers."

One of the more light-hearted challenges was exemplified by the RAF's participation in the Bleriot Anniversary Air Race from Marble Arch in London to the Arc de Triomphe in Paris. The air race was held from July 13-23, 1959, and a few days beforehand officers and men assisting the race team began to assemble at the RAF Fighter Command Station at Duxford, to make their plans for the assault. On July 11 and 12, most of those concerned moved to RAF Biggin Hill, the chosen United Kingdom base for the team, and to Villacoublay, the French base.

Competitors in the race were Group Captain Ryder, the Station Commander at RAF Duxford; Squadron Leader C.C. Maughan, the Officer Commanding 56 (Hunter) Squadron at Duxford; Flight Lieutenant Williams, a pilot from the same squadron, and Under Officer Volkers, a cadet from Cranwell. After much detailed planning it was finally decided that competing pilots should travel on the pillions of RAF motorcycles from Marble Arch to the Thames embankment near Chelsea Bridge, from there down a slippery pole onto a mud bank (which meant that the state of the tide dictated the time of the flight) where a helicopter would be waiting for a quick flight to RAF Biggin Hill. The RAF team had worked out that precious time and energy could be saved if a Hunter two-seat fighter was used so that the pilot could be taxying for take-off while the competitor was still strapping himself in and getting his breath back after the motorcycle and helicopter dash from the city centre. Competing officers were therefore supported by a team of Hunter pilots, co-ordinating officers, air traffic control officers and ground servicing staff, and their narrow victory was the result of careful planning and an extremely high standard of team work.

From RAF Biggin Hill the flight was by Hunter T.7 to Villacoublay, from where the competitors flew by helicopter to Issy heliport on the left bank of the Seine, leaving a four-minute motorcycle dash to the Arc de Triomphe. The journeys in the opposite direction were done over the same route and this proved eventually to be the faster direction. Squadron

Leader Maughan finally put up the best time of 40 minutes 44 seconds. Flight Lieutenant Williams achieved the second fastest time, but was disqualified as his motor cycle driver failed to notice a red traffic light in London when he went cruising past at about eighty mph. Prizes were presented at Marble Arch on July 22 by Lord Rothermere, Chairman of the Associated Newspaper Group. The RAF's £5,000 prize money was subsequently divided by the Air Council between the RAF Benevolent Fund, The Soldiers' Sailors' and Airmen's Families Association and Paraplegics Sports Endowment Fund.

Some other events of historic importance during these two years were the upgrading in November, 1958 of 90 Signals Group at Medmenham, Bucks, to become RAF Signals Command; the disbandment in April, 1958 of RAF Home Command and transfer of the Air Training Corps to RAF Training Command; the formation in November, 1959 of the first Royal Auxiliary Air Force Maritime Headquarters at Edinburgh; the entry to service with 99 Squadron at Lyneham in June, 1959 of the Britannia prop-jet transport aircraft; and of the Jet Provost for ab initio flying training in September of the same year. In July, 1959, a Valiant of 214 Squadron captained by Wing Commander M.J. Beetham carried out the first non-stop flight from the United Kingdom to Cape Town (6,060 miles in 11 hours 28 minutes with air-to-air refuelling), and in October, 1959, British Forces Arabian Peninsula was set up in Aden under the command of Air Chief Marshal Sir Hubert Patch as the first major tri-Service command since the Second World War.

One other event of these years is believed to be unique in the annals of any of the Armed Services. On October 19, 1958, St. Clement Danes in the Strand was re-consecrated as the Church of the Royal Air Force by the Archbishop of Canterbury, in the presence of Her Majesty Queen Elizabeth II and HRH The Duke of Edinburgh. It is the only Service church not linked with a particular military unit. It was on May 10, 1941 that this church, built by Sir Christopher Wren in 1682, on the foundations of far older churches (the first of which had been built by Danes who were married to English women in the time of Alfred the Great) was reduced to a charred ruin by incendiary bombs. After the war, funds were raised by the RAF and by Commonwealth and Allied air forces for its restoration. More than 700 squadron and unit badges made of Welsh slate have been let into the floor, together with a memorial to Polish squadrons. Beneath the north gallery is a memorial to the 19,000 members of the United States Air Force who gave their lives while flying from British soil. In the simple chapel in the crypt, the black granite font came from the Royal Norwegian Air Force, the paschal candelabrum from the Royal Belgian Air Force and the stone altar was the gift of the Royal Netherlands Air Force. The RAF Church of St. Clement Danes is thus a fitting memorial to the men and women of many countries who fought and flew with the RAF during the Second World War.

Our Special Duty

'This is our special duty; that if anyone specially seeks our help, we should give him such help to the utmost of our power' CICERO

On July 31, 1960, the emergency in Malaya, 'Operation Firedog', was officially declared at an end. From the start of operations in 1948, aircraft of the Far East Air Force had flown some 47 million miles in operations against the terrorists and in support of military and police forces on the ground. Seventy per cent of Malaya's 50,000 square miles consists of jungle-covered mountains inhabited by aborigines, with little or no communication on the ground, except by river or jungle track. All forms of air support from troop movement, supply and casualty evacuation to reconnaissance and ground attack were not only decisive in the ultimate success of the long drawn-out anti-terrorist operations, but without them it is most unlikely that the communist inspired insurrection could have been contained at all. Now that the campaign was over, military and civil authorities in Malaya considered it essential if the improved internal security situation was to be maintained, to continue to use the RAF in providing armed support, in supply dropping operations and in maintaining communications with remote police forts and with detached units of the Commonwealth Brigade.

In the same month that the emergency in Malaya was declared ended, the RAF was called upon to assist the United Nations in the Congo. After the sudden granting of independence to the Congo by the Belgian Government in June, 1960, the mineral-rich province of Katanga declared itself an independent state, tribal disturbances broke out in the capital city of Leopoldville and in other parts of the country, and the 25,000-strong national security force mutinied in many places, expelled its white officers and started plundering Europeans' property. The newly formed Congolese Central Government called urgently for United Nations assistance to restore order.

The response by member states was prompt and impressive, and the United Nations force that emerged was one of the most polyglot in history, surpassing the number of different national forces that had served under the United Nations' flag in Korea. The problem was how to get them quickly from their different countries into the middle of Africa. The Commander of the Ghanaian Brigade, which had been offered by Ghana to the Congo Government, was General Alexander, a seconded British Army officer. Not unnaturally, therefore, the RAF was asked for help to move this force. Initially an airlift was requested for the transport of about 1,500 troops and police with vehicles and supplies, from Accra to Leopoldville. The first stage of the airlift, completed by the end of July, was carried out by Comets, Britannias and Beverleys which flew out from the United Kingdom and carried Belgian and some British refugees on their return flights. Aircraft of Middle East Air Force and of British Forces Arabian Peninsular were also used to fly food and supplies to the Congo and to evacuate refugees. In August, an RAF detached flight was based at Accra. Two Hastings from 114 Squadron at RAF Colerne were allocated for this duty. Despite difficult flying conditions with low cloud base and severe turbulence and political difficulties such as the temporary closing of Leopoldville airport, the detached flight maintained regular schedules in support of the United Nations' forces with few cancellations. After the evacuation of Ghanaian police and Embassy staff from Leopoldville had been successfully completed, General Alexander sent a personal message to the RAF expressing his thanks for their prompt action.

The next large scale emergency involving the RAF occurred about mid-way between the Congo and Malaya and more than 3,000 miles from both — in Kuwait. In 1961, some forty per cent of the United Kingdom's oil came from Kuwait and it was not surprising, therefore, that when in June General Kassem of Iraq threatened to seize the newly independent Emirate and intelligence reports confirmed the move of Iraqi troops, the British Cabinet reacted sharply. On June 28 all forces earmarked in accordance with prepared contingency plans were ordered to stand by. On June 30 the Emir appealed for help, the British Cabinet approved and Commander-in-Chief Middle East ordered landings to start as soon as possible after dawn the next day.

A Beverley from Aden was the first military aircraft to touch down, on July 1, at Kuwait's civil airfield, a sand covered strip in a sea of sand, six miles south of the town. It had on board the ground crew of 8 Squadron, whose fighter ground-attack Hunters arrived from Aden ten minutes later in a sand storm and 1,000 yards visibility. They were closely followed by another Hunter squadron from Aden. From then on the airlift of supplies from Bahrain to Kuwait continued in spite of sand storms; and further reinforcements arrived both at Aden and Bahrain direct from the United Kingdom, including more men to man the early warning radar.

Transport Command's first task in this operation was to lift a parachute battalion from Cyprus to Bahrain, and supporting units and stores from England. At the same time, further transport aircraft flew 24 Brigade and 45 and 42 Marine Commandos from Aden to Kuwait. The latter Commando had been landed at Aden from HMS *Bulwark* which, fortuitously, had been on passage in the Indian ocean at the start of the emergency. Within four days of the order, the major part of the force was in position. Within six days the positioning operation was complete, twenty-four hours ahead of the timetable. Thereafter, air transport kept the force supplied.

The variety of RAF support for this operation may be gauged from the many different types of aircraft involved; long-range Comets and Britannias from England, Beverley and Valetta tactical transport aircraft from Aden and Nairobi, reinforced by Beverleys from 38 Group in the UK; Pembrokes and Twin Pioneers from Aden and Bahrain, Hastings from Far East and England, fighter-ground attack and fighter-reconnaissance Hunters from Aden, Canberra bombers from Germany and photographic reconnaissance Canberras from Cyprus.

Meanwhile at the forward airstrip, in ground temperatures rising to 130 degrees, activity had been intense. The Hunters having arrived fully armed with guns and rockets were back in the air again as soon as refuelled, patrolling forward areas at the Iraq frontier where British and Kuwait troops were digging in. An RAF signal squadron had set up an airfield control organisation, including a portable direction-finding station to help 'home' aircraft in poor visibility. They also provided a telephone network, radio, teleprinter and morse circuits with the Bahrain air-head. An air movements team from RAF Khormaksar worked non-stop with Army movements, unloading troops and equipment. With the main airlift complete, life at the forward air-strip became less feverish and officers and men off duty were able to relax in air-conditioned civilian clubs and swimming pools.

Two of the lessons learned during the Kuwait operation were the need for more and larger transport aircraft and for lighter and more modern air-portable equipment. The Beverley, with its spacious fuselage and ability to lift nineteen tons from 3/400 yard roughly prepared airstrips, was a good work-horse for comparatively short journeys in the tactical area, but it could not carry the bulkier army equipment that might have to go by air, and the RAF still had no bulk carrier capable of long range strategic operations. Nevertheless, on the final count, when all moves were complete, nearly 10,000 men and 850 tons of freight had been air lifted. The total cost of the operation was reported as £900,000, and at the time that seemed little enough to pay for the security of nearly half of Britain's oil.

In October of the same year the RAF was called upon to help in a very different sort of operation in the Caribbean. On the night of October 31, hurricane 'Hattie' struck the principal town of British Honduras. Throughout the night the hurricane raged, at one time reaching a speed of 200 mph, gusting to 240 mph. The damage was increased both by tidal waves and torrential rain in the days immediately following the hurricane. The result was the almost complete destruction of Belize. Further south, the town of Stann Creek was virtually wiped off the map. The magnitude of the damage far exceeded that of previous hurricanes.

On November 2, at the request of the Colonial Office, aircraft of both Coastal and Transport Commands started flying supplies into Belize via Kingston, Jamaica. On November 4, an RAF medical team flew to Belize. Commanded by an RAF doctor, Squadron Leader B.A.J. Barrow, the team was composed of two nursing officers of Princess Mary's RAF Nursing Service, Flight Officer D. Hutchins and Flying Officer Iris Rawlings, and four male air ambulance attendants. An Air Transport Operations Centre, provided by 38 Group Transport Command, was established at Kingston to control and co-ordinate all the RAF Operations.

Squadron Leader Barrow reported how on Sunday November 5, he and his medical team moved into Belize town and saw for the first time the effects of 'Hattie's' savagery, and the appalling havoc she had left in her wake. "The ruined town assailed our noses", he later reported, "long before we had actually arrived from the airport. A heavy, nauseating, penetrating stench overhung the ruins, and the characteristic smell of death intruded in the vicinity of collapsed buildings containing the bodies of those trapped in their homes during the hurricane. By dark, an unusual quiet descended on the town and we learned that a strict night curfew was in force to prevent looting which had broken out soon after the hurricane had passed." The arrival by air of British troops and the introduction of martial law quickly corrected the situation.

The RAF medical team took over a large but severely damaged house in Belize, and although living and working under appalling conditions, they inspired and encouraged the locally recruited staff and labour gangs to convert a ruin into a hospital for sixty-five patients who were fed, clothed, treated and nursed — and lived or died — under a roof, instead of on the streets. As its adjutant, the team had a Flying Officer Pinks, an RAF officer born in British Honduras, who had flown with them to Belize to seek the survivors of his family. On his return to Belize, after seventeen years in England, he met many of his school friends, who were able to give invaluable assistance in converting the house to a hospital. Squadron Leader Barrow concluded his report by saying that the next twelve days were some of the busiest of his life. Compressed into this short space of time they inoculated the survivors with TAB, visited the sick, performed minor surgery, inspected and tested the water supply and advised on the salvage operations. The medical authorities in Belize reported afterwards that the work of the RAF medical team was a vital factor in the prevention of an outbreak of typhoid during the chaotic conditions following the hurricane.

Belize was only one of several mercy operations carried out by the RAF during those two years. In 1960, Shackletons of 224 Squadron, with aircraft of many other countries, flew help to Agadir in Morocco when more than 12,000 people were killed and thousands more injured in one of the most violent earthquakes of modern times. News of the tragedy reached the RAF in Gibraltar some 500 miles NNE of Agadir about mid-day on March 1. Crews of 224 (Shackleton) Squadron were brought to immediate readiness and efforts intensified to make all aircraft serviceable. Supplies of tents, blankets and medical material were delivered to the airfield from Army sources throughout the day and loaded on to all available aircraft. Within one hour of receiving a message from the British

Embassy in Morocco, asking for help, the already loaded aircraft were airborne on the morning of March 2.

Mercifully the airfield at Agadir, five miles south east of the town, was still serviceable although the control tower had to be abandoned because of cracks in the walls. Into this airfield came an international airlift composed of aircraft of French, American, British, Spanish and many other nationalities, the speed of whose organisation and diversity of whose loads was probably unprecedented. From the air it could be seen that almost all of the old native quarter of Agadir was destroyed and more than half of the modern European and tourist centre. But the air view told only part of the story for many of the apparently intact commercial buildings, flats and hotels had collapsed inwards, crushing the occupants. The British Red Cross team, who were also carried by RAF Shackleton from Gibraltar, arrived on March 4, and had a great deal of hard work ahead of them.

Early in 1961, the RAF brought relief to tribesmen in the Northern provinces of Kenya where serious famine had resulted from failure of the rains the previous year. In Operation 'Maize Bag' detachments of Beverley aircraft from 47, 50 and 30 Squadrons flew thirty-one sorties dropping over 300,000lb of maize, 20,000lb of dried meat and 2,000lb of dried milk. The supplies were dropped in 100lb containers, in an area virtually inaccessible to overland transport. Ironically, in the autumn of the same year, RAF transport aircraft from the United Kingdom and Middle East were again called upon to help Kenyan Africans now cut off by floods. Known as Operation 'Tana Flood' and later extended to Somalia, some 6 million pounds of food were dropped from the air.

A quite different requirement for the saving of lives by the RAF had occurred off the coast of Cyprus in 1960. With a gale blowing, the Yugoslav motor vessel *Snjeznik* had got into difficulties during an attempt to refloat the Japanese motor vessel *Nagato Maru*. In response to an SOS call, three Sycamore helicopters from 103 Squadron at Nicosia flew to the aid of the ship now in serious peril on a lee shore. One of the helicopters winched a French speaking RAF officer onto the deck of the *Snjeznik* to brief the crew on air rescue procedures. Thirteen men were then taken off by helicopter. In the rough and gusty conditions, one helicopter approached too close to the mast of the ship which was struck by its rotor blades, causing the aircraft to fall into the sea. Fortunately, both pilot and winch operator were quickly picked up by a second helicopter.

Turning from deeds in the field to words in Parliament, we find the 1960 Report on Defence emphasising that, as military aircraft and their weapons became more complex, more power was required from ancillary equipment. Whereas a Wellington bomber during the last war used some five kilowatts of electric power for ancillary equipment, the V-bomber was using about 140 kilowatts. This in turn meant that the men and women who maintained and operated such equipment must possess higher standards of scientific and technical knowledge and skill. To meet this requirement, the RAF was all the time improving its training resources. In the five years prior to 1960, for instance, the proportion of highly skilled tradesmen in the RAF had gone up by fifty per cent and more RAF officers had been sent on degree courses. An important by-product of the raised standard of skill and knowledge was that retiring Servicemen could command better employment on return to civil life, and consequently contribute more to the national wealth.

During the early 1960s, work study and allied techniques were being introduced on an increasing scale. Studies in aircraft servicing in Bomber Command, for example, had increased aircraft availability by ten per cent and resulted in much higher utilisation of manpower. Similarly in Fighter Command the time taken to refuel, rearm and check a Hunter fighter had been cut by half, as had the number of men required to do it.

In 1960, a new officer career structure had been introduced following recommendations made in 1958 by the Advisory Committee on recruiting. This committee had proposed that the career structure of officers should be redesigned so that as far as possible they should have the choice of retirement before age forty or employment to as near age sixty as practicable. As a result, the RAF introduced a scheme whereby all full career officers had an opting-out point at age thirty-eight, but if they did not choose to return to civilian life at that time, they could continue their career to at least age fifty-five, irrespective of rank attained.

Also in the 1960 Report on Defence, the Government affirmed that they could not foresee a time when the United Kingdom would not need highly trained professional forces to help the country play its part in world affairs. "In a more peaceful world," the report stated, "it was visualised that these forces might eventually take on a wider international role, but the need for them would remain." Notwithstanding this statement on the future, we find in 1961 the Secretary of State for Air, Mr. Julian Amery, saying to the Preston Branch of the RAF Association that the RAF was not getting enough pilots and navigators of the high standard needed. It was "only a question of a few hundred men," he said, "but unless they come forward the sharp end of the Service would be blunted." Mr Amery went on to say that he did not think young men were discouraged from coming forward by the knowledge that only the best of them would be accepted; he believed the root of the trouble was "the widespread belief that there is no future in flying and that in a few years the Air Force will have nothing but ground-based missiles." This, he commented, could not be further from the truth; missiles with which we planned to maintain our contribution to the deterrent would be mounted on aircraft — in the first instance on the V-bombers; and the decision to build the TSR.2 means that "we intend to have manned combat aircraft in service as far ahead as anyone can foresee. Meanwhile, Transport Command has undergone a three-fold expansion and I don't doubt is destined to grow still further." Lack of enough of the right kind of aircrew was the only shadow on the RAF recruiting horizon; overall recruiting was going well and, said the Minister: "we fully expect to reach our manpower target of 135,000 officers and men by 1963."

91

It was to help overcome the aircrew shortage that a new type of commission was introduced in 1961. Short Service Commissions for aircrew had been given up after the war because of the greatly increased cost of training. Most post-war aircrew officers (except a small number of National Servicemen selected for pilot training), were committed to a pensionable period of service to the age of thirty-eight, or extending over sixteen years, whichever was the longer. The new 1961 scheme provided aircrew with the option of ending their service after eight years (with a £1,500 gratuity) or after twelve years (with a £4,000 gratuity). Those not exercising their options but completing the full term of service would qualify for the normal rate of retired pay and terminal grant. Officers entering on the new type of commission were guaranteed service to the age of thirty-eight by the RAF, the option to leave earlier was on their side only. In addition, there were to be good opportunities of selection for a full career to the age of fifty-five for those who earned it and wanted it.

Moving on from aircrew to aircraft, 1960 saw the first English Electric Lightning single-seat all-weather supersonic fighter enter service with 74 Squadron at RAF Coltishall. Speaking to the Press when they visited the Squadron, Squadron Leader John Howe, the Squadron Commander, said: "We know we can catch the bombers and, going on past experience, we know we can outfight any fighter equivalent to the USAF Century-Series. The performance of the aircraft, coupled with the ease with which it is flown, gives the pilots confidence, and the fact that it is felt to be the best fighter in operational service in the world today gives our Lightning pilots the highest possible morale."

The Lightning F.Mk 1 was first introduced into squadron service in the autumn of 1960, supplementing the two-seat Javelin which it would eventually replace. Powered by two Rolls-Royce Avon turbojets with reheat, it had three times the thrust of the Hunter and could fly twice as fast. It could scramble to operational height in three minutes and was still effective above 60,000 ft.

It was also in the autumn of 1960 that the RAF took delivery of the first three Westland Belvedere helicopters. Belvederes were the first turbine-powered helicopter (with twin Napier Gazelle engines), the first twin-engined and the first twin-rotor helicopters to go into RAF service. Operational trials were carried out during 1960/61 by the Belvedere Trials Unit at RAF Odiham. In November 1961, the first Argosy entered service with the Transport Command Operational Conversion Unit at RAF Benson in Oxfordshire.

Looking to the future, there was much talk in 1961 of the RAF requirement for a Short Take-off and Landing (STOL) transport aircraft to support future V/STOL combat aircraft and to handle airlifts into inaccessible locations. Mr. W.J. Taylor, the Under Secretary of State for Air, had already made reference in the House of Commons to an operational requirement for a V/STOL ground-attack aircraft. Mr. Taylor said that following the Minister of Defence's recent meeting with the German Minister of Defence, there was to be joint development of an aircraft based on the Hawker P.1127.

In rounding off the first two years of this new decade, brief mention must be made of several other events of rather more than purely historic interest. In July 1960, for instance, the RAF ensign was hauled down for the last time at Katunayake airfield in Ceylon and, except for Air Commodore Barker who was seconded to command the Royal Ceylon Air Force, the last RAF men left Ceylon by air for Singapore. In October of the same year, Far East Air Force officially completed its move out of RAF Kuala Lumpur, on the conclusion of the longest campaign involving British forces — twelve years — since the Napoleonic wars, and handed over the airfield to the Royal Malaysian Air Force. In March 1961, RAF Gan, the coral island airfield in the Indian Ocean which had taken the place of Katunayake, completed its first year of operations as an RAF staging post. During its first twelve months of operation, Gan had handled 630 aircraft, over 12,000 passengers and 1½ million pounds of freight.

In August 1960, Cyprus became a Republic and the Air Officer Commanding-in-Chief Middle East Air Force (renamed Near East Air Force in 1961, with British Forces Arabian Peninsular assuming the title of Middle East Air Force at the same time) became responsible for the administration of the Sovereign Base Areas of Akrotiri (containing the RAF airfield and the HQ at Episkopi) and Dhekelia. In UK in 1960, 38 Group was re-formed (with Air Vice-Marshal P.G. Wykeham as Air Officer Commanding) as a self contained tactical Group within Transport Command, containing fully mobile transport and fighter squadrons capable of moving to any part of the world in support of the Army's strategic reserve.

In December 1960, the Minister of Defence had announced a radical departure from traditional UK air defence policy. Henceforward, the United Kingdom would form one of four NATO air defence regions and RAF Fighter Command would operate under the Supreme Allied Commander Europe (SACEUR) based in Paris. In effect, ever since the air defence 'Exercise Dividend' in 1954 had demonstrated the dependence of the UK on the NATO early warning system, there had been close collaboration between the UK and the NATO northern, central and southern air defence regions. But it had taken some years to overcome Fighter Command's reluctance to be placed under the operational command of SACEUR. This was understandable, because many still serving could not forget the situation that existed just before the fall of France in 1940. Fighter Command's resources in pilots and aircraft had been seriously depleted by sending reinforcements to France in desperate and unsuccessful attempts to stem the German advance. But for the continuous pleas of Air Chief Marshal Dowding, AOC-in-C Fighter Command — in writing to the Air Ministry and in person to the assembled Cabinet — to send no more, it is doubtful whether his Command would have been left with just sufficient resources to win the Battle of Britain, the critical turning point in the war. But by 1960, with the greatly increased speed of jet bombers compared with the bombers of twenty years earlier, the situation had completely changed. Britain's *only* hope of successful air defence, if the threat from the East materialised, was to operate as a fully integrated member of the NATO air defence system. Alone we would certainly fall, together we would have a chance to stand. The Air Officer Commanding-in-Chief Fighter Command (Air Marshal Sir Hector McGregor) thus assumed the additional title of Commander United Kingdom Air Defence Region.

Amongst record flights in 1960 was one of 8,110 miles non-stop to Singapore by a Valiant of 214 Squadron, involving refuelling in the air over Cyprus and Karachi. Another record flight in 1961 was by a Vulcan of 617 Squadron, flying 11,500 miles non-stop to Australia, involving an additional air-to-air refuelling rendezvous over Singapore.

In June 1961, with an eye to the future, a Group Captain was appointed to the new post of Deputy Director of Operational Requirements Space under the Assistant Chief of Air Staff (OR). The 'Blue Streak' long range offensive ballistic missile was the RAF's first space project. After deletion from the RAF's weapon programme on grounds of cost, its rocket motor became the basis for the European Launcher Development Organisation (ELDO) space rocket. (In the 1970s it was dropped from this European programme also).

Meanwhile, not forgetting the past, in July 1961, a bronze memorial statue to the late Marshal of the Royal Air Force, the Viscount Trenchard, the first Chief of the Air Staff, was unveiled in Victoria Embankment Gardens by the Prime Minister, Mr. Harold MacMillan, and dedicated by the Archbishop of Canterbury.

Deeds Not Words

Motto of No 20 Squadron

In June 1962, the Royal Air Force celebrated the 50th Anniversary of military aviation in the United Kingdom with a flying display at RAF Upavon, which, as the cradle of the infant flying service in 1912, was a uniquely appropriate venue for the celebration. Amongst 75,000 visitors were Marshal of the RAF Sir John Salmond and Air Chief Marshal Sir Arthur Longmore and many others who had been in at the start. The Duke of Edinburgh unveiled a commemorative plaque in the partly constructed new building for HQ Transport Command and afterwards lunched in the RAF's oldest Officers' Mess, dating from the days of the newly formed Central Flying School of the Royal Flying Corps.

The flying programme started, in brilliant sunshine, with the ascent of an "R" type observation balloon. This was followed by First World War aircraft from the Shuttleworth Trust: the Avro 504K, Sopwith Pup, SE5A and Bristol Fighter. Then by the Bristol Bulldog, one of the front-line aircraft of the early 1930s, the Avro Tutor basic training aircraft, the Hawker Hart light bomber and Gloster Gladiator fighter, all representing the middle and late 1930s, and a Fleet Air Arm Swordfish which had been still a front-line aircraft in the early years of the Second World War.

Other Second World War aircraft that flew were the Spitfire and Hurricane, the Fairey Fulmar and de Havilland Mosquito. The final fly-past of Shackleton, Argosy and Britannia, Comets Mark 2 and 4, the three V-bombers — Valiant, Vulcan and Victor — and the Canberra, the Sea Vixen and Scimitar from the Fleet Air Arm, the Javelin and Lightning from Fighter Command, brought the display into the 1960s. It seemed unlikely that such a variety of military aircraft, old and new, would ever fly together again, although the establishment of the Shuttleworth Trust should ensure that a few of the vintage types will be preserved in a condition in which it would still be safe for them (from time to time) to "slip the surly bonds of earth" and take to the air.

In the previous month, about 600 former members of the Royal Flying Corps and the Royal Naval Air Service had come together from many parts of the world to attend a reception at Lancaster House in London to celebrate the Golden Jubilee. The following day, at a service in the RAF Church of St. Clement Danes, the Chaplain-in-Chief of the RAF dedicated a Book of Remembrance containing the names of 13,945 men and women of the RFC and the RAF (including the Air Battalion Royal Engineers) who had died *before* 11 a.m. on September 2, 1939, when Prime Minister Neville Chamberlain announced on the BBC, that a state of war would exist between Great Britain and Hitler's Germany.

The Government took the opportunity presented by this anniversary of reiterating in their Statement on Defence that manned aircraft would remain essential to the successful performance by the RAF of all its principal roles: nuclear deterrence, provision of strategic and tactical airlift for all three Services, air defence, strategic and tactical reconnaissance, all forms of support for the Army in the field and long-range maritime reconnaissance and strike. The massive deterrent effect of nuclear striking power, they emphassed, was a fact which, if the West maintained an effective balance of force, provided a justifiable hope of holding the peace until disarmament provided a more lasting solution. The RAF's use of conventional air power in the Berlin airlift, in Malaya, in the Middle East and Africa in the years since the end of the war, had also made an important contribution to reducing international tensions and limiting local conflicts. It was necessary, the Government considered, for the United Kingdom to continue to make it clear to potential aggressors and local trouble-makers, that it would strike back with all the means it judged appropriate. But if the United Kingdom had nothing but nuclear forces, this policy would not be credible. A balance had to be maintained, therefore, between conventional and nuclear strength.

Ironically, it was in October of that RAF anniversary year that America and her Western allies came dangerously close to the brink of a third World War, in the Cuban missile crisis. Air reconnaissance had shown unmistakably that launching sites were being prepared in Cuba for ballistic missiles. Some of the missiles and their crews had already arrived, more were on their way in Russian ships already at sea. On October 24, the United States Navy started a blockade of this largest of the West Indies islands. All NATO forces and also the RAF V-bomber force were alerted. Four days later Russia agreed to dismantle her missile bases in Cuba; but the American President, upon whose shoulders the main weight of decision had lain during these critical days, was assassinated the following year, before the Western World had appreciated the new era in East-West relations that his courage and firmness had initiated.

One of the main lessons of the Cuba crisis, an American newspaper has pointed out, was that: "In the nuclear age it is even more important to have good communication between antagonists than between allies. During that crisis President Kennedy and Prime Minister Khrushchev had communicated through diplomatic channels that required several hours for the transmission of each message. By contrast, missiles carrying thermonuclear warheads could span the distance in a few minutes. It was conceivable that, in another crisis, both nations would be destroyed unless the words travelled faster than the missiles." Consequently, the so-called

Plate 11 During the confrontation with Indonesia (1965/1966) an RAF Whirlwind helicopter lands on a football pitch at Kuching, Sarawak, to bring a sick woman to hospital from a remote village.

Plate 12 Westland Belvedere helicopters flew on trooping and casualty evacuation missions during the confrontation with Indonesia and also, in visiting remote villages in the jungles of Malaysia, played an important part in the 'hearts and minds' campaign.

Plate 13 No 20 Squadron lined up on the tarmac at RAF Tengah, Singapore in 1959. Aircraft are Hunter FGA 9s, a T.7 and four Single Pioneers which were used for Forward Air Control.

Plate 14 A RAF Belvedere helicopter brings up supplies for a Ghurkha outpost on the North Borneo-Indonesian frontier during the confrontation.

Plate 15 A Blue Steel stand-off guided missile about to be loaded onto a Vulcan strategic bomber of the RAF's V-Force.

Plate 16 Two Vulcan bombers (blacksmith of the Gods) flying over the Ballistic Missile
Early Warning Unit at RAF Fylingdales on the Yorkshire moors.

Plate 17 TSR2 – the revolutionary low-level strike/reconnaissance aircraft on a successful
test flight in 1964, before cancellation on grounds of cost.

'hot line' was set up as a rapid communications link between Washington and Moscow. (It has since demonstrated its value on a number of occasions when international tension has been high). Similar communications links were thereafter set up between London and Moscow and between Paris and Moscow.

During 1962/63, the RAF's nuclear capability consumed only about 10% of the United Kingdom's defence resources, and although in December 1962, the American Skybolt project was cancelled and the RAF Vulcan Trials Force was withdrawn from Eglin Air Force Base in Florida, the British Blue Steel powered 'Stand-Off' bomb had been successfully introduced into the V-force. In May 1963, the V-bomber force had been assigned to NATO and had become fully integrated into SACEUR's war organisation. By the end of the year, the V-force had reached its peak strength, although re-equipment of Vulcan 2s and Victor 2s with Blue Steel would not be completed until the end of 1964. The latest airborne electronic counter-measures were also being installed to reduce the effectiveness of enemy defences, and other special measures were being taken and planned to improve the operational capability of the V-bombers. When British Polaris submarines entered service, in the 1970s, it was hoped that their long-range (1,500 miles) missiles, capable of being launched under water, would make up to some extent for the loss of the Skybolt air-launched missile.

Meanwhile, Blue Steel had exceeded its specification in range, accuracy and reliability of components, and its nuclear warhead was in the megaton range. The missile had a Bristol-Siddeley Stentor rocket engine, using liquid propellants, giving it a speed several times that of sound. After launching from the carrier aircraft, the automatic built-in navigation system guided it to the target. The missile had small delta-shaped fore-planes for pitch control, a rear mounted delta wing with inboard ailerons, and a pair of stabilizing fins. The airframe was similar to that of an aircraft and the wing structure also followed normal aircraft practice, but with special precautions to combat the intense aerodynamic heating which occurs at high supersonic speed.

During the first part of an operational flight, the missile's navigation system would be integrated with that of the carrying aircraft, the heading being monitored continuously and the position accurately determined by radar in the parent V-bomber. At the moment of release, outside the enemy's defence zone, the missile's computer (which already "knows" the target location) is automatically given the exact position from which it is starting, its speed and direction of heading. Released, Blue Steel falls freely at first and then, after a few seconds delay for safety, the rocket motor fires and the missile accelerates and begins to climb. From this point onwards, it would be under command of its inertial navigator which computes every change of velocity (from ultra-sensitive acceleration measurements made within the missile) with reference to the position at which it has left the carrier. The flight is programmed, and once launched Blue Steel operates

97

under its own orders. Requiring no signals from outside, it cannot be jammed or diverted by counter-measures during flight.

Plans for extending the V-bomber capability included the further development of a nuclear weapon which had been intended in the first place for tactical operations with the Buccaneer and TSR.2. It was particularly suited to exploiting to the full the capacity of modern aircraft to fly fast at low level — low enough to be under enemy radar cover. In addition, it had been found that this weapon could be adapted speedily and cheaply for strategic use. It would extend the life of the V-bombers because it could be used at low level and used tactically, and would be the complement to Blue Steel. Under an arrangement between the Canadian and British Governments, therefore, V-bomber crews were in turn spending eight days at the Royal Canadian Air Force base at Goose Bay in Labrador before the end of 1963. During their stay each crew was flying three or four low-level routes over some of the wildest terrain in the world, so providing highly realistic navigation training in the sort of conditions, both climatic and topographical, that they would be likely to face in the heartland of Europe over Russia.

Training and accidents are always closely related subjects, and in May of 1963, information of considerable importance was published as a result of a statistical survey that had been carried out in the early 1960s to discover if there was any relationship between 'pilot error' accidents and the age and experience of the pilot. The main conclusion was that those RAF pilots who are in constant flying practice are much less accident prone than those who fly 100 hours or less in a given year. The constant flying practice factor, it appeared, was of greater significance than either age or total flying experience. These findings were to influence future policy regarding provision of flying refresher courses for pilots who had been employed for some time in ground appointments which offered little opportunity to remain in flying practice.

In the field of air transport, by 1962, the closest liaison had been established in training and operations between RAF Transport Command and formations of the Army's Strategic Reserve. The degree of air mobility which the forces had achieved had been well demonstrated in the Kuwait operation of the previous year. The policy now was steadily to increase the strength of the RAF air transport force by the addition of new aircraft. The Comet 4 was entering service in 1962 and orders had been placed for both the VC.10 and Belfast. Two crews had already been selected to train with BOAC crew members on the VC.10. Argosies were being delivered to reinforce the medium range transport force, and that year the decision was taken to order a military version of the Hawker Siddeley (ex-Avro) 748, for short range transport, and the Wessex helicopter for carriage of troops and casualty evacuation from the front line.

As an essential ingredient of the extremely close liaison developing between the Services in the 1960s, a new Joint Service Staff was set up in the Ministry of Defence to serve a committee comprising representatives of the Navy, Army, RAF and Central Defence staffs, to advise the Chiefs of Staff upon all aspects of Joint Service operations including training; but close liaison was not confined to the military field, for one of the most significant developments in British aviation in 1962 was the formation of the Headquarters National Air Traffic Control Services, as the first step in the creation of a common system of control for both civil and military air traffic. The Headquarters United Kingdom Air Traffic Services, which was the operational Headquarters of the RAF organisation for air traffic control, was renamed Headquarters Military Air Traffic Operations and was brought under the operational direction of the civilian Controller of National Air Traffic Control Services. Meanwhile, work on a new radar system to meet the requirements of air traffic control and air defence was making good progress.

Turning from affairs at home to overseas, 1962 was nearly at an end when reports were received at Headquarters Far East Air Force that revolt had broken out in the small British Protectorate of Brunei in North Borneo. Fortunately the RAF had aircraft of 209 Squadron (twin and single-engined Pioneers) already operating anti-piracy patrols from Labuan Island, a few miles off the west coast of North Borneo. The rest of the squadron's aircraft were airborne on the 100-mile flight from Singapore to Labuan within hours of the first news of the trouble. The RAF's first task was to get troops to the Shell oil refinery at Seria which was reported to be held by 5,000 rebels who had already taken hostages. The plan was to land troops on each side of Seria town. On one side, at Anduki, was a small airstrip and on the other some level, if rough, ground where it was hoped the Pioneers could land.

Beverleys of 34 Squadron from RAF Seletar flew troops to the waterlogged airstrip at Anduki, the leading aircraft collecting bullet holes in its twin fins. The Twin Pioneers landed their armed passengers on the rough ground at Pananya without opposition. At both places the troops moved off to immediate action and quickly and successfully regained possession of the Seria oil fields. From then on 209 Squadron Pioneers were kept fully occupied flying troops to a dozen different parts of the Protectorate, carrying out reconnaissance, dropping leaflets to retreating rebels and helping to carry prisoners to jail.

Hunters from the 20 Squadron detachment at Labuan carried out visual reconnaissance over possible escape routes, particularly the Baram and Limbang Rivers, which ran along the Western and Eastern borders of the Brunei Protectorate respectively. The squadron had only recently returned from a six-month stay at Chieng Mai in Tailand where they had flown at short notice in May 1962, at the request of the Thai Government. Singapore radio had announced in an early morning news broadcast on May 16 that: "Bodies of troops from Laos have been reported crossing the river Mekong into Thailand." The Thai Government fearing a full-scale invasion had appealed to its South East Asia Treaty Organisation allies for assistance. No 20 Squadron was the United Kingdom's immediate response. Of six Thai airfields, two were allocated to air transport forces, one to the Australians, one to the US Marine Corps, one to the United States Air Force and Chieng Mai to the RAF. The RAF ground party found on arrival nothing but a 7,000ft concrete runway. Everything else, fire engine, ambulance, radar control caravan, tents, kitchen equipment and ammunition) had to come by air in Beverley and Hastings transport aircraft.

When, after the South West monsoon had come and gone, the squadron received orders to return to Singapore, the Mayor of Chieng Mai gave a farewell dinner for the officers. In his speech he said that "the noise of the aeroplanes made it quite plain that we had protection in the sky above us," and in commenting upon the RAF's good relations with the local people, he added, "it is just as if they are brothers belonging to the same country."

In Brunei, the 20 Squadron aircraft had arrived just in time to save the British Resident from an unknown fate at the hands of the rebels, by creating a noisy low-flying diversion over the small town of Lawas, where as a prisoner of the rebels his life was being threatened. Also active in the second phase of the Brunei campaign were photographic-reconnaissance Canberras of 45 Squadron and Belvedere helicopters of 66 Squadron. The latter had achieved the longest helicopter sea crossing up to that time by flying from their base at Singapore island some 400 miles across the South China sea to Kuching in Sarawak. Then, after refuelling, they flew another 500 miles over dense forest and mangrove swamp, to Labuan Island off North Borneo.

Reports of possible trouble had also been received from Tawau, a small port on the east coast of North Borneo, where a short but adequate runway for Beverleys existed. Because of the possibility of snipers, the aim of 34 Squadron's Beverleys which brought reinforcements was to spend the minimum time on the ground. The pilot of the first Beverley, said: "We dropped down, banged the doors open, dumped the ramp and our Landrovers and trailers poured out. So did the troops. Then we pulled everything shut, opened up the engines and took off. From start to finish the disembarkation took two and a half minutes." All subsequent turn-rounds took less than five minutes.

Tawau had also been selected as an advanced base for a RAF rescue/target towing launch of 1124 Marine Craft Unit from which to conduct anti-piracy patrols in the Celebes Sea. Captained by a squadron leader of the RAF Marine Branch and armed with a 20mm Oerlikon gun borrowed from the Royal Navy, and provided with a gun crew and a shore patrol party by 62 Field Squadron RAF Regiment from Tengah, the launch was ready for anything.

The first daily patrol out of Tawau was to the south east, and although 212 miles were covered no vessels were seen except for some Japanese fishing trawlers. The second day was more successful, when several local craft crowded with illegal immigrants were found many miles from land.

Each craft was turned back and the captain warned not to try to land in British North Borneo.

Apart from deterring pirates, one of the principal objects of the operations was to show the flag and assist in restoring the morale of the inhabitants, particularly of those living in villages which had been attacked by raiders. Wherever it called, the launch was welcomed by the village elders, or at the larger settlements by the District Officer or Senior Police Official.

Soon after the marine craft's arrival, the anti-piracy forces in the area between Sandakan and Tawau were reinforced by a Shackleton of 205 Squadron, and two Royal Navy minesweepers. On arrival the Shackleton made a supply drop of rations for the Marine Craft's crew and in the course of the next four days in co-operation with the aircraft, seven suspicious craft were intercepted. By the time that Her Majesty's Air Force vessel No 2755 returned to her home port in Singapore, she had covered a distance of some 4,300 miles.

It soon became clear that Indonesia would take advantage of the unrest in Brunei to oppose the concept of Malaysia, uniting Malaya, Sarawak, Borneo and Singapore. By January 1963, President Sukarno had coined the word 'confrontation'. Indonesian guerrillas moved into Sarawak and with the help of Chinese communists attacked villages and police stations killing and capturing local people. British and Malayan forces were immediately committed to safeguarding the Sarawak border with Indonesia. In the first phase of confrontation RAF transport squadrons were mainly concerned with the build-up of troops, vehicles, RAF ground staff and equipment and with with re-supply of troops already on the ground in North Borneo and Sarawak. Belvedere helicopters were flying right up to the front line on trooping and casualty evacuation and reconnaissance, while three Sycamore helicopters were flown to Labuan (an island airfield on the west coast of North Borneo) in two Beverleys, reassembled, and were flying on operations the following day.

In April 1963, the Indonesian guerrillas stepped-up their raids into the North Borneo territories of Sabah and Sarawak, but the worst violence did not occur until after the state of Malaysia was established on September 16. The next day thousands of Indonesian demonstrators stormed the British and Malaysian Embassies in Djakarta and the Consulates of the two countries in North Sumatra were sacked. The British Amabssador in Djakarta recommended all British women and children to leave, and with the consent of the Indonesian authorities an airlift began, operated by Beverleys of 34 Squadron and other RAF transport aircraft. In twenty-four hours more than 400 women and children were flown to Singapore.

On September 18, Britain informed the Prime Minister of Malaya that she was ready to assist in defending Malaysia's independence under the terms of the Mutual Assistance Treaty. The build-up of forces continued and by the end of the year the British and Commonwealth forces were fully prepared to react to the Indonesian confrontation. It was not only in the

Far East but also in India that help was required from the RAF during those years. When hostilities broke out between Chinese and Indian troops on the north-east borders of India in the autumn of 1962, British tea planters and their families were evacuated in RAF transport aircraft which flew to Assam from Singapore. In the autumn of the following year, an RAF Javelin squadron flew from the United Kingdom to an airfield near Calcutta to exercise and assist the Indian air defence organisation. They stayed in India for three weeks and were flight-refuelled by Valiant tankers on their outward and return journeys, between overnight stops at Cyprus and Bahrain.

In November 1963, in the longest military airlift ever undertaken by British forces, the first Battalion Royal Ulster Rifles were flown 12,000 miles from the United Kingdom to Australia in seven RAF Britannias to take part in training with the Australian Army. In the same year, 78 Squadron, equipped with Twin Pioneers, completed seven years unbroken service in Aden. Based at RAF Khormaksar, they had operated in support of Army units throughout the federation of South Arabia, and apart from their primary role of short-range transport, had done much to stimulate Anglo-Arab friendship by carrying out mercy missions including flying dangerously ill children and Arab soldiers to hospital. No request for help had been ignored and by day and night one of the squadron's aircraft and crews had always been at stand-by, thus living up to the Squadron's motto; *Nemo non paratus* — 'Always Ready'.

Typifying the RAF's world-wide capability, in the summer of 1963, Transport Command Britannias flew men of the Second Battalion, the Green Jackets, to British Guiana, where they were required because of a "deterioration in the security situation". In November 1963, Hastings aircraft from 24 and 36 Squadrons, which had flown more than 1½ million miles supporting Ghanaian and Nigerian Army United Nations units in the Congo, returned to the United Kingdom after three years of operating in Central Africa. Although not officially United Nations personnel, the RAF men had found it advisable to wear the United Nations beret and scarf for identification purposes in confused and often dangerous situations.

As for the manpower required to support these multitudinous activities around the world, during 1962/3 there had been no major recruitment problems in the RAF, and except for the Engineer Branch, which suffered from the national shortage of engineers, requirements were broadly met in all fields. The disbandment of Thor missile squadrons in 1962 had so reduced the requirement for tradesmen that it had been decided to enlist very few adult males in the ground trades during 1963, though youths and women were still required. The resulting run-down of the recruiting organisation later proved to be a serious mistake because it took some years to recover.

The year 1963 had seen the first University Cadetship Awards made by the Royal Air Force; this was a new scheme whereby a boy who obtained the offer of a place at University (or was already an undergraduate) instead of applying for a cadetship at the RAF College Cranwell, could apply for sponsorship by the RAF at University.

This year had also seen the introduction of a new aircrew category, that of Air Quartermaster. Hitherto the air quartermaster posts in RAF transport aircraft had been filled by corporals and sergeants of the Supply Trade Group, thus helping to ensure good liaison with Air Movements sections (manned by the Equipment Branch). Later, volunteers were accepted from all trade groups. These volunteers served well, but with the increasing size and range of transport aircraft their responsibilities and flying hours increased. In the cause both of justice and increased professionalism, it was recognised — belatedly — in 1962 that they must have aircrew status and pay. The introduction of this new aircrew category meant that, for the first time in peace, women could serve as aircrew. They were in fact of particular value in dealing with female and young passengers. In the strategic trooping role, the AQM's main task was to liaise with Air Movements sections, to compile or check aircraft trim sheets and passenger and cargo manifests and en route, to prepare and provide meals for passengers and generally look after their welfare. In the tactical role, where only men are employed, they also act as despatchers of paratroops and of supplies dropped from the air.

Another event of some significance during these years was the amalgamation of the Aircrew Selection Centre from RAF Hornchurch with the Ground Officer Selection Centre at RAF Biggin Hill. Henceforward selection for NCO aircrew and for commissioned service in flying and ground branches would be carried out at one place. Apart from the economies it achieved, this move was important in recognising the fact that many good officers came to the RAF Ground Branches because, for medical or aptitude reasons, they could not be accepted for aircrew training.

Also in 1963, RAF Maintenance Command celebrated its Silver Jubilee with a dinner at the Command Headquarters at Andover, attended by the Chief of the Air Staff and five of the former seven Commanders-in-Chief. Maintenance Command was formed at Andover on April 1, 1938, exactly twenty years after the RAF itself. By the end of the Second World War the Commander-in-Chief was referred to as "managing director of one of the greatest business undertakings in the world". At the peak of its wartime activity the Command controlled some 200 Maintenance Units in Britain. In 1963, the number of Maintenance Units was down to seventeen (supplying aircraft, vehicles, explosives and equipment); two large engineering units, two repair and salvage units, six bomb disposal flights and an airfield construction depot. Their work also involved air testing aircraft after major modification or overhaul, ferrying aircraft between contractors and aircraft storage units, and the major servicing of V-bombers. Maintanence Command had now entered the world of computers in a big way with the installation of an automatic data processing system at the RAF Supply Control Centre at Hendon. This specially designed computer kept a record of 750,000 different items of equipment used by the RAF, and greatly simplified and expedited supply of RAF units wherever in the world they were operating.

In mid-March 1963, three of the last five Lincoln bombers in RAF service carried out a farewell fly-past over East Anglia and Central England, saluting the cities of York and Lincoln as they flew by. They had operated on special duties in Signals Command since 1949 and were now due for retirement. Lincolns had entered RAF service in 1945 and were destined (when VJ-day came) for attacks on Japan. The last piston-engined bombers in the RAF, they had seen active service in operations against the Mau Mau in Kenya and in anti-terrorist operations in Malaya.

On September 1, 1963, Air Chief Marshal Sir Charles Elworthy took over as Chief of Air Staff from Marshal of the RAF Sir Thomas Pike. Born in New Zealand, the new CAS graduated from Cambridge with an honours degree in Law and was called to the bar in 1935. His keen legal brain was to serve the RAF well in a difficult period of agonizing re-appraisal of the requirements of the Armed Services, after the Labour Government came to power in 1965. Marshal of the RAF Sir Thomas Pike thereafter became Deputy to the Supreme Commander Allied Powers Europe.

Amongst errands of mercy in those years one of the most outstanding was the rescue of the crew of the French trawler *Jeanne Gougy* which, in November 1963, was driven onto the rocks off Lands End. Reefs and gale force winds prevented the lifeboat from approaching the wreck and a number of crew members, severely weakened and unable to use a breeches buoy, were in imminent danger of drowning. A Whirlwind helicopter from 22 Squadron detachment at Chivenor flew out to the rescue. Air Signaller Sergeant Alec Smith was first lowered into the sea and although repeatedly submerged by breaking waves secured the body of a crew member who had been swept overboard and brought it up to the aircraft. Four men were taken off the wreck by means of cliff rescue gear, but the fifth, too weak and exhausted, remained in the wheel-house. Sergeant Smith was lowered through the wheel-house door and succeeded in reaching the seaman and in dragging him into a position from where he was winched to safety. Lowered again he discovered another exhausted seaman; then, despite his own exhaustion and nausea, he made two further descents to see if there were any more survivors. For his tenacious courage and utter disregard of his own safety, this 28-year old Sergeant Air Signaller received the award of the George Medal.

Throughout the severe winter of 1962, RAF rescue helicopters flew daily missions in many parts of the west and north of the United Kingdom providing fodder for cattle and food for villagers, many of whom had been completely cut off by heavy snow. They also flew GPO engineers to discover and repair breaks in telephone lines and Electricity Board officials for the repair of electricity grid lines.

On a unique mission, in April 1962, a Belvedere helicopter of 72 Squadron lowered the eighty-foot high spire onto the roof of Sir Basil Spence's newly constructed Coventry Cathedral, built upon the ashes of the old Cathedral that had been burnt to the ground in a devastating air raid upon Coventry in 1942.

In bringing this chapter to a close, several other events of importance must be mentioned. In May 1962, HQ Near East Command had been disbanded and the Air Officer Commanding-in-Chief had become both AOC-in-C Near East Air Force and Commander British Forces Cyprus. In July of the same year, the Founder's Medal of the Air League (awarded for outstanding contributions to British Aviation) was presented to the RAF's Central Flying School (where flying instructors are trained for the RAF and other Services) on the 50th anniversary of its formation. Also in July, No 2 Field Squadron of the RAF Regiment converted to the parachuting role as part of the United Kingdom's Strategic Reserve. In November, three Vulcans (from 27, 83 and 617 Squadrons) set out on a flight round the world, to coincide with the opening of the Commonwealth Games in Australia and celebration in New Zealand of the 25th anniversary of the Royal New Zealand Air Force.

In April 1963, the Air Ministry Directorate-General of Works (formed as AMWD in 1919) became part of the Ministry of Public Buildings and Works, and in June of the same year Princess Margaret presented standards to 203, 204, and 210 Squadrons at RAF Ballykelly in Northern Ireland, while on July 31, 1963, the RAF Station at Netheravon near Salisbury closed exactly fifty years after it had opened.

By the end of 1963, Fighter Command had undergone a considerable transformation. The two Group Headquarters of Battle of Britain fame — Nos 11 and 12 — had been disbanded and replaced by Sectors. The Sectors were concerned with day-to-day operational control of all fighters, anti-aircraft missiles and radar units in their respective areas of responsibility, while HQ Fighter Command at Stanmore retained overall control of the UK air defence region under the Supreme Allied Commander, Europe. Furthermore, the *administration* of all units in the Command, previously shared between the two Group Headquarters, was henceforward centralised at Fighter Command HQ, thereby achieving considerable economies in manpower.

Provident Fear

'Early and provident fear is the mother of safety' BURKE

In January 1964, the Ballistic Missile Early Warning Unit at RAF Fylingdales on the Yorkshire moors became fully operational. RAF Fylingdales was the third BMEWU to become fully operational, its companion units operated by the United States Air Force were at Thule in Greenland and Clear in Alaska. Together they spread a blanket of radar beams some 3,000 miles across Europe and Asia to provide almost instant warning should ballistic missiles be launched against the United Kingdom or North America. In the event of the UK being threatened, Fylingdales would ensure sufficient warning for V-force aircraft to take off before destruction on the ground. This was considered to be the worst situation, assuming the minimum warning period of four minutes to which Bomber Command alert procedure was geared. A non-belligerent defence system, the BMEW system was regarded as an effective deterrent to war, since it was a reminder to any potential attacker that the nations of the Free World would have time to get their own missiles and bombers on the way for retaliation before the aggressors' missiles hit their targets.

From the three Stations, information on what the radars saw in their surveillance areas flowed constantly by multiple communication channels into the Combat Operations Centre of the North American Air Defence Command (NORAD) at Colorado Springs. From NORAD, it was relayed instantly to other key defence installations such as the US Strategic Air Command in Nebraska and US Air Force Headquarters at the Pentagon in Washington. In 1964, data from Fylingdales was fed to RAF Fighter Command's Control Centre at Stanmore, to Bomber Command and to the Air Ministry. The RAF was also linked directly with NORAD for data from the other units. The rearward communications network flashed information automatically over some 225,000 miles of cable and radio circuits at the speed of light. Each of the detection sites being connected by a complex of land and under-sea telephone cable, microwave radio relay and tropospheric scatter transmission systems, and it took only ten seconds for an alert message to be received at the end of the chain.

At Fylingdales, the heart of the unit was a cluster of three large (140-ft diameter) domes sheltering three 84-ft rotating antennas. These radars, thrusting their beams out through their protective spheres made of paper, glass-fibre and plastic, were capable of both detecting and tracking missiles at ranges of thousands of miles.

Computers played a vital role in the system. They automatically analysed radar return signals and interpreted them, and activated display panels at all of the Command and Control Centres, where the progress of the oncoming attackers would be shown in lights on large wall maps of the top of the world. Thus they computed target trajectories and compared trajectories with observed satellites, the characteristics of aurora, and the characteristics of meteor trails to prevent erroneous identification. A Display Information Processer at Fylingdales also appraised the Intermediate Range Ballistic Missile threat level and transmitted this to the RAF Operations Centres for cor-relation with other warning information and activities. One of the most important contributions to the system's reliability was the automatic check-out and monitoring equipment.

Although the job done by RAF Fylingdales would not be possible without the aid of computers and automated monitoring systems, the final responsibility was that of the RAF Duty Officers. In the 1960s, they were members of the Fighter Control specialisation of the General Duties (Ground) Branch (or sometimes aircrew officers in a ground appointment). In their work, these men, along with their colleagues in the RAF and US Air Force Commands concerned, were making their contribution — night and day — to a safer world. And the BMEWS also had a peaceful role as space trackers. They continuously tracked satellites and fed data into the Space Detection and Tracking System at the North American Air Defence Command Headquarters, where a detailed catalogue was maintained of all space activity.

The Defence White Paper published in February 1964 re-affirmed that the keystone of British defence policy was the prevention of major war and that if, together with their allies, they failed in this aim, none of their other objectives could be attained. Nuclear weapons, the Government reiterated, were so devastating that, unless their use could be prevented, it would not be possible to secure the homeland or carry out obligations to friends and allies. Yet, until true disarmament became a reality, it was the overwhelming power of these very weapons and the determination of the nations not to provoke their own destruction that kept the peace. The year 1964 was the nineteenth in which this truth was demonstrated; and in the state of the world that then existed no other realistic policy was apparent. "Early and provident fear" was indeed "the mother of safety", as Burke had said nearly two centuries earlier.

The argument for an independent British deterrent rested, in the Government's view, on the fact that, if no power in Europe was capable of inflicting unacceptable damage on a potential enemy, he might be tempted to attack in the mistaken belief that the United States would not act unless America herself were attacked. In 1964, RAF V-bombers by themselves were considered capable of inflicting greater damage than any potential aggressor would consider acceptable. But concern was increasing about the vulnerability of V-bombers to ground-to-air guided missiles at high altitude. Increasing emphasis was therefore being given to training V-bomber crews in the low-level role, using the Blue Steel stand-off missile and Bomber Command invited the press to RAF Wittering to hear all about it.

It was 139 (Jamaica) Squadron that was on show to the press at Wittering, the first Victor 2 squadron to convert to Blue Steel from free-fall weapons, although Vulcan squadrons had been flying with the missile for about two years. The tactic would be for Victors and Vulcans to approach high, thereby conserving fuel, drop quickly to fly separately below the enemy radar cover, releasing the Blue Steel missile outside the highly defended target areas. "It gives us" said Mr Hugh Fraser, Secretary of State for Air, "an expanded range of options." Penetration of enemy territory depended, explained Air Marshal Sir John Grandy, the Air Officer Commander-in-Chief, on six factors: aircraft performance, evasive routing (with or without air refuelling), high and low level capability, electronic counter measures, the success of earlier strikes on enemy defences, and stand-off weapons.

The new tactics had been proved in a number of "100% effective" low-level firings of Blue Steel on the Woomera Range in Australia. A proportion of Bomber Command crews were already trained in the low-level role and would become more proficient before the end of the year. The modifications required to Blue Steel for firing at low level were not extensive and the missile's range was not affected. The carrier bomber range was of course reduced at low level, but as Sir John Grandy pointed out, the intention would not be to fly the whole mission low down, but to come down when it was tactically advantageous to do so. The modifications necessary in the aircraft were also small and could be done in the course of normal maintenance, and V-bombers would have their upper surfaces camouflaged so that they would be difficult to see by patrolling fighters from above.

Bomber Command had four states of alert, Air Marshal Sir John Grandy told the press. Alert Condition 4 was in operation as he spoke. In this state, a proportion of the force was fuelled, armed and ready to scramble. Alert Crews were on duty together for twenty-four hours, living and sleeping always within earshot of the alarm bell, with everything ready for take-off in the aircraft. They had frequently demonstrated their ability to get airborne within four minutes. So even at this lowest state of alert, the minimum warning of a missile attack from the BMEWU would be sufficient. If the international situation rendered it advisable, however, the entire force would be brought to Condition 1 and dispersed in pairs to a large number of different airfields.

The type of warning the Command would receive was two-fold. Strategic warning from intelligence and political sources fed direct to

Headquarters Bomber Command; and tactical warnings of possibly hostile aircraft from the whole NATO early warning system, and of missiles whose trajectory threatened the UK or America from the three BMEWUs linked with the North American Air Defence Command as well as with the NATO air defence system in Europe. In the worst situation of the missile threat, Britain would get from four to eight minutes warning, depending upon the site from which ballistic missiles were fired. But if the enemy attack was planned to hit UK and American targets simultaneously, because of the greater distance of American targets, the UK would receive fifteen minutes warning.

Turning to limited war, non-nuclear capabilities of the V-force, the Air Marshal showed a map displaying the areas covered by the radii of action of Vulcans and Victors operating from established British bases overseas, with air refuelling. It was notable that every recurrent trouble-spot for Britain in the past few years fell within the V-bomber radius of action. The standard non-nuclear weapon for the V-force was the 1,000lb HE bomb, of which the Victor could carry thirty-five and the Vulcans and Valiants could each carry twenty-one.

Early in 1964, the work of the V-force had become better known to the general public through the medium of a TV documentary film. Viewers saw the navigator's radar-scope photographs of the ground, compared with his map; his preparations for radar identification of the target area by tracing prominent features onto transparent film; his ability to control the aircraft's movement in the critical run-up to the target with a small control column on his desk, linked with the automatic pilot. During a discussion on the effects of atomic flash, a pilot demonstrated the use of an eye patch, donned before weapon release, to shelter one eye so that it would remain effective if the other was temporarily blinded by flash. Finally, from a discussion of their great responsibilities, the film left the clear impression that the V-bomber crews were highly professional yet modest men and simple livers, who liked peace and were happy in a homely way. On duty and off, they preserved the nerve for action and the spark of indignation. Because of their devotion to their task they hoped and believed that zero hour might never be signalled, but if it was, they would indeed be leaders and wielders of power.

Although by the end of 1964 the first of the V-bombers — the Valiant — was taken out of service some years ahead of schedule because of fatigue cracks, Victors replaced them in the in-flight refuelling role the following year. Valiants had lived up to their name in the course of the nine years service they had rendered, and in their final year of operations, three Valiants of the RAF's Radar and Photographic Reconnaissance Squadron had photographed in eleven weeks some 400,000 square miles of the Rhodesias (an area greater than the UK, France and Germany together) and another two aircraft completed an earlier unfinished air survey of Trinidad and British Guiana, British Honduras and Jamaica. In the same year, 202 Hastings Squadron, one of the oldest in the RAF, which for nearly eighteen years had specialised in daily meteorological sorties 800 miles out into the Atlantic — was disbanded. With computers and other improved techniques assisting forecasting, the additional information obtained by these flights no longer justified their cost.

In October 1965, the Air Officer Commanding-in-Chief of RAF Flying Training Command, Sir Patrick Dunn, held a reception at his Headquarters near Reading to celebrate the 25th anniversary of the Command, at which he entertained six of his predecessors. In the previous year a milestone had been reached in the RAF's flying training policy when, on September 11, 1964, three young offices graduated from the Operational Conversion Unit at RAF Coltishall to become the first pilots to fly the Lightning straight from flying training. With increasingly complex and expensive aircraft entering the RAF in the 1960s, ever higher standards of skill and experience were required to fly them and to make the most of their performance and sophisticated weapon systems. The easiest way of ensuring high standards was to use pilots who had already carried out at least one tour in the same role. By 1964, this was no longer proving practical. It was decided, therefore, to select above average pilots from those who had completed their 160 hours of basic and 70 hours of advanced flying training, give them a further 70 hours lead-in training on Hunters and then a fifteen week flying course at the Lightning OCU, which included 44 hours in the Lightning flight simulator. The experiment was a success, but no Lightning squadron would initially have more than a small proportion of these 'first tourists' on its strength. This was considered important at that time, because the higher performance Lightning F.3 was handed over to the Air Development Squadron of the Aeroplane and Armament Experimental Establishment in January 1964, and would ultimately replace all the earlier Lightnings then in squadron service. With greater fuel capacity and longer range, the F.3 would carry two of the Hawker Siddeley Dynamics Red Top collision-course air-to-air missiles in place of the existing Fire Streak pursuit-course missile.

It was in March 1964 that the cost of modern weapons was emphasised by a small item published in the Auditor General's Air Services Appropriation Account. This showed a loss to the public funds of £10,850 due to a Fire Streak missile being accidentally released from beneath a Javelin and damaged beyond repair!

In the field of technical training, in December 1965, a new building was opened at the RAF School of Photography at RAF Cosford by Air Chief Marshal Sir Alfred Earle, Vice-Chief of the Defence Staff. Designed to improve the School's training capacity, the new building housed some of the most advanced photographic processing equipment available, making it one of the most up-to-date establishments of its kind in Europe. The school had its origin in the Army School of Ballooning, formed in 1912. As early as September 1914, Royal Flying Corps squadrons were making operational photographic sorties in France, while in January 1915, Lieutenant J.T.C. Moore-Brabazon (later Lord Brabazon of Tara) was

110

placed in command of the Experimental Photographic Section Southern Aircraft Reserve Depot attached to No 1 Wing RFC. Then, on January 1, 1917, the School of Photography came into being at Farnborough as a training unit of the RFC. In 1963, the School moved to RAF Cosford where, in 1965, it was responsible for the training of all apprentice and adult RAF photographers, and a wide range of new equipment was being introduced to keep pace with the more exacting photographic techniques. The new building also housed a comprehensive historical section which recorded the highlights of the Branch's history. One of the principal exhibits was a manual of air-to-ground photographs taken unofficially over the enemy lines in 1914 by Moore-Brabazon, in an effort to convince his initially sceptical superiors of the immense potential of aerial reconnaissance.

Now automatic high-speed processing of air film was carried out on cassette loading machines at speeds of up to forty feet per minute. These production speeds had been made possible by dispensing with the time-consuming immersion operation. In its place, developer and stabiliser solutions, at near maximum temperatures, were sprayed on to the fast-moving film as it passed through the machine. Although similar equipment had been employed by the RAF for some time, this was the first time it had been used for training purposes and it represented a considerable advance on previous equipment which had a processing capacity of only four feet per minute. Air Chief Marshal Earle was a particularly appropriate person to perform the opening ceremony at a school which had trained so many apprentices, as he himself had entered the RAF through an apprenticeship at Halton and made his way to the top of his profession.

It was in October of the same year that a new Technician Apprentice scheme replaced the Aircraft Apprentice scheme which had provided the backbone of the RAF's servicing organisation ever since February 1920, when the RAF Apprentice School at Halton was established by Trenchard. At the same time, a new Craft Apprentice Scheme replaced the Boy Entrant scheme that had been in existence since September 1934. Under the new scheme, Technician Apprentices would continue to be trained at Halton for those posts which required the highest level of skill. Entering the Service on completing GCE at ages of between 15½ and 18, they would receive three years training which, for aircraft and electronic technicians, could qualify them for the Ordinary National Certificate in Engineering after two years. The Aircraft Technician would become the RAF's trouble-shooter on propulsion and airframe sub-systems; the Electronic Technician (Air) would deal with the increasingly complex airborne electronic systems; the Electronic Technician (Ground) would deal with similar ground-based systems and the Dental Technician would, like his civil counterpart, provide the essential technical backing for the RAF Dental Services.

The Craft Apprentice in a List 1 trade, after two years training, would become a competent tradesman of the 'fitter' type, well qualified to develop and improve his knowledge and ability as his career progressed and his experience increased. He would be trained in one of ten different specialisations; propulsion, weapons, airframes, air radar, navigational instruments, air communications, ground radar, ground communications, aircraft electrical systems and ground based electrical systems. Apprentices who trained in one of the trades in List II would then be called either Craft Apprentices, i.e. Cooks, or Administrative Apprentices, i.e. Clerk Secretarial and Supplier General. For this category of apprentice the training course would last for one year.

By July 1964, the surplus of tradesmen resulting from disbandment of Thor missile squadrons had been re-trained as far as possible for other trades, and recruiting of adult airmen started up again. It was at this point that the RAF regretted having allowed the recruiting organisation to run down, for the impetus had been lost and starting up again proved to be a slow business. Also in 1964, difficulty was experienced in meeting aircrew recruiting targets, but this was largely a hangover from the loss of confidence in the future of the manned military aircraft after the emphasis on missiles in the 1957 White Paper on Defence. The 7½% average pay rise which came into effect on April 1, 1964 could not, it appeared, by itself resolve recruiting problems.

In 1965, the RAF was making increasing efforts to economise in both manpower and equipment and one way of doing this was to place more effort into the protection of the lives of those already in the Service, and their increasingly expensive aircraft, by improved flight safety and good leadership. Lord Wavell had once said that "good leadership is the reflection of a Commander's personality on his troops." "If we are good enough and proud enough of our professional skill," an article in *Air Clues* emphasised, "we will forestall the errors which could later become accidents. This *is* good leadership."

Nevertheless, flight safety has never been a safety first affair. As long as the RAF required all weather operations, tactical formations, tight fuel margins, low flying and weapons exercises, there were bound to be some accidents. For those unfortunate enough to be involved, therefore, the RAF had established in 1950 a Medical Rehabilitation Unit at Headley Court in the Surrey countryside. Believed to be the first rehabilitation unit in the world to be designed specifically for the purpose, by 1965 it had treated over 6,000 patients from the Navy and Army as well as the RAF. Full-time rehabilitation ensured the quickest possible recovery from illness or accident. In addition to RAF doctors, a RAF Physical Fitness Officer, remedial gymnasts, physiotherapists and PT instructors were available to provide for the individual needs of each patient.

Switching from consideration of the sick to the activities of the particularly fit, it was in the autumn of 1964 that an RAF squadron leader and NCO photographer participated in a tri-Service expedition to the Island of South Georgia in the Antarctic, some 1,100 miles east of Cape

112

Horn. In the course of four months they re-traced the late Sir Ernest Shackleton's route, made successful ascents of the island's two highest mountains and carried out a survey on behalf of the Royal Geographical Society. After four months over difficult and dangerous terrain in appalling weather, the team returned to England feeling they had contributed another chapter to the long history of joint-Service endeavour and co-operation.

It was in the spirit of the times to demonstrate how closely the three Services worked together, for in April of the same year, a Unified Ministry of Defence was formed, with authority and responsibility vested in a single Secretary of State for Defence. On April 1, 1964, the Air Ministry became the Air Force Department of the Ministry of Defence, the Air Council became the Air Force Board, and the Secretary of State for Air, the Minister of Defence for the RAF.

It was not only policy, but the demands of military operations overseas that stimulated ever closer co-ordination between the Services in those years. In Asia and Africa, in all the under-developed regions, there were in the 1960s powerful pressures for change. It was for Britain both an interest and a responsibility to help the change to take place with a minimum of violence. This was in Britain's interest because violence in all its forms is contagious and can quickly threaten the healthy society as a whole; it was Britain's responsibility because in so many parts of the world formerly dependent states looked to Britain for help in establishing themselves and making their own way in peace. Nowhere was this more true in 1964 than in the Far East, where the threat and actuality of violence was acute. The United Kingdom had a special responsibility for helping Malaysia to establish and consolidate its independence, and increasing calls had been made upon UK military resources for this purpose. The creation of a unified command in the Far East had helped in this respect and the build-up of RAF airlift capacity had also made an important contribution.

In the early months of 1964, the Indonesian Air Force started air supplying its guerrilla troops still in Borneo by night as well as day. Javelin all-weather fighters of 60 Squadron were therefore deployed to Kuching and Labuan, together with Ground Control Interception (GCI) facilities to cover the threat along a total frontier of some 1,600 miles, and to reinforce 20 (Hunter) Squadron. At the same time, RAF fighter units in Malaysia were called to a high state of alert. The Singapore, Malaya and Borneo areas were declared an air identification zone and all unidentified aircraft were to be intercepted. By February 1964, British air effort in Borneo had built up to a level that necessitated the appointment of Air Commodore A.V.R. Johnstone as Air Officer Commanding British Air Forces Borneo. In addition to air defence and reconnaissance patrols, Whirlwind, Wessex and Belvedere helicopters operating from bases in Sarawak and Sabah greatly assisted the mobility of Army and Royal Marine detachments, and RAF Twin Pioneers provided tactical and transport support in the forward areas. These operations had successfully contained the threat to Eastern Malaysia and had notably demonstrated the value of inter-Service co-operation, and the value of and the need for more helicopters.

After the Indonesian landings in Malaysia itself in September 1964, theatre air forces were reinforced by detachments of V-bombers and additional Canberras, Shackletons and Javelins. The main value of these reinforcements had been as a deterrent, but reconnaissance operations had helped to locate the invaders and Hunters had carried out air strikes in support of ground forces.

In the Middle East, unification of command was already working well, but in no other theatre were the defence problems more complex. During 1964 in the wild and mountainous area of the Radfan, thirty-five miles north of Aden, dissident tribesmen supported, supplied and encouraged from the Yemen, had effectively closed the Dhala Road which was one of the main trade routes from the Yemen to Aden, by mining and ambushing traffic, and the Federal Government had asked for British assistance. A Brigade Headquarters was formed and a small Brigade Air Support Operations Organisation was attached to it early in the planning stage. Radforce, which was a combined Federal Regular Army/British Force, was given the task of making the Dhala Road safe for traffic and gaining control of the Radfan. Plans called for the maximum use of air tranport, with Hunters and Shackletons giving armed support. Mr Hugh Fraser, then Minister of Defence (RAF) commented to Air Vice-Marshal J.E. Johnson, the Air Officer Commanding Air Forces Middle East, when he visited the area: "I think it amazing that the troops in the forward areas have been calling down RAF fighters to strike dissident strongholds only twenty-five yards from their own positions. This not only emphasises the extreme skill of the Hunter pilots, but also underlines the confidence of the troops in the pilots' ability to press home their attack with pinpoint accuracy."

Middle East Headquarters' responsibilities extended to East Africa where, early in 1964, there were mutinies in local forces and Commonwealth governments sought the assistance of the British Government. In addition to ground forces, Shackletons and Canberra reconnaissance aircraft, as well as Hunters, had been deployed to Kenya and 38 (Field) Squadron of the RAF Regiment was flown from Aden to take part in the Kenya operations. The Army Units were flown to Kenya and Uganda in medium range tranport aircraft. Kenya's own forces depended upon British Army and RAF units for logistic support in their internal security operations in the North East of Kenya until, in December 1964, the last British troops left Kenya on the final winding up of the British base there.

The following year, the National Liberation Front in the Aden Protectorate mounted a terrorist campaign primarily against Servicemen and the local police force, but also affecting civilians, using guns, bombs, grenades and rocket-launchers. The monthly average of incidents rose to thirty-one by the beginning of September 1965 compared with nine over the last three months of 1964. The garrison in Aden was therefore reinforced with two major Army units, one of which included members of the Territorial Army Emergency Reserve, and with a squadron of the RAF Regiment. RAF maritime reconnaissance aircraft were used to patrol the Persian Gulf to help prevent the smuggling of arms and the infiltration of rebels into the Gulf States and the South Arabian Federation.

The next problem that Middle East Forces had to deal with resulted from the illegal declaration of independence by Rhodesia when, at the request of the Zambian Government, arrangements were made to provide for the air defence of Zambia. HMS *Eagle*, coming from Singapore together with escorting destroyers and logistic support-ships, sailed to a position off the East Coast of Africa where she was available to launch her aircraft into Zambia. An RAF Javelin squadron, together with radar control and communications units, was also held ready in Aden. In the event, the Javelin squadron, which was better suited to the air defence task, was used and HMS *Eagle* was released to her normal duties. A squadron of the RAF Regiment was flown to Zambia from the United Kingdom to safeguard RAF units on the ground, and Britannia aircraft of Transport Command were also used to fly fuel from Dar-es-Salaam to Zambia in support of the Zambian economy. By the end of the year, the rate of air supply of fuel into Zambia by the RAF exceeded 100 tons a day. Also during 1965, a company of infantry was flown by the RAF to Francistown (Bechuanaland) to guard the BBC relay station there. When, in May 1965, civil disturbances in Mauritius placed the local police force under severe strain, it was from Aden that a company of infantry was flown by the RAF to reinforce the police.

During these years, the RAF was active in other parts of the world, providing help to the local populace after a cyclone in Ceylon and typhoon Ruby in Hong Kong; and in spite of their military preoccupations in Aden and other parts of the South Arabian Federation, the RAF and Army provided help after severe flooding had caused a local economic and agricultural disaster in the Federation.

Nearer home, in the Mediterranean, six major army units and three armoured car squadrons had been flown to Cyprus by RAF Transport Command when serious trouble again broke out between the Greek and Turkish communities. This British peace-keeping force was superseded at the end of March 1964 by the United Nations Force in Cyprus, for which the RAF's contribution included helicopters. The RAF also provided an airlift for the rotation of the Danish contingent to the United Nations force.

Finally, on the other side of the Atlantic, law and order could not have been maintained in British Guiana during these years without the presence of British troops, and in May 1964 the garrison had been reinforced by the 1st Battalion Devon and Dorset Regiment, which had been flown out by Transport Command. A combined force of Army and RAF helicopters had been established to help in supporting troops in patrolling the country and in helping the police in their search for arms and explosives.

When the Labour Government came to power towards the end of 1964, they considered that they had inherited defence forces which were seriously over-stretched and in some respects dangerously under-equipped. Mr Denis Healey's first Statement on Defence emphasised that expenditure of over £20,000 million since 1952 had failed to provide the necessary incentive for voluntary recruitment in some important areas, or to produce all the weapons needed for current tasks. Political commitments had not been matched by military resources, nor had resources made available for defence been related to the economic circumstances of the nation. The plans for 1965/66 inherited from the previous government would have made necessary a further increase in defence expenditure, the White Paper pointed out, and to continue along these lines would have meant imposing an increasing burden on the British people which none of their competitors in world trade were carrying. It would have meant that Britain was steadily raising the percentage of her national income devoted to defence at a time when Russia and the United States were reducing theirs. The new Government, therefore, set in train a series of studies on Defence policy.

In February 1965 the new Prime Minister announced cancellation of the P.1154 VTOL supersonic interceptor and ground-attack aircraft in favour of the American Phantom, and of the Hawker Siddeley 681 (STOL transport) in favour of the American Hercules transport aircraft. It was decided, however, to continue developing the P.1127 Kestrel VTOL fighter, which later became the Harrier. The RAF version of the McDonnell Douglas Phantom was to be powered by two Rolls-Royce Spey engines, giving a speed range up to 1,600 mph. In the ground attack and strike roles, it could carry up to ten tons of weapons. The Hercules C.1 was the RAF version of the Lockheed C-130E medium range transport used by the USAF. With four Alison turboprop engines, it could carry infantry, paratroops, casualties, or freight. It would eventually replace both the Hastings and Beverley.

On April 6, 1965, the Budget speech announced cancellation of the revolutionary British Aircraft Corporation Tactical Strike Reconnaissance 2 aircraft which had flown for the first time the previous year. Development of the TSR.2 was one of Britain's longest and saddest stories in the field of military aviation. It had started on the desk of a Wing Commander in the Operational Requirements (OR) Branch of the Air Ministry some thirteen years earlier. He had been tasked with writing the operational requirement for a highly sophisticated, supersonic, tactical nuclear strike aircraft with a subsidiary conventional bombing role. The Wing Commander and his staff produced — and had rejected — many draft specifications. Years passed and new OR staffs came and went before the Tactical Strike and Reconnaissance 2 requirement was accepted by Air Ministry and other Government departments concerned and passed to the aircraft industry. Once on the drawing board, developing engine, airframe and electronic technology made it clear that an aircraft could be produced with extremely high performane and load carrying capability, and that the RAF would have at its disposal a piloted yet highly automated nuclear weapon delivery system for *strategic* as well as tactical use, in other words, a successor not only to the Canberra low-level interdicter bomber, but also to the V-bombers.

As a strategic bomber, it would have flown at high altitude subsonically (to conserve fuel and increase range) until approaching hostile airspace, when it could have made a high-level supersonic approach to and escape from the target area. Alternatively, before entering enemy radar coverage, it could have dived down and, with the help of terrain-following radar and auto-control for low-level flight, it could have penetrated below the radar screen, no more than 200 feet or so above the tree tops and just below the speed of sound, to deliver a guided weapon from outside a highly defended target area. If it had entered squadron service, TSR.2 would have been the biggest leap forward in the history of fighting aircraft in the Royal Air Force. But it was not to be. From about 1961 onwards, development costs escalated dramatically. Hardly a month went by without the Minister having to be told either that another £15 million was required by the British Aircraft Corporation, or another £5 million by Rolls-Royce, or another £2 million for the electronic equipment. The British economy could no longer stand the heavy costs of 'going it alone' on a new aircraft development of so revolutionary and complex a character.

It is easy to be wise after the event, but in the economic climate of 1965, no British Government regardless of complexion, could have accepted the costs of equipping even one or two RAF squadrons with this magnificent aircraft. The Air Staff in fact were wise enough to realise this at the time. There were three aircraft already in production that might provide a less costly substitute for TSR.2 (in its tactical role) and which could be in service with the RAF much earlier. The possible British alternative was the Blackburn (later Hawker Siddeley) Buccaneer. Specially designed for low-level flight at a maximum speed just below that of sound, it was able to carry nuclear or conventional weapons, or cameras for reconnaissance. Consideration was being given to developing the Buccaneer to give it a supersonic capability at low level. A French alternative was the Dassault Mirage IVA two-seat medium range light bomber, which was already entering service with the Armee de l'Air's nuclear strike force. It's maximum speed at 40,000 feet was about 1,500 mph and its tactical radius of action (flying to the target supersonically and returning just below the speed of sound) was about 800 miles. It was equipped with advanced electronic counter-measures against anti-aircraft guided missile defences. The third possibility was the American General Dynamics F-111 swing-wing supersonic nuclear strike and conventional attack aircraft, which was already in production for the United States Air

Force. The Royal Australian Air Force had already opted for the American F-111 instead of TSR.2. Cancellation of the latter, therefore, although a severe blow to the British Aircraft industry, did not leave the RAF without several more cost effective alternatives.

On the credit side in 1965 were the conversion of some Victor bombers to tankers for in-flight refuelling (in place of the phased out Valiants) and the arrival at RAF Gutersloh in Germany of Lightnings for 19 and 92 Squadrons, the first Lightnings to be based overseas.

Two committees whose findings were to have important implications for future RAF policy reported during 1965. One had been examining the role, nature and organisation of higher defence studies and as a result of its recommendations consideration was being given to means of encouraging the universities to play a more active role in higher defence studies and to stimulate academic awareness of defence problems. Proposals included the creation of up to six Fellowships to be awarded annually in universities to selected senior officers to allow them to pursue some appropriate course of advanced study or research. Support was also being considered for the creation, in selected universities, of an additional post of lecturer in an existing faculty, to specialise in the defence aspects of its discipline.

In the same year, a committee under the chairmanship of Field Marshal Sir Gerald Templer, which had examined the rationalisation of air power, reported certain recommendations relating principally to the inter-operability of aircraft, training and logistic support. In due course, the Air Force Department took over the handling of fuels (POL) for all three Services and started also to take over responsibility for domestic equipment in messes and married accommodation for all three Services.

In the international sphere the RAF — in the middle 1960s — was working ever more closely with the Air Forces of its allies. In October 1964, for instance, a tripartite Kestrel evaluation squadron was formed. Based at RAF West Raynham in Norfolk and commanded by Wing Commander D. McL. Scrimgeour, RAF, the squadron was equipped with nine Kestrel (HS.1127) fighter-ground-attack aircraft to assess the various aspects of V/STOL operations, their control and logistics. Four British, four American and two German pilots comprised the aircrew strength of the unit and each nation also contributed ground and technical staff.

Earlier the same year, 74 Squadron of the RAF (which has a Tiger as its squadron badge) spent four days at a French Air Force base with French, American and Belgian 'Tiger' Squadrons to train together, exchange experience and wine and dine together. Then in August 1965, the Royal Air Force gained top points in both the day and night phases of NATO's annual photographic reconnaissance competition with 31 Squadron, flying Canberras, judged the outstanding day reconnaissance squadron, and a crew from 17 Canberra Squadron being judged the outstanding night-reconnaissance crew. On September 19, 1965, The Queen and Prince Philip attended a Thanksgiving Service in Westminster Abbey for the 25th anniversary of the Battle of Britain.

The year 1965 cannot be allowed to pass without mention of the death of Sir Winston Churchill. As Marshal of the RAF, Sir John Salmond wrote at the time: "In his passing, the RAF lost a distinguished friend and supporter; as Secretary of State for both War and Air in 1919, it was Churchill who backed Trenchard in the fight for the very existence of the young Air Force; and it was Churchill who supported Trenchard's proposal that Mesopotamia should be controlled by air power. In Winston's own words, this proved in a manner patent to all intelligent minds, the immense part which the air would play not only in war but in peace.

"On the 25th anniversary of the formation of the Royal Air Force he had completed over 30,000 miles flying on duty as Prime Minister; and he was delighted to accept honorary pilot's wings, the RAF flying badge, presented by the Air Council in recognition of the debt owed him by the Service. He was proud to wear the wings on his uniform as honorary Air Commodore of 615 County of Surrey Squadron Royal Auxiliary Air Force.

"In the maelstrom of politics it was far from easy, even for one as far-seeing and resolute as Churchill, to run counter to the views of the most powerful in pressing the claims of a new Service. Nevertheless, he did just this. In the 1930s, his was an unpopular voice calling for the rebuilding of British air power. He was a great champion of the RAF, although he first cherished the RNAS. He was among the first to appreciate how vital it was for the separate expertise of the three Services to be launched in co-operative action when the biggest blows had to be struck.

During the Second World War, he seemed to become particularly identified with the RAF outlook. We shall remember him with special affection; he, too, always 'reached for the stars'."

The Long Hard Look

'That which is to be established once for all should be considered long' PUBLIUS SYRUS

The years 1966/67 were for the Royal Air Force (not to mention the other two Services) a period of agonising re-appraisal. In its review of defence in 1966, the Government emphasised that military strength was of little value if it was achieved at the expense of economic health. On taking office in October 1964, the Labour Government had, therefore, decided to carry out a far-reaching examination of the Nation's defence needs, and had set a financial target of £2,000 million at 1964 prices (for all three Services combined) to be reached by 1969/70.

Although by 1966 political commitments had become fewer, larger military tasks had been imposed by those that remained because the military power of certain countries had been increased, particularly by supplies of modern weapons from abroad. As a result, British forces outside Europe had been continuously tied down in the early 1960s by operational tasks in many parts of the world. As far as the RAF was concerned, this had involved many emergency moves to overseas theatres including detachments from both flying squadrons and the RAF Regiment. In 1966, for example, twenty-six RAF units and 157 aircraft were involved in operational moves to overseas trouble spots.

Also in the 1966 defence review the Government had stressed that developments in weapons technology, by changing the nature of military strategy and tactics, constantly influenced the options open to a Government in its foreign policy. Because it takes at least ten years to develop and introduce a major new weapon system, and at least five years to produce base facilities abroad, the Government was compelled to plan the main features of defence policy more than a decade ahead. Yet there could never be certainty either about political or technological developments in the intervening period. Defence policy, therefore, had to be based on assumptions which must be constantly revised and which were less certain the further ahead one looked. The fate of the 1957 Defence White Paper, in which it was assumed that missiles would take over from manned military aircraft, illustrated the danger of being over-dogmatic about weapon and political developments. In short, therefore, the Government had to look ten years ahead and decide what sort of military capability was then likely to make political sense.

In 1966, Britain was already making a major contribution to the United Nations Force in Cyprus, and had offered further units for logistic support of any United Nations force, wherever this might be required in future. Nevertheless, Britain had to continue living in a world in which the United Nations had not yet assumed effective responsibility for keeping the peace and in which the arms race had not yet been halted. In such a world, the first purpose of armed forces would continue to be the defence of the British people. The security of the United Kingdom still depended primarily on preventing war in Europe. For this reason the continuation of the North Atlantic alliance was vital to survival.

Broad guide-lines governing the possible recourse by NATO to nuclear weapons in self-defence had been agreed at the Athens meeting of the NATO Council in 1962. The nuclear deterrent was still a credible policy, but the way in which a decision would be taken in a crisis and the strategic doctrine which should determine their employment required further study. Once nuclear weapons were employed in Europe, where several thousand were available, it was considered certain that unless the aggressor quickly decided to stop fighting, the conflict would escalate to a general nuclear exchange, in which the whole of America's nuclear forces would be engaged. The United Kingdom, therefore, had at this time recommended to the alliance the abandonment of those military preparations which rested on the assumption that a general war in Europe might last for several months. On the other hand, it was agreed that NATO, and therefore the RAF, must maintain enough conventional forces to deal with small-scale conflicts in the European theatre, without automatic resort to nuclear weapons. Thus, by December 1967, NATO Ministers had agreed to the adoption of a new strategic plan based on a more flexible and balanced range of appropriate responses to all levels of aggression, confined in the first instance to the use of conventional weapons, and only escalating the response to include the use of nuclear weapons as an absolute last resort.

At first sight, a direct threat to Britain's survival seemed less likely outside Europe. Although Britain had important economic interests in the Middle East, Asia and elsewhere, military force was not considered the most suitable means of protecting them. The United Kingdom, however, had a number of obligations which could not be relinquished unilaterally or at short notice and some of these obligations would still exist in the 1970s. In addition, Britain shared with other countries a general interest in seeing peace maintained, so far as possible, throughout the world. It was this interest above all which justified Britain's military presence outside Europe.

At this time, much of Africa, the Middle East and Asia was going through a period of revolutionary change, which sometimes spilled across international frontiers. In recent years, the threat to peace had been far greater outside Europe than within it. When such instability led to open war, it imperilled not only economic interests in the area, but even world peace. Recent experience in Africa and elsewhere had shown that the UK's ability to give rapid help to friendly governments, with even small British forces, could prevent large-scale catastrophies.

Nevertheless, to maintain all current military tasks and capabilities outside Europe imposed an unacceptable strain on over-stretched forces, and bore too heavily both on domestic economy and on reserves for foreign exchange. For all these reasons it had been decided that, while Britain should retain a major military capability outside Europe, she should in future be subject to certain general limitations. First, Britain would not undertake major operations of war except in co-operation with allies. Secondly, she would not accept an obligation to provide another country with military assistance unless the country concerned was prepared to provide facilities to make such assistance effective in time. Finally, there would be no attempt to maintain defence facilities in an independent country against its wishes. Future policy would therefore be to keep a higher proportion of Britain's Forces in the United Kingdom, and to rely on quick reinforcement by air.

By 1967, the Government had become particularly concerned to settle the size and shape of the Services for the next decade in a way that would provide the maximum possible stability for the men and women who were making their careers in them, yet in July of that year, a Supplementary Defence White Paper announced a personnel redundancy scheme! Meanwhile, good progress had been made with the RAF re-equipment programme. In particular, foundations had been laid for collaboration between Britain and France in a variable-geometry aircraft, as well as in the Jaguar aircraft and the Martel air-to-ground missile; the two Governments had also agreed on the joint production of a family of helicopters which would meet requirements of all three Services throughout the 1970s, and the Tiger-Cat ground-to-air missile had been ordered for the RAF Regiment. The broad shape of the future programme of Service aircraft had been settled for the next ten years or so, and it was considered that industry should now be able to plan its future with confidence. Where it had been decided to obtain aircraft from abroad, it was planned to incorporate British equipment in such aircraft as far as possible.

All these plans would come to nought, however, unless manpower shortages could be overcome. Early in 1967, therefore, a major enquiry had been started into the social and demographic factors which were likely to govern the supply of manpower required in the long-term by the Services. The intention was to relate Service plans more closely to national manpower resources and the demand on them; to provide data for better use of manpower; and to enable the recruiting effort to be more precisely directed. The investigation was to take account of the enquiry into the effectiveness of paid recruiting publicity.

On January 1, 1966, the total strength of the Royal Air Force was 127,000 and by January 1967 it had fallen to 124,000. The results of the 1965

University Cadetship competition had been disappointing; although there were more applicants than in previous years, fewer were of the quality required. With an extension of the scheme to include the Equipment, Secretarial, Education and Catering Branches in addition to the Flying and Engineer Branches, far more high quality candidates would be required in future years.

Although in these two years sufficient pilots had been recruited, navigator recruitment targets had not been met and there was a serious short-fall in recruitment to the Engineer Branch and to the aircraft and fighter control specialisations of the General Duties (Ground) Branch. Although the Equipment and Secretarial Branches and the RAF Regiment were not so badly affected, recruiting to these Branches was nevertheless far from satisfactory.

On a slightly happier note, recruiting of adult airmen for the mechanical and electrical engineering trades was going well, but there was still a shortage of men for the less popular trades, such as gunner, firemen, steward and supplier. Similarly, entries into engineering apprenticeships were sufficient but more recruits were wanted for apprenticeships in the administrative trades. Women's Royal Air Force officer recruiting had been excellent in practically all branches and recruitment of non-commissioned women had also been good, but there was a need for a number of older and more mature women to fill both commissioned and NCO posts.

Probably the most serious manning weakness was the inadequate rate of re-engagement amongst serving airmen. If this situation continued it would lead to a steady drain of experienced men and a shortage of senior NCOs of the skill and experience needed to fill higher posts; and the training bill would go up because more replacements would have to be trained. It was estimated, on current trends, that only about 55% of those required would be prepared to extend their service. In addition, more officers were retiring voluntarily.

It was believed that the two principal reasons for the fall in re-engagement and for the increase in voluntary retirement of officers were the tempo at which overstretched Forces were continually operating and the disturbance to family life, with long periods of separation which this entailed. One of the objects of the Defence Review was to bring commitments into line with resources. At the same time, it was considered by the Government that conditions of Service — pay and allowances, careers and housing — must be attractive and take account of the special conditions of Service life.

Since the Government's statement on the defence estimates was published in February 1967, further consideration had been given to the money and manpower requirements in the 1970s, both in relation to anticipated commitments and to the resources which the country was likely to be able to afford for defence. For some time it had been argued that a Soviet attack in Europe was unlikely and the United Kingdom should probably receive ample warning of any change in the threat. Some of the forces required in Germany in an emergency, therefore, could be held elsewhere in peacetime, provided that they could be returned promptly if a crisis occurred. It had therefore been proposed to Britain's allies in NATO and Western European Union (WEU) that one brigade of BAOR and one squadron of RAF Germany should be re-deployed to the UK early in 1968. This would lead to a foreign exchange saving of about £5½ million a year.

Outside Europe, it was considered that in the next decade new transport and tanker aircraft would make it possible to move forces across the world faster and in larger numbers than was possible even a few years previously, and the military strength of the United Kingdom's friends and allies was growing. Plans had therefore been revised for deployment outside Europe to enable major reductions to be made in the size and cost of British forces as a whole. Plans to reduce forces in the Mediterranean, the South Atlantic and the Caribbean were already being implemented. The British intention to withdraw from South Arabia and the Aden base by January 1968 had also been announced.

In the Far East, it had been decided to reach a reduction of about half the forces deployed in Singapore and Malaysia during 1970/71. As far as the RAF was concerned, although its basic role would be unchanged, the size of the front line would be reduced. More aircraft would be concentrated in Britain; the increased range made possible by refuelling in flight, higher performance and resulting greater mobility of the new aircraft rendered this greater concentration practical. The reductions up to 1971 would occur mainly in the Far East, Aden and Malta; with four squadrons of aircraft being moved from Aden to the Persian Gulf.

To understand how British forces in general and the RAF in particular were deployed outside the UK, some explanation of overseas commitments at this time is necessary. Obligations in the defence of other countries derived essentially from three sources: international treaties, bilateral agreements and the residue of colonial responsibilities. All were consistent with obligations under the United Nations Charter. The UK was a member of the North Atlantic, Central and South East Asia Treaty Organisations (NATO, CENTO and SEATO). Although Berlin was outside the area defined in the North Atlantic Treaty, it was accepted that an attack on Berlin would be equivalent to an attack on the Treaty area. Under the Baghdad Pact of 1955, which gave rise to the Central Treaty Organisation, the UK was committed to co-operate with Iran, Pakistan and Turkey for "security and defence". Finally, under the Manila Treaty of 1954 which established the South East Asia Treaty Organisation, the UK was committed to "act to meet the common danger" in the event of an attack against any of the parties to the Treaty, which included Pakistan, the Philippines, Thailand, Australia, New Zealand, France and the USA.

The UK also had certain specific obligations arising from bilateral agreements with foreign and Commonwealth countries and with the

Persian Gulf States. In the Mediterranean, the UK was committed to "assist" in the defence of Malta and to "consult and co-operate" in the defence of Cyprus. Under the Anglo-Libyan Treaty of 1953, the UK was committed to go to the aid of Libya in the event of her being engaged in war or armed conflict. The UK was responsible for the protection of the Federation of South Arabia and of certain unfederated states in the same area. In the Persian Gulf, the UK had a number of written and implicit understandings, some of them dating back many years, which amounted to an obligation to support Bahrain, Qatar, Muscat and Oman, and the Trucial States against external attack. Under the Simonstown agreement of 1955, HM Government and the South African government made arrangements for continued use by the UK of the Simonstown naval base "to ensure the safety of the sea routes around Southern Africa". In the Far East, the UK had treaties of 1957 and 1963 to afford "such assistance as the Government of the Federation of Malaysia may required for the external defence of its territory". Independent Singapore accepted these treaties as binding on her too, and responsibility had also been assumed for the protection of the Sultanate of Brunei.

The UK was responsible for the external defence and internal security of such territories as Gibraltar, Aden, the High Commission Territories in Southern Africa, British Guiana, British Honduras, Mauritius, the Seychelles, the Falkland Islands and Hong Kong. Finally, as a member of the United Nations, the UK had accepted an obligation to provide, in certain circumstances, Armed Forces for maintaining international peace and security. For example, the UK contributed substantially to the UN Force in Cyprus.

The new and more economical approach to all these commitments was to have in overseas theatres the minimum forces considered essential and hold ready in the UK the Army strategic reserve and operational squadrons and supporting units of the RAF, with strategic and tactical air transport and tanker aircraft.

During 1966-67 the RAF had deployed within the United Kingdom bomber, reconnaissance, tanker and air-defence forces; strategic and tactical transport squadrons and ground-attack squadrons of Transport Command; maritime reconnaissance squadrons of Coastal Command, and squadrons of the RAF Regiment. Plans for improving the RAF command structure in the UK had been announced on June 16, 1967. One bomber Group headquarters would close before the end of 1967, and in 1968 Fighter and Bomber Commands would merge into the new Strike Command, and Flying Training and Technical Training Commands would combine to form Training Command. These measures were expected to give better command and control and save manpower.

In Europe the RAF had a Tactical Air Force, including light bomber, reconnaissance and air defence squadrons; fighter reconnaissance aircraft and support helicopters. In the Mediterranean the RAF had light bomber, reconnaissance and tactical transport squadrons and air-defence forces;

also a flight of helicopters in support of the United Nations in Cyprus.

In the Middle East, the RAF's responsibility at this time covered an area west of a line down the centre of the Indian Ocean and included the islands of the Western Indian Ocean; East, Central and Southern Africa; the Arabian Peninsular and the Persian Gulf. A unified command was operating, and in support of some 17,500 troops the Air Force had units in Aden including ground-attack, fighter-reconnaissance, tactical transport, maritime-reconnaissance squadrons and a squadron of the RAF Regiment all based at or in the vicinity of Aden, while at Bahrain there were ground-attack and tactical transport squadrons.

In the Far East the RAF had light bomber squadrons, reconnaissance aircraft, air defence forces (including Bloodhound Mark II mobile air defence missile squadrons), ground-attack and medium and short range tactical transport squadrons, RAF Regiment squadrons and V-bombers which deployed on rotation. Units of the RAAF and RNZAF also formed part of FEAF.

Discussion during these years of the aircraft required to discharge the RAF's wide-ranging responsibilities inevitably re-introduced the debate about carrier-borne aircraft versus land-based aircraft. The Government agreed that of the then existing force of five carriers, only three would continue to be available throughout the 1970s. The total cost of such a force would be some £1,400 million over a ten-year period. For this price, it would be possible to have only one carrier permanently stationed in the Far East, with another normally available at up to fifteen days' notice. It was not considered that this could give sufficient operational return for the expenditure.

It was also considered that the tasks for which carrier-borne aircraft might be required in the later 1970s could be performed more economically in other ways. It was the Government's plan, therefore, that in the future aircraft operating from land bases should take over the strike-reconnaissance and air-defence functions of the carrier on the reduced scale which commitments would require after the mid-1970s. Close anti-submarine protection of the naval force would be supplied by helicopters operating from ships other than carriers. Airborne early warning aircraft would continue to be operated from existing carriers, and subsequently from land bases. Guided missiles could largely replace both guns and aircraft for close anti-aircraft defence of ships and for attack against enemy ships.

In discussing a replacement for the RAF's Canberra — both the interdictor bomber (BI.8) and the photographic reconnaissance version (PR.9) — it was argued that the key to the deterrent power of our armed forces was the ability to obtain early warning of an enemy's intentions from air reconnaissance and other intelligence sources and to strike at his offensive forces, fuel supplies, reinforcements and airfields, well behind the front line. This role, known as 'interdiction' had been assigned to the RAF's Mark 8 Canberra low-level interdictor squadrons in Germany since the early 1950s, but this aircraft could not safely continue after 1970. By the mid-1970s, it was intended that the Anglo-French variable-geometry aircraft should begin to take over this and some other roles including reconnaissance. Meanwhile, if the RAF was not to be lacking in a most critical part of its capability for some five years, some arrangement had to be made for bridging the gap. In February 1966, therefore, it had been decided to buy fifty of the General Dynamics F-111 aircraft from the United States. Until the Anglo-French variable-geometry aircraft was available, the F-111A would be supplemented in the strike role by the V-bombers, which would cease to form part of the contribution to the *strategic* forces of NATO when the Polaris submarine came into service, and which would penetrate enemy territory at low level.

It was considered at this time that no other aircraft could be available by 1970 to match the performance of the F-111A. The only two competitors were a possible development of the French Mirage IVA with two Rolls-Royce Spey engines and a developed version of the Buccaneer Mk II. In April 1965, therefore, an arrangement had been made with the US Government for the F-111A. The British Government later decided to place an immediate order for ten F-111As, to be followed in April, 1967, with an order for forty more.

The Air Staff considered that the F-111A would meet nearly all the requirements of the recently cancelled TSR.2, and it could be in RAF service much earlier. One of the most interesting features of the F-111 aircraft was its variable-sweep wing. This enabled the aircraft to fly at high supersonic speeds at high altitudes with its wings swept back at an angle of 72.5°, and to achieve a supersonic dash close to the ground. With wings forward (with only 16° of sweep) and using high-lift devices such as flaps and slats, it had a good take-off and landing capability using short, comparatively easily prepared airstrips in the tactical area. To be able to swing the wings from 16 to 72.5° in flight meant that the designers had to provide a single hinge point strong enough to transfer all the wing loads to the aircraft fuselage. In a ground attack and nuclear strike aircraft capable of near-sonic and supersonic speeds at low level, the wing (and the hinge around which it pivoted) had to be capable of withstanding lift forces up to eight times the weight of the aircraft to ensure sufficient manoeuverability for its low-level role. Also, because most of the F-111's weapons are carried beneath the wings, the pylons on which they are carried also had to pivot to maintain an attitude parallel to the line of flight, whether the wings were fully forward or fully swept.

Wing Commander Geoffrey Fletcher who, in 1965, commanded the RAF Bomber and Maritime Flight Test Squadron at Boscombe Down, had been sent by the RAF to fly the F-111 at the General Dynamics airfield at Fort Worth in Texas and at Edwards Air Force Base in California, to advise on its suitability as a substitute for TSR.2. He was duly impressed. He reported that he felt virtually no change in the trim of the aircraft when the wings were swept back, but that because you lose lift and reduce drag, you have to raise the nose to maintain height. He also observed that, going really fast the fuselage itself could give enough lift without any wings at all, "but you can't tuck them away completely." Most impressive of all was the F-111's automatic terrain following capability at high speeds at low level. From Edwards Air Force base he flew low-level through the Sierra Nevada mountains. "On auto pilot," he reported, "you select the height you want to fly above the ground, and the radars and computers control the aeroplane at the required height." Similarly, navigation is handled by a self-contained aircraft navigation system which relies on no external radio directions. The pilot simply sets his required destination on the computer, and the computer gives the necessary steering instructions to get there. The system can operate, therefore, anywhere in the world.

As for the radar, the faster the aircraft is flying, the further the radar looks ahead. Flying supersonically at low level there is not time to dive down into every valley at high speeds, therefore the radar disregards the narrower valleys for computing purposes and concentrates on clearing the next mountain range. "To see a mountainside coming at you at several miles a minute is exhilerating, to put it mildly", Wing Commander Fletcher commented, "and the duplication of all the vital equipment, together with the outstanding performance of the aircraft and the radar, soon gives you great confidence in the entire system."

In the mid-1960s, the RAF's air defence fighters were the Gloster Javelin, a two-seat all-weather intercepter, and the English Electric Lightning single-seat fighter. The Javelin was due to be phased out in the next few years as more Lightnings came into service. The ground-attack aircraft providing close-support for the army was the single-seat Hunter FGA9 and this had to be replaced by 1970. When it had been seen in early 1965 that its intended replacement, the supersonic P.1154, would be too costly and come into service too late, the project was abandoned. It was planned to use instead a combination of American McDonnell Douglas Phantoms and the British subsonic V/STOL P.1127 (the Harrier). Later, it was proposed to take a strike version of the Anglo-French Jaguar in order to release Phantoms to replace Lightnings in the air defence role. Meanwhile, the first of the long-range Lightnings (Mk 6) arrived at RAF Binbrook in April 1966.

There was also a firm production commitment for a development of the Comet (Nimrod) to replace the Shackleton Mk II in the maritime reconnaissance role, at the end of the 1960s. As for air transport, British strategy would rely increasingly on air mobility as overseas bases were given up. Thus it was decided in 1966 to purchase some American C-130s (Hercules) aircraft, which were already in service with the USAF. Built by Lockheed and powered by four Allison turboprop engines, the Hercules was a rugged multi-purpose military transport aircraft well suited for the paratroop assault role, for carriage of troops into airstrips in the tactical area and for the normal carriage or air dropping of freight. The British overall programme provided for continued production in the UK of the

Plate 18 At a ceremonial parade at RAF Akrotiri, Cyprus, in January 1968, the last Near East Air Force 'Strike' Canberra wears the badges of the disbanding Squadrons – Nos 6, 32, 75 and 249 – when their multiple responsibilities were handed over to two Vulcan Squadrons – Nos 9 and 35.

Plate 19 RAF Buccaneers in the maritime support role for the Royal Navy. Ship is a Russian 'Kanin' class destroyer.

Plate 20 The Transatlantic Air Race 1969, Squadron Leader Graham Williams arrives in his Hawker Siddeley Harrier at the disused coal yard at St. Pancras Station.

Plate 21 The 50th Anniversary of the Royal Air Force College, Cranwell in 1970. Cranwell is now the RAF's post-graduate college.

Plate 22 Three members of the RAF's 'Falcon' free-fall parachute display team 'showing the flag' while falling earthwards at 120 mph.

Plate 23 Nimrod – the 'Mighty Hunter'. The world's first turbojet-engined maritime reconnaissance aircraft shadowing a Russian 'Kiev' class helicopter carrier.

Plate 24 Phantoms of RAF Germany flying past Schloss Hohenzollen (1971).

Plate 25 A Phantom interceptor of 43 Squadron (the 'Fighting Cocks') flies alongside a Soviet Tupolev Tu-95 reconnaissance aircraft. Phantoms and Lightnings have frequently been scrambled to intercept such intruders over the North Sea to escort them out of British Airspace.

Lightning, Buccaneer, Andover, Basset, Jet Provost, VC.10 and Belfast. Delivery of Belfast strategic freighters to 53 Squadron and of VC.10 strategic troop and passenger carriers to 10 Squadron — both at RAF Brise Norton near Oxford — started in the early months of 1966.

With higher performance and more complex aircraft due to enter the Service in the next few years, adjustments became necessary in the pattern of flying training. By the beginning of 1966, for example, the RAF had returned to the idea of using light piston-engined aircraft for preliminary flying training before ab initio pilots started basic flying training on the Jet Provost. Plans were also made to replace the more powerful version of the Jet Provost, the T.4 which was used in the second stage of basic flying training, with a pressurised MK 5 version. This would permit more realistic training at higher altitudes.

At the RAF College, Cranwell, it was decided in 1966 that advanced flying training for pilot and navigator cadets should no longer be given at the College; instead, they would join their ex-university and direct entrant colleagues at the advanced pilot and navigation schools. This would shorten the Cranwell course by six months to two-and-a-half years, and save money by centralising training on the more advanced types of aircraft.

Other training developments in these years included replacement of the Sycamore basic helicopter training aircraft by the Sioux (Bell 47). The handling of the new trainer being much more like that of the current operational helicopters would give a better initial introduction to helicopter flying than its predecessor. Training in flying and operating helicopters in mountainous terrain continued to be done from the RAF Central Flying School's special unit located at Valley in Anglesey, and helicopters of all three Services used the unit and together evolved a common doctrine for operations in this type of country.

The introduction of the Dominie T MK 1 (with twin rear-mounted Viper turbojets) at the beginning of 1966 was a significant development in the training of navigators. With its ability to fly at 400 knots at 40,000 ft and its comprehensive modern navigation equipment, the Dominie was an essential supplement to the Varsity trainer.

Following a review of the requirements in aircrew training, other than pilot and navigator, it was decided in 1966 that all airmen aircrew would complete an initial course of five weeks to prepare them for their responsibilities. No more air signallers would be trained and air electronics officers and senior NCOs would now undergo a common course of 50 weeks duration. The new Air Engineers Course had been increased to 48 weeks to include 44 hours flying for each student. After the five-week initial course, air quartermasters would continue to receive their specialist training in Transport Command; from 1970, however, they would have the opportunity to train also as helicopter winchmen/crewmen.

In the increasingly complex field of RAF supply, with American fighter and transport aircraft and French helicopters entering RAF service in increasing numbers during the next few years, the programming of the computer at the RAF Supply Control Centre at Hendon was already being overtaken by events. By the end of 1966 the computer had about 250,000 different items under control. By 1969, it was expected to have the entire range, as well as the majority of Naval air stores, on the computer. Initially, the computer would record and control centrally all stocks of equipment, whether held in depots or on Stations and this would enable requirements to be met more speedily. At the same time, the computer would be accumulating and recording the data which would enable more advanced methods and formulae for provisioning and distribution to be evolved.

Plans were also well advanced to introduce computers into equipment supply depots. They would replace the keyboard and document-writing machines; cut operating costs, simplify procedure and save staff. The depot computers would be linked to the central computer, performing not only work dictated by that computer but also some equipment accounting and depot management tasks, which the Hendon computer was unable to carry out.

The RAF was also developing a computer system to provide technical maintenance data for both the Service and the aircraft industry. Its main purpose would be to improve reliability and operational effectiveness in front-line technical equipments. It would be able to monitor and analyse 2.5 million defects a year. In addition, it should lead to better management of manpower and technical support and a reduction in maintenance costs. The maintenance data would be linked with the supply computer to give early indication of abnormal requirements for spares. New techniques for non-destructive testing, which employed dye-penetrant, X-ray ultrasonic and eddy current techniques, were being used increasingly to service aircraft. With these techniques, tests could be made and cracks and flaws in castings and forgings could be detected without stripping down. This saved a lot of expensive manpower.

Turning to the RAF's involvement in active operations overseas, the Bangkok agreement between the Malaysian and Indonesian Governments was signed on August 11, 1966, marking the official ending of 'confrontation', a trial of military strength which started in Sarawak in September 1963. The campaign was fought by British Forces in support of Malaysia's own forces, with important contributions from Australia and New Zealand; their task being to help Malaysia preserve her independence and territorial integrity, using no more force than was essential. In spite of the vast area involved and the number and variety of the forces available to the two sides, operations throughout were under the strictest political and military control. Confrontation was never allowed to escalate above the level of local conflict and comparatively few lives were lost. The campaign, on two fronts more than 1,000 miles apart, was a model of inter-Service and inter-allied co-operation. Commonwealth air and naval forces controlled more than 3,000 miles of coastline and the air space above it. Ground forces, involved in jungle warfare, were continuously supported from the air and were almost entirely dependent for speedy movement and

130

supply on helicopters and STOL aircraft, for which suitable landing sites and radio communications had to be developed.

In the last twenty-one months of confrontation transport aircraft and helicopters of the RAF, the RAAF and the RMAF carried 31,000 tons of freight and nearly 250,000 men. Much of the flying was carried out in exacting and dangerous conditions over poorly-mapped mountainous jungle, with only the barest navigational aids, and often under enemy fire. Helicopter crews had been particularly active and the fact that the vast majority of their loads, human and freight, were safely delivered, often into difficult landing and dropping zones, was proof of a high standard of training and of flying and navigating skills.

In addition to air transport and air defence, the RAF had provided maritime and photographic reconnaissance and ground attack missions in close support of the army. In one particular incident, strike Canberras were used to flush out Indonesian paratroopers dropped by night on the Malaysian mainland sixty miles north of Singpore, so that the army and internal security forces could deal with them. Finally, the long-range conventional attack and nuclear strike potential of the V-bomber detachments on Singapore island was not lost on Indonesian leaders. It was undoubtedly a major factor in deterring the threatened Indonesian attack on Royal Navy ships passing between Java and Sumatra. As a result of close and continuous air support, therefore, ground forces were able to dominate more than 1,000 miles of frontier jungle in Borneo for three years against guerrilla action by hostile forces that were always superior in numbers. But this achievement would not have been possible if the Commonwealth troops, British, Australian and New Zealand and those of Malaysia and Singapore, had not won and held the confidence of the local inhabitants of many of whom had lived in remote areas until then with little contact with the 20th century. The 'Hearts and Minds' campaign was as critical to Commonwealth success as the continuous jungle patrols and the system of helicopter supply. Lasting lessons were learnt about the use of military forces to help people in their everyday lives.

By the middle of 1967, the bulk of our air and ground forces had withdrawn from Eastern Malaysia. In the Mediterranean theatre, in Cyprus, the RAF was withdrawing from the airfield at Nicosia and concentrating on the airfield at Akrotiri and in the Near East Air Force Headquarters complex at Episkopi. In Libya, the RAF staging post at Idris had been closed, and with the withdrawal of the Shackleton maritime reconnaissance squadron from Gibraltar in Otober 1966, the RAF HQ was disbanded although the airfield was retained as a staging post.

In the Middle East, during 1966, terrorism increased, particularly in and around the town and port of Aden. The number of incidents increased even beyond the total of the preceding year. During the long, hot summer, following an attack by Egyptian MiG-19s from Yemen on the town of Nagub 130 miles north-east of Aden, Hunter FGA.9s of the RAF Khormaksar strike wing were sent to the airfield of Beihan, near the

Yemen frontier. It is worth noting that the Wing Commander in charge of the Strike Wing at this time had, in addition to a Distinguished Flying Cross, a degree in philosophy, politics and economics. All three disciplines, he considered, were valuable in his job, the first perhaps the most. From day to day anything could happen. Apart from internal security problems — shooting in back streets, hand grenades hurled through windows — the RAF was concerned with helping the army maintain the integrity of more than 1,000 miles of frontier with three different countries: Yemen, Saudi Arabia, and Muscat and Oman. Within the 113 square miles of the Aden Federation more than twenty different Sultans, Emirs and Sheiks had treaty connections with the British and in numerous quarrels amongst them, the British played a pacifying role. Rival tribes encouraged with Russian rifles and Egyptian grenades were never too particular against whom they used them so long as there was chance of profit. In Aden town, young RAF officers, with volunteers from amongst their men, took turns to relieve hard pressed army units on security patrols and received their share of hostile grenades.

Also early in 1966, a small force of five Shackleton aircraft had assembled at Majunga on the Island of Malagasy off the east coast of Africa, to co-operate with the Navy in continuous reconnaissance of the Mozambique channel, preventing oil tankers from carrying fuel to the illegal regime in Rhodesia. Early in the following year, four PR.9 Canberras from 13 Squadron detached from Malta completed a photographic survey of 90,000 square miles of the southern half of Kenya.

The RAF in the United Kingdom had its share of active operations during these years. For example, in the week ending October 29, 1966 alone, on sixteen separate occasions, Lightnings of Fighter Command intercepted and escorted out of UK airspace Soviet *Bison* four-jet reconnaissance bombers over the North Sea. In the following year the wreck of the *Torey Canyon* tanker on the Seven Stones Reef off Lands End provided realistic target practice for both ground attack and reconnaissance squadrons. Hunters from RAF West Raynham used fire bombs and 3-inch rockets and others from RAF Chivenor dropped 100 gallon fuel tanks with the object — only partially successful — of burning the vast quantities of escaping oil before it polluted the British and French coastlines. Extensive reconnaissance patrols flown by RAF Victors, Canberras and Shackletons at least ensured that all concerned were kept fully informed of the movement of the oil slicks so that measures could be taken to minimise the damage when it was washed ashore.

The years 1966 and 1967 were also periods of important organisational changes. In January 1966, the RAF Technical College moved from Henlow to amalgamate with RAF College Cranwell where officer cadets for the GD (Flying) Branch, the Equipment and Secretarial Branches and the RAF Regiment were trained. For the first time in the history of the RAF, officer cadets for full careers in the RAF's five principal branches would live and train together and thereby, it was hoped, form friendships

132

early in their careers and attain a better understanding of their different specialisations.

In October of the same year, the RAF Technical Branch shed its rather old-fashioned name and became the Engineer Branch, while in April the RAF's Airfield Construction Branch disbanded. Its officers and men either transferred to other RAF branches or to the army Royal Engineers.

In August 1967, Transport Command was renamed Air Support Command. Belfasts, built by Short Brothers in Northern Ireland, were already entering the Command. They could carry 150 to 200 fully armed troops, three Wessex or four Whirlwind helicopters, three Saladin armoured cars or two Polaris missiles. VC.10s, with the ability to carry more than 100 passengers from Britain to Singapore in 18 hours flying time, were entering squadron service, as were the first of 66 Lockheed Hercules tactical transport aircraft, designed for paratroop operations and for carriage of troops or freight into short, easily prepared airstrips. The Andover CC.2, military version of the Hawker Siddeley 748 which had a good short-take-off-and-landing (STOL) and rough airstrip performance, was already operating in its tactical transport and VIP transport roles. The newly named Air Support Command would, by the end of the year, be able to assume increased responsibility for all forms of air support.

On May 3, 1967, evacuation of Service families from Aden began. Six months later, all British troops and aircraft had left the Federation for ever. The entire evacuation was a triumph of most careful planning and an event of historic importance as the biggest RAF airlift since Berlin. A brief description of the RAF's part in the operation will therefore provide a fitting conclusion to this chapter. There were, as usual, complicating factors: a distinct possiblity that the final stages might turn into a 'fighting withdrawal'; the looming crisis between Turkey and Greece over Cyprus — a vital staging post on the strategic air route — and finally the need to retain flexibility in the timing of each phase of the operation.

Two Squadron Leaders from Headquarters Air Support Command were given the task of working out the strategic and tactical airlift plans in detail, the latter being done on the spot in Aden. The final two stages of the withdrawal consisted of a concentrated period in which forces were reduced to the minimum necessary to hold the base for a limited period, and a tactical phase during which Army and RAF forces were completely withdrawn under a security umbrella provided by a Royal Navy task force. The tactical airlift from Aden in the final three days of withdrawal was provided by Hercules and Britannia aircraft flying a 1,000-mile leg to RAF Muharraq on Bahrain Island. Here troops handed in their weapons, fed and bathed before re-embarking for the strategic airlift by VC.10s and Britannias to the United Kingdom. With the worsening situation in Cyprus, the Hercules force was deployed from UK to Bahrain earlier than planned, with other aircraft flying in from Singapore. The standard load for each Hercules was 75 passengers and 4,500lb of baggage. New techniques were developed to ensure minimum turn-round time at Aden

(RAF Khormaksar), leaving port-side engines running and loading from the starboard side was a good example. Hercules aircraft achieved a turn-round time of nine minutes, and at the peak of the lift 100 men were being flown out every hour. One of the secrets of the success of the whole operation was the positioning, at Aden and Bahrain, of two Air Support Command operation cells to work in conjunction with the forward Air Transport Operations Centre. Two Belfast aircraft were also employed in the operation as well as 105 Squadron Argosies which carried out six shuttle flights each day between RAF Khormaksar and all gulf airfields. For defence, Hunters based at Khormaksar were available for close support and reconnaissance, while RAF helicopters with machine guns manned by RAF Regiment gunners in their doors and Royal Navy helicopters operating from a Commando carrier, patrolled the airfield perimeter round the clock, using batteries of lights for illuminating the ground by night.

After the last RAF aircraft had left, an ominous silence descended upon Khormaksar airfield and upon the port of Aden, which, since its capture by the East India Company in 1839, had become the greatest oil bunkering port in the world with about 500 vessels calling each month. The RAF's own link with Aden dated from the 1914/18 war, when aircraft operated against the Turks from a rudimentary landing ground. From now on the future of Aden would be in the hands of its own people, but it should not be forgotten that it was the British who raised it from a village of about 400 inhabitants and gave it back its ancient prosperity, and British officers and men who, from the beginning to the end, had served the Colony and Federation honourably and well. There were many Arabs whose enthusiasm for the Arab cause was tempered by a liking for the British, by gratitude for RAF mercy flights, and by a realisation of material benefits brought by the rule of law supported as a last resort by a highly discriminating use of force.

The Future Hour

'We men, who in our morn of youth defied
the elements, mush vanish; be it so!
Enough, if something from our hands have power
to live, and act, and sense the future hour' WORDSWORTH

It was in 1968 that sweeping defence cuts were introduced in the RAF and her sister Services, not so much as part of a planned defence policy, but forced upon the Government as a result of the economic crisis. RAF cuts included cancellation of the 50 American F-111s which were to have made up for earlier cancellation of the TSR.2. It was at the same time decided to accelerate withdrawal of forces from Malaysia, Singapore and the Persian Gulf and complete it by the end of 1971. All this would involve an accelerated run-down of RAF manpower. Yet by the beginning of the following year it was possible to see the light at the end of the tunnel, 'to sense the future hour'. The final report of the Hodgkinson Committee on RAF officer structure had been completed and its recommendations were being studied by the Air Force Board. This Committee had been set up early in 1968 under the Chairmanship of Air Vice-Marshal W.D. Hodgkinson, to undertake a deep and thorough review of the officer structure of the Royal Air Force, in order that it could be reshaped, as necessary, to fit it for the tasks of the next decade and beyond.

A momentous decision in the field of personnel policy was announced in Parliament just before Christmas 1968. After 1970, the RAF College, Cranwell, established by Trenchard in 1920, would no longer take boys direct from school. Instead, the RAF would sponsor its cadets at university and on completion of their degree studies they would go to Cranwell for officer training and as much as possible of their professional training. So the Cranwell tradition would be carried on into the RAF's second half-century with Cranwell having the increased status of a post-graduate college.

This decision, made with courage and foresight in the midst of these difficult years, marked the most important change in officer recruiting policy in the 48 years since Cranwell had been established, and was an act of faith in the future. It was a change dictated by the developing pattern of education which had resulted in a doubling of the numbers at universities in the UK in the 1960s, and by the ever-increasing complexity of political, economic, technological, strategic, administrative and human problems that senior officers would be called upon to resolve in future years. For the former reason, the same sort of young men who in the past had entered

Cranwell direct from school, would increasingly be found in the universities and polytechnics and, therefore, only able and willing to start their careers on completion of their degree studies. This in turn would serve the further purpose of increasing the proportion of graduates — men whose intellect had been developed by many different academic disciplines — amongst the career officers of the RAF. In this same year, it was decided that in future officers of the Women's Royal Air Force should have the same rank titles as RAF officers, and in the following year, one of the largest and most technically advanced computers in the world was installed at RAF Insworth near Gloucester, to take over all the RAF's personnel records.

During 1968, the RAF continued to play its part in peace keeping and mercy operations in widely separated parts of the world. In Hong Kong, RAF helicopters continued to assist the garrison and the police in their internal security operations and training, while Flights attached from the RAF Regiment in Singapore and visits by RAF fighters helped to maintain public confidence. When communal disorders broke out in Mauritius, a company from the 3rd Battalion the Light Infantry was flown by the RAF to assist in maintaining law and order on the island. Shackleton aircraft of Coastal Command and Far East Air Force continued to patrol the Mozambique Channel to prevent the arrival in East Africa of oil destined for Rhodesia. In the Persian Gulf, Shackletons assisted the British officered Trucial Oman Scouts by searching for dissident tribesmen and illegal immigrants, and a detachment of four Canberra PR.9 aircraft from Malta carried out an aerial photographic survey of Muscat and Oman, the Trucial States, Qatar and Bahrain, covering an area of over 138,000 square miles in about 100 flights.

After violent rioting had occurred in Bermuda in April 1968, Air Support Command aircraft flew a tactical Battalion HQ and a company of the 1st Battalion the Royal Irish Rangers to the island. Victor aircraft of the UK reconnaissance force completed a survey of Denmark that had been started in 1967, and in the course of the year, RAF Shackletons, marine craft and helicopters of Coastal Command and volunteers of the RAF Mountain Rescue team rescued 26 servicemen and 176 civilians, while a further 72 civilians were flown by helicopter to hospital. A high spot for the RAF rescue service had occurred in June, 1968, when a Shackleton found the solo yachtsman Jan de Kat in a dinghy in mid-Atlantic, despite the fact that he was 200 miles away from his reported position. Search and rescue forces from Cyprus took part in the hunt for the Israeli submarine *Dakar* and for missing Jordanian and Egyptian airliners; bodies from the latter were recovered from the sea and taken to Alexandria by RAF marine craft. During the same year, a helicopter rescued the crew of the Greek motor vessel *Prodromos*, after which a RAF marine craft returned to the vessel and the RAF crew made it seaworthy enough to be towed to Cyprus. Before the end of the year, the Ministry of Defence had distributed a pamphlet to civil authorities and organisations in the UK, to let them know what assistance, both emergency and routine, the Services may be able to offer, and how it should be sought.

In the United Kingdom, on April 30, 1968, two historic Commands, Bomber and Fighter, stood down and were merged to form Strike Command. Coastal and Signals Commands were also absorbed by Strike Command in November of the following year. These fundamental changes in the structure of the Royal Air Force had their origins in the early part of the decade, when the Air Council had foreseen, even before the three single Service Ministries were integrated within the Ministry of Defence, the need for reorganisation to meet changing circumstances. Air Vice-Marshal Spotswood, who by 1968 was Air Chief Marshal Sir Denis Spotswood, Air Officer Commanding-in-Chief, RAF Strike Command, had been appointed in 1963 to study the long-term future of the RAF. He had been required to consider the shape and size of the front line and changes necessary to improve efficiency. As a result of this study two operational Commands took the place of four, and the front line 'teeth' forces of the Royal Air Force in the United Kingdom would in future be found either in Strike or Air Support Commands.

From April 1968, therefore, Strike Command's responsibilities included command and control of the nuclear strike and conventional attack forces, strategic reconnaissance, air defence, long-range maritime reconnaissance, air-to-air refuelling and of certain calibration and electronic warfare flying units. Air Support Command's responsibilities included control of those tactical reconnaissance, close support and transport support forces which operated mainly in support of the land forces. Basic thinking behind these changes stemmed from the fact that whereas in the past front-line bomber, fighter and maritime forces comprised a large number of airfields, squadrons and men, with each single unit have a single, clear cut task to fulfil, commitments in future although still covering the full range of options open to air power, would have to be met by a significantly smaller force. Multi-role weapons systems had therefore been introduced, comprising versatile aircraft of high performance like the McDonnell Douglas Phantom, so providing a flexibility greater than ever before.

Strike Command, with its headquarters at High Wycombe, consisted of six Groups by November 1969. No 1 (Bomber) Group, responsible for day-to-day operational control and training of the V-bomber and air-to-air refuelling forces; No 11 (Fighter) Group, controlling the air defence squadrons of Lightnings, Phantoms and Bloodhound missiles, with their associated communications and ground environment radars, including the Ballistic Missile Early Warning unit at Fylingdales; the Central Reconnaissance Establishment, operating all strategic reconnaissance forces based in UK; the Military Air Traffic Operations organisation (MATO) with its Headquarters at Uxbridge; No 90 (Signals) Group, which assumed Signal Command's worldwide responsibilities covering the whole field of communications, air traffic control, air defence radar systems and ground based navigational aids; and No 18 (Maritime) Group, which had assumed Coastal Command's responsibilities for long-range maritime reconnaissance, anti-submarine warfare, and search and rescue.

In the course of his visit to RAF Scampton on April 29, 1968, the Secretary of State for Defence the Right Honourable Denis Healey had said:

"The successors of the men who fought in the Battle of Britain, the Battle of the Atlantic and the Battle of Germany will soon be combined into one Command, and will go forward together, to even greater heights. the men are the same and their outstanding professional expertise will now be harnessed to a single purpose. All that will then remain to do, is that the new Command should learn how to use its formidable muscles."

A year later, the Air Officer Commanding-in-Chief summarized (in a special report) some of the achievements of the first twelve months of the new Command. In May 1968, four Lightnings of 11 Group flew, with the help of of 1 Group's Victor tankers, on what was at the time the longest non-stop fighter deployment ever carried out by the RAF, 4,000 miles to Bahrain in eight hours and two minutes. In January 1969, ten Lightning F.6s of 11 Squadron from RAF Binbrook flew to Singapore and back, a distance of 19,500 miles. Landing only at Bahrain and on the island of Gan in the Indian ocean, the fighters were refuelled by sixteen UK-based Victors pre-positioned along the route. More than 160,000 gallons of fuel were transferred in over 200 air-to-air contacts and more than 400 men — reserve aircrew, air traffic controllers and servicing men — were deployed in Britannias and Belfasts of Air Support Command to support each stage of the operation, including exercises in the Far East with the Royal Navy and Singapore air defence forces.

Lightnings had also flown to Canada in one hop to take part in the Toronto air show. No 44 Squadron had flown its Vulcans 'westabout' via America to Singapore and Australia for three weeks of exercises with Far East Air Force, the Royal Australian Air Force, the Royal New Zealand Air Force and again the Royal Navy. A detachment of strategic reconnaissance Victors of 543 Squadron had operated from Lima, capital of Peru, for more than three months and, in the course of the detachment, carried out some remarkable full-range flights in order to collect high altitude air samples and so monitor nuclear fall-out from the French H-bomb explosion in the Pacific. By April 1969, the Ballistic Missile Early Warning unit at Fylingdales had operated continuously and without any degradation in its cover for over 450 days, a record for a unit of this complexity. During its first year, Strike Command had also taken part in some 175 air displays around the world.

"The exercise of modern air power," Air Chief Marshal Sir Denis Spotswood's 1969 report concluded, "is becoming increasingly more complicated. The very tools of our trade are growing in complexity and, in so doing, are calling for ever higher standards from our aircrew, our engineers, our suppliers, administrators and all whose task it is to make a modern air force work. Increasing complexity and the ever-present requirement for cost effectiveness make more and more serious the consequences of misdirection and bad planning. I am, personally, in no doubt whatsoever that a large or, rather, a comprehensive headquarters serving a single commander and itself controlling functional Groups, must offer the best solution to the problems of the age. It is a solution that allows us to concentrate instead of dissipating those two invaluable assets — expertise and experience."

When RAF Coastal Command re-formed on November 28, 1969, as No 18 (Maritime) Group of Strike Command, it brought to the new Command a thirty-year tradition as guardian of the skies over the seas that surround Britain and of the sea lanes that throughout history have been her lifeline to the rest of the world. Coastal Command's then two existing Groups, No 19 Group at RAF Mount Batten, Plymouth and No 18 Group at RAF Pitreavie Castle, Fife, re-formed as Headquarters Southern Maritime Air Region and Headquarters Northern Maritime Air Region respectively. No 18 (Maritime) Group's Headquarters remained at Northwood, Middlesex, alongside the Royal Navy's Western Fleet Headquarters, with whom it worked closely, and the Group Commander assumed the NATO posts held hitherto by the Air Officer Commanding-in-Chief, RAF Coastal Command, those of Commander Maritime Air Eastern Atlantic Area and Commander Maritime Air Channel Command.

Only three decades earlier, in 1940, the submarine menace had been on Britain's doorstep critically threatening her lifeline with the world. Gradually, the Command's Catalinas, Hudsons, Liberators and Sunderlands had forced the enemy away from the shores of Britain to operate in mid-Atlantic, and by 1943 it was rare for a sinking to take place less than 500 miles away from the coast. By that time, the Command was operating from Spitzbergen to the Caribbean, and as far South as the river Orinoco in Venezuela. For a time in 1942, the Command operated in North Russia in support of allied convoys to Russia. Also in the Mediterranean and South Atlantic, the men of Coastal Command had hunted the submarine. In addition to sinking 184 U-boats on its own, the RAF shared with the Royal Navy in the sinking of another twenty-one, and had damaged a further 285. Between March, 1941, and the end of the war, nearly 480,000 tons of enemy shipping were destroyed by the RAF alone.

By 1969, Coastal Command's Shackletons had become better known for their photography of Russian warships, and of trawlers carrying more aerials than were required for fishing, and also for the activities of the air-sea rescue helicopters. Although the primary task of the helicopters was for RAF and civil aircraft rescue, in the first ten years after they entered service with the RAF, helicopters had saved more than 1,000 lives, many of whom were yachtsmen and swimmers in difficulty at sea and critically ill civilians ashore. As for the ageing Shackletons, in the Autumn of 1969, conversion training of their crews at RAF St. Mawgan had started on the Nimrod, the world's first pure-jet engined maritime reconnaissance aircraft. Developed from the de Havilland Comet Mk 4c, it was powered by four Rolls-Royce Spey turbofan engines giving a much higher performance and a greater radius of action than the Shackleton.

On July 2, 1969, the London *Times* contained the following cryptic note under the head of "Nuclear Change". "Britain's strategic nuclear deterrent, which for the past twelve years has been in the hands of the Royal Air Force was handed over yesterday to the Royal Navy." The RAF, speaking through Strike Command, made it quite clear, however, that although the Quick Reaction Alert role (Britain's nuclear deterrent response) had passed to the Royal Navy, this in no way altered the constitution of the RAF nuclear deterrent force. Its Vulcans, which with the Victors (now transferred to the reconnaissance and flight refuelling roles) had upheld Britain's contribution to the deterrent forces since 1957, was still the only aircraft based in Europe capable of penetrating enemy defences at long range. Carrying the Blue Steel stand-off weapon, or a 21,000lb conventional bomb load, or a nuclear device, Vulcans still had both high and low level capability, using terrain-following radar for the latter, upon which most emphasis was now placed. Strike Command's Buccaneers were designed specifically for the low-level role and could carry a variety of weapons including the Martel stand-off missile, rockets and HE or nuclear bombs. Canberras of the RAF's 2nd Tactical Air Force in Germany, as well as Phantom ground attack aircraft in Air Support Command, were also capable of carrying nuclear weapons should the need arise.

As for Air Support Command, 1969 proved to be another record year. More than 450,000 passengers were carried, of whom over 2,000 were aeromedical patients. Aircraft of the Command flew some 56 million miles (equivalent to more than 2,000 circuits of the circumference of the earth at the equator). Fixed wing tactical aircraft of No 38 Group carried 80,000 troops and dropped over 1,300 paratroops and 200 tons of supplies on exercises. A further 2,700 training parachute drops were made. Helicopters of the Group lifted over 100,000 men and 3,000 tons of freight. The growth of the RAF's strategic air transport base at Brize Norton was demonstrated by its handling of 130,000 pasengers and 8,400 tons of cargo during 1969, compared with 155,000 passengers and 17,000 tons of cargo handled by the Command's tactical base at RAF Lyneham. A good idea of the continuing world-wide activities of the Command can be gained from the following list of the overseas countries in which its aircraft supported Army units during 1969: Belgium, British Honduras, The Caribbean, Canada, Cyprus, Denmark, Ethiopia, Fiji, France, Germany, Gibraltar, Hong Kong, Iceland, Italy, Malaysia, Malta, New Zealand, Netherlands, Norway, Persian Gulf, Solomon Islands and the United States. It is clear from this list of twenty-two countries that during the 1960s, RAF aircrew were still seeing more of the world in twelve months than most civilians see in a lifetime.

The RAF's first Phantom Squadron, No 6, was declared fully operational in August 1969 as a ground-attack and offensive support squadron within No 38 Group of Air Support Command, after their crews had converted from Canberras at RAF Coningsby in Lincolnshire. It had already made its public debut leading the RAF fly-past over Caernarvon Castle after the investiture of the Prince of Wales in July. By the end of the year, the second Phantom squadron, No 54, was also working up to operational standard at Coningsby. The tactical air element of No 38 Group, which provided support for the Army Strategic Reserve, was already replacing its Hawker Hunter FGA.9s with a mixed force of Rolls-Royce Spey-engined Phantom FGR. Mk IIs and Hawker Siddeley Harriers. The Mk I Phantom was allocated to Strike Command in the air defence role, the Mk II to Air Support Command and RAF Germany in the ground-attack and reconnaissance roles. In the mid-1970s, it would be replaced in the latter roles by the Anglo-French Jaguar, powered by two Rolls-Royce/Turbomeca Adour turbofan engines. Phantoms would then replace the Lightnings in the interceptor role.

Versatility was the outstanding feature of the Phantom. It could carry up to five tons warload — almost twice the load of a Canberra — at speeds up to Mach 2 and had better radar and greater endurance than the Lightning. Loads which could be carried in various permutations included eleven 1,000lb free-fall or retarded bombs, more than 100 armour piercing rockets, a 20mm Vulcan gun firing 100 rounds a second, four Sparrow radar-guided air-to-air missiles, four Sidewinder infra-red air-to-air missiles and a reconnaissance pod with cameras and radar equipment. With a British designed and manufactured inertial navigation and attack system, its navigation and weapons aiming capabilities were extremely accurate.

Some aspects of the Harrier's performance, with its ability to hover and to land and take-off vertically, were even more remarkable, and at the beginning of 1969, No 1 Squadron was selected to be the first to convert to this aircraft. A Harrier conversion team had been set up at Dunsfold consisting of four qualified flying instructors with long experience on Hunters, in the care of Hawker Siddeley Aviation's Deputy Chief Test Pilot, Mr Duncan Simpson. Ground training included systems courses at Hawker Siddeley, Rolls-Royce (Bristol Engine Division) and Ferranti. Visits were also made to Specto Avionics to study the Head Up Display unit for instrument flying, to Miles Aviation on the simulator, and to the Royal Naval Air Weapons Group at Whale Island on computerised weapons systems.

Six hours of helicopter flying were made a pre-requisite for all pilots before flying the Harrier. Although there was not much similarity between hovering a helicopter and a Harrier, it was considered important that a prospective Harrier pilot should appreciate that an aircraft could be designed to lose all forward speed without falling out of the sky. The newly converted pilots were unanimous in their praise of the Harrier as a worthy successor to the Hunter. "It is tremendous fun," one of them commented, "and most exhilarating to fly, but one must be absolutely clear in one's own mind exactly what to do with brain, hands and feet before opening the throttle at the start of a vertical or short take-off exercise." The final exercise on the conversion course was a landing on a fifty foot square pad amongst the trees. This called for a degree of accuracy in flying comparable to that required in formation aerobatics.

By the end of 1969, the first RAF squadron to operate the Buccaneer S.2, No 12, formerly a Vulcan B.2 squadron, was re-forming and converting at RAF Honington. It had been announced that all four RAF Buccaneer squadrons would be committed to the NATO alliance, and that when the Royal Navy fixed-wing carriers were retired, the RAF would take over their Buccaneer aircraft also and assume responsibility for maritime attack and air defence operations. Some squadrons would replace the Canberras in Germany as part of the 2nd Allied Tactical Air Force, to provide a tactical ground attack, nuclear strike and reconnaissance contribution to the Supreme Allied Commander Europe. It was considered that the SACEUR-assigned squadrons would be suitable for their low-level penetration role until the late 1970s, when it was planned that the new, swing-wing, Multi-Role Combat Aircraft (MRCA), being developed jointly by Britain, Germany and Italy, would be available to replace them.

The Buccaneer had been designed to exploit a loop-hole in all known radar defence systems, the inability of radar to see over the horizon. It would approach its targets at speeds around Mach 0.85 hugging the ground at about 200 ft, and even when close to hostile radar would receive some protection from 'clutter' caused by nearby trees, hills and buildings. Remaining sub-sonic, it would avoid the spiralling problem of rapidly mounting drag and fuel consumption reducing range and load-carrying capability. As in the Phantom, the doppler navigation system incorporated a computer and rolling map display giving a continuous indication of the aircraft's position, while forward-looking radar, by giving a picture of the terrain ahead, could both warn the pilot of obstructions and assist in location of the target.

The RAF would operate the Buccaneer on low-level attack and reconnaissance missions over land and sea and, by fitting an under-wing pod containing hose and drogue and extra fuel tanks in the bomb-bay, it could also be used as a tanker aircraft for air-to-air refuelling. A total load of 8,000 lb — a combination of bombs, rockets, flares and the Martel Anglo-French television-guided missile — could be carried under-wing and in an under-belly bomb-bay that rotated through 180 degrees. The bomb could be either conventional (TNT) or nuclear. For reconnaissance, the bomb-bay could be fitted with a pod containing several cameras. In the low-level role, therefore, the Buccaneer would be highly flexible, although the Phantom, because of its excellent supersonic performance at high level and in the climb, would be even more so.

Both Buccaneer and Phantom heralded an era of increasing importance for the navigator. Even more than in the wartime nightfighters, the pilot was utterly dependent on his navigator, not only for keeping track of the aircraft's position, but also for helping him identify the target and select the appropriate weapons. Th navigator in the two-man aircraft would be doing a job that in the V-force was done by a navigator-plotter and a navigator-radar operator together. At the high speeds and low levels involved, his task was only rendered practical with the help he could expect to receive from radar and from the computerised navigation and weapons aiming systems.

In January, 1968, the Handley Page Hastings was retired from Air support Command after twenty years service, and in June, the last pre-war aircraft in the RAF, the Avro Anson, was withdrawn from service. With old aircraft giving place to new it is worth recording that, as guests in a NATO competition in the summer of 1969, four Hunters of 1 and 54 Squadrons of Air Support Command, came first in two of the events and second in another, in competition with the most up-to-date aircraft of eleven NATO Air Forces. They won first place in the combined results for rocketry, skip-bombing and strafing and in an event involving Forward Air Controlles on the ground. The achievement was the more remarkable because the rules required nomination by serial number, the day before the competition started, of the four aircraft to be flown. It says much for the soundness of Rolls-Royce engines and Hawker airframes and the high standards of RAF maintenance crews, that fifteen-year old Hunters could compete so successfully with many more modern types.

The other old aircraft which in 1969 were giving place to new, were the Valetta, the Scottish Aviation Twin Pioneer and the Belvedere helicopter. Based on the Viking, itself a development of the wartime Vickers Wellington, the Valetta had started taking over from the famous Douglas Dakota in the troop carrier, paratrooping, glider tug and air ambulance roles at the end of the 1940s. Some 263 Valettas were built and many of them operated with the RAF throughout the Malayan emergency and at Suez and Kuwait. A 'flying classroom' version appeared in 1950 and was used in Air Navigation Schools and at Cranwell until it gave way in the late 1960s to the Vickers Varsity. The Twin Pioneer was retired after eleven years service notably again in the Malayan emergency, during confrontation with Indonesia, in operations against the Mau Mau in Kenya and in Bahrain, Kuwait and the Aden Federation. The Bristol Belvedere HC.1, the RAF's first and only twin-rotor helicopter had entered service with 66 Squadron at Odiham in 1961, the two further squadrons, 26 and 72, had been formed in 1962. During the rebellion in Tanganyika (now Tanzania) in 1965, 26 Squadron Belvederes had operated from the Commando carrier HMS *Centaur*, and later they supported the army in the Radfan operations when based in Aden. No 66 Squadron played an important part during and after confrontation with Indonesia from 1962 to 1966, operating from Labuan Island off Borneo, carrying troops and supplies over difficult mountainous terrain and jungle. The last of the Belvedere Squadrons, 66, disbanded in Singapore in March 1969.

Further squadron disbandments occurred at Akrotiri in Cyprus in January 1969, when the Canberra Squadrons 6, 32, 73 and 249 forming the Akrotiri Strike Wing handed over their multiple responsibilities, including provision of strike power for the Central Treaty Organisation, to two squadrons of Vulcan B.2s, Nos 9 and 35, transferred from Cottesmore in the United Kingdom. No 6 Squadron's Standard was then transferred to the first RAF Phantom squadron, while 32 Squadron gave their number to the RAF Metropolitan Communications Squadron at Northolt. At the Akrotiri ceremonial parade, the squadrons carried their Standards emblazoned with a total of fourteen campaign and Battle Honours for operations in the Middle and Near East ranging from Malta to India, over a period spanning nearly fifty years. In October, 1969, the first maritime reconnaissance Nimrod arrived at RAF St. Mawgan in Cornwall, for service with the Maritime Operational Training Unit. In the field of communications, in January 1969, Signals Command became No 90 (Signals) Group within RAF Strike Command, and on November 21 of the same year, the Skynet communications satellite — with the operation of which the RAF would be very much concerned — was launched from Cape Kennedy in Florida. In the same year, but in the field of medicine, an RAF medical team had set up the Maxillo Facial Unit in Nigeria, and for this work they were subsequently awarded the Wilkinson Sword of Peace.

When, in December 1969, the new regime in Libya called for the early withdrawal of British forces from El Adem and Tobruk, arrangements were made to bring out heavy military equipment by sea, and some 1,700 British Servicemen and their families in aircraft of Air Support Command. The closing down of the RAF airfield at El Adem and its associated air weapons ranges in the surrounding desert, gave added importance to RAF Akrotiri as the only RAF base in the Eastern Mediterranean to which RAF squadrons from the United Kingdom and Germany could now go for high intensity weapons and navigation training in the good Mediterranean weather. It was also now the main RAF air defence, ground attack, strike, reconnaissance and air/sea rescue base on the southern flank of NATO, and provided support in depth for CENTO, as well as local air support for the United Nations peace keeping force in Cyprus itself. And it was in these years that there was a marked increase in Russian military activity in Egypt and continued activity of Russian war ships and maritime aircraft in the Mediterranean.

Much nearer home, in August 1969, serious communal violence had broken out in Northern Ireland. The danger had been anticipated and in April Argosies, Hercules and Britannias of Air Support Command had transported the first reinforcing battalion to Northern Ireland and continued to maintain subsequent reinforcement and supply flights. A Wing of the RAF Regiment took its turn in the rotation of units on security duties in Northern Ireland throughout the year. Also throughout the year RAF fighters had been stationed in Gibraltar to help maintain confidence when the frontier with Spain had been closed by the Spanish authorities.

Further afield, two companies of the 2nd Battalion the Parachute Regiment, together with a detachment of Metropolitan Police, were flown in Air Support Command aircraft to the West Indies island of Anguilla to restore peace and stability. Hercules aircraft continued to support the troops and police on the island direct from the United Kingdom and a RAF Andover aircraft was based in the area to maintain communications locally.

Air Support Command aircraft also carried supplies and helped in rescue operations in the flood disasters that occurred in Algeria and Tunisia in the autumn of 1969. There was one chance to help in that year that the RAF was particularly glad to take. During the Second World War, a Malaysian civilian had transported British families to safety during the Japanese advance through Malaya. He had refused any award or official recognition for his bravery saying that he liked British people and their country and it was his duty to help. In the summer of 1969, he was completely paralysed when a tree crashed on his car. The RAF flew him to England and took him by RAF ambulance to Stoke Mandeville hospital. A debt repaid after a quarter of a century.

It was in May of 1969 that the Transatlantic Air Race sponsored by the Daily Mail had provided more cheerful breakfast table reading in the British (and New York) press. RAF entrants included a VC.10 (on a routine training flight) a Victor bomber and, most newsworthy of all, two Hawker Siddeley Harrier V/STOL fighters. The aim was to achieve the fastest time between the Post Office tower in the centre of London and the Empire State building in the centre of New York, in either direction. The Royal Navy achieved the fastest New York to London time — five hours eleven minutes and twenty-two seconds — in an 892 Squadron Phantom, refuelled in the air by RAF Victor Tankers. Squadron Leader Lecky-Thompson in a Harrier achieved the best time — six hours eleven minutes and fifty-seven seconds — in the London to New York direction, although because of the normally helpful westerly winds, Squadron Leader Williams achieved a better 'Harrier' time — five hours forty-nine minutes and fifty-eight seconds in the other direction. There was much publicity attending the successful flights of these two Harrier pilots, flying their single Rolls-Royce engined aircraft between the United Nations East River pier alongside the skyscrapers of Manhattan, and the disused coal yard alongside St Pancras Station. No doubt this all helped the sale of Harriers to the United States Marine Corps, which added some £200 million to Britain's export earnings. When Squadron Leader Williams took off from New York, the rain was pouring down, and the surrounding skyscrapers disappeared into cloud — as he did — a few hundred feet only above the ground! With one of his blind flying instruments — the artificial horizon — unserviceable, he finally broke clear of cloud at about 36,000 feet. "And what a marvellous sight it was," he said afterwards, "to see the Victor tanker flying along in and out of cloud ahead of me at the appointed rendezvous." His second refuelling rendezvous was over Gander in

145

Newfoundland. The upper cloud had disappeared and, bang on time, four Victor tankers in close formation swung in front of me without my having to make the slightest alteration in course or speed."

It was also in May 1969, that the RAF's No 1 Parachute Training School at Abingdon celebrated its millionth parachute drop. The Central Landing Establishment as it was incongruously first called when Winston Churchill ordered the formation of an airborne force in April 1940, was formed at RAF Ringway, near Manchester. Its main task in 1969 was still the basic parachute training of airborne forces, but the school had also trained men from the Royal Navy, Marines, Army (including Special Air Services), the RAF College, Cranwell and the RAF Regiment, as well as troops and instructors from other countries. The staff of the school, officers and NCOs, were by 1969 all members of the Physical Fitness Branch of the RAF. The following month, Her Majesty the Queen presented the Queen's Colour to the RAF Central Flying School at Little Rissington. Both these establishments were now units within RAF Training Command which was the name given in June 1968 to the new Command created by the amalgamation of Flying and Technical Training Commands. As an interjection in a paragraph describing highlights in the field of RAF training, it is worth mentioning that, in 1969, the RAF became the first of the Services to use a new driving tuition simulator developed from the pilot's link trainer, to help training Mechanical Transport drivers in the safety of the class-room. In the sphere of staff training, important changes were being implemented or planned in those two years. On December 4, 1969, the RAF Staff College at Andover was amalgamated with the RAF Staff College at Bracknell after forty-seven years existence. In the same year, it was decided that in 1971 the Imperial Defence College, where senior officers and civil servants studied strategy, international relations and major issues of defence policy, should be re-named the Royal College of Defence Studies, with more emphasis being placed on the study of European problems in greater depth. At the same time, the Joint-Services Staff College would be re-named the National Defence College, and here, in the middle of their careers, officers would study to fill key posts in the direction of defence.

These changes were timely for the defence cuts of 1968, coinciding with the first period for many years in which British forces were not involved in actual fighting, had produced a situation in which the whole purpose of defence forces and of NATO was in doubt in the minds of large sections of the British public, and this in turn had produced an unfavourable recruiting climate. In 1968, therefore, although the RAF achieved its reduced targets for pilots and navigators, recruitment to the main officer ground branches and to many of the airmen trades, as well as to craft and administrative apprenticeships, suffered a serious shortfall.

Unexpectedly, in August 1968, Russia moved a quarter of a million men into Czechoslovakia in three days. The older generation could not fail to be

146

reminded of another Czechoslovakian crisis which had immediately preceded the second World War.

A leading article in the London *Times* said of the Czechoslovakian crisis that: "It certainly served as a timely reminder that the use of force to achieve political objectives is still a very acceptable technique to the leaders in the Kremlin." It was not without significance, therefore, that in the spring of 1969, the Government Defence White Paper announced that in future Britain's defence effort would be concentrated mainly in Europe and the North Atlantic area. It went on to say that, although no major forces would be retained East of Suez after withdrawal from Singapore and the Persian Gulf, a general capability would be retained in Europe and the United Kingdom for deployment overseas when national or treaty interests demanded it and also in support of United Nations operations. Finally it emphasised that the increasing study of defence problems outside the Government was helping to create a better awareness in the country as a whole of the value of the Armed Forces. "We are working closely with the universities in many fields," the White Paper recorded. Five defence lectureships had been established with Ministry of Defence support at the universities of Aberdeen, Edinburgh, London, Oxford and Southampton.

The 1969 White Paper on defence concluded its statement of general policy with these words:

"The basic aim of our defence policy is now fully established. It is to ensure the security of Britain by concentrating our major effort on the Western Alliance. This aim is sensible, stable and vital. It is sensible because it recognises the basic realities of our economic and political interests in the world today. It is stable because the task is irreducible, we can withdraw from East of Suez but not from our situation in Europe, on which our national security depends. It is vital because, without the security which comes from the strength to deter aggression, we put at risk the achievement of all our other national purposes."

The Recurring Nightmare

'History is a nightmare from which I am trying to awake' JAMES JOYCE

The year 1970 marked the start of a new and the end of an old decade. The 1960s had seen the death of Blue Streak, the only Intercontinental Ballistic Missile designed and built in Britain, and the disbandment of RAF Thor intermediate-range ballistic missile squadrons. Neither event brought many tears to the eyes of flying men. Cancellation of the American Skybolt airborne target seeking missile, which was intended to extend the viability of the V-Force by enabling bombers to strike at targets from outside the range of their anti-aircraft guided missile defences, was a more serious blow, but meanwhile the Bristol Blue Steel powered 'stand-off' bomb had been successfully introduced in the V-force, although its range was considerably less than that of Skybolt.

In 1964, the three separate Service Ministries had been abolished and a unified Ministry of Defence had been formed. As Michael Howard wrote in 1970: "The abolition of the Service Ministries and the co-location of their successor Departments within the Ministry of Defence was not only the first step in the gradual construction of an integrated bureaucracy but a spectacular achievement in itself." The new Ministry contained a Central Defence Staff, 'The Centre', a Navy Department (in place of the Admiralty), an Army Department (in place of the War Office) and an Air Force Department (in place of the Air Ministry). The Air Council was renamed the Air Force Board (of the Defence Council). The Chief of Air Staff, however, still remained Head of the RAF and responsible for its day to day operations and administration, and with his Navy and Army colleagues, was a member of the Chiefs of Staff Committee chaired by the Chief of the Defence Staff. By 1967, the Service Ministers were downgraded to Parliamentary Under-Secretaries of State.

From 1964, therefore, responsibility for plans and operations, the defence programme and budget and the research and development programme for all three Services was concentrated within the new Department. Requirements for new equipment were henceforward considered by a unified Operational Requirements Committee, and had to be justified against the overall strategic concepts envisaged for the period when the equipment would be in service. The committee was assisted by a defence operational analysis staff which examined the cost effectiveness of all new proposals.

That strong control of defence expenditure was vital to ensure cost effectiveness in a Service that was dependent more than any other on advanced technology, was demonstrated by the death of the revolutionary tactical strike and reconnaissance aircraft (TSR.2) whose cancellation after successful early flights was announced in the Budget speech of 1965. As *Flight International* has pointed out: "TSR.2 did not die in vain." Its death taught that cost is the enemy of technology. The old wartime dictum "never mind the cost, get it right", had persisted too long! Nevertheless, its demise heralded the end of an era for the RAF. It meant that when the Vulcans become obsolete before the end of the 1970s (when their ability to penetrate the increasingly effective anti-aircraft guided missile defences will have become increasingly dubious) the RAF may have no aircraft capable of attacking targets at the V-bomber's radius of action.

In other words, although th RAF would have no *strategic* bomber to take the place of the V-bombers, since the advent of the new generation of anti-aircraft missiles, not even a supersonic strategic bomber could survive at high altitude over the territory of an enemy armed with such missiles. The penalty in terms of a fantastic rate of fuel consumption when flying supersonically at low level meant that, for all practical purposes, the low-level mission would be limited in range to the tactical area. This did not mean that the RAF no longer believed in the doctrine that the best form of defence was the threat of strategic offence, but simply that the NATO alliance must henceforward depend on America's strategic missiles alone to fill the gap in the West's deterrent policy. To ensure that America would be prepared to continue to provide this vital element of deterrence, therefore, it was all the more important that the United Kingdom, together with her other European allies, should clearly demonstrate to America their preparedness to bear their fair share of the defence of Europe within the North Atlantic Treaty Organisation.

This, therefore, is the moment in our stocktaking at the start of a new decade, when we should remind ourselves of several fundamental facts about Britain's defence policy for the 1970s. First, as stated in Denis Healey's last Defence White Paper, after five years as Minister of Defence in the Labour Government: "Britain enters the 70s with an overall military capability which no other West European power can surpass," and that: "the next decade is likely to see changes in the international situation which strengthen the powerful arguments for closer European Defence Co-operation". Second, as confirmed in the Conservative Government's first full Statement on Defence in 1971: "Britain's basic security continues to depend on the strength of the North Atlantic Alliance and it is to NATO that by far the greater part of Britain's military forces is committed." Third, as Gordon Lee of *The Economist* has pointed out: "The security of Western Europe depends upon the American nuclear guarantee and upon the continuing presence of some American troops in Europe;" and he goes on to explain how with the growth of air power, the creation of vast nuclear armouries, the rise of super powers and the relative decline of Britain's economic strength, we can no longer "pursue an independent strategy".

We must, however, also remind ourselves, and the world (for what use is a deterrent to war unless the whole world knows of its existence?) that we entered the 1970s as the third strongest nuclear power, not limited to a single Polaris submarine on patrol at a particular time, but possessing the biggest stock of nuclear bombs and missiles outside the USA and Russia, with around 200 combat aircraft capable of delivering them should the need ever arise. Finally, we should repeat what was said in the prologue to this book, that one aircraft can deliver, in a single attack, destructive power fifty times greater than all the bombs dropped by RAF Bomber Command on Germany in six years of war.

The commitment of North America to the defence of Western Europe has been the foundation of NATO's strength. Because of it, the Alliance has, since 1949, maintained the balance of power and hence the peace of Europe. Britain's and the RAF's contribution to NATO is now our most important defence commitment, but because of our pattern of trade, the obligations and sentiment involved in the old and new British Commonwealth, and in treaties with old friends around the world, Britain more than other west European power continues to be concerned with what happens outside Europe.

The defence dilemma which faced Britain at the start of the new decade, therefore, was how much effort should be devoted to Europe and how much to East of Suez. The Labour Government, prompted by the 1970 economic crisis and devaluation, made Europe Britain's primary defence commitment, decided on withdrawal of virtually all forces from East of Suez by the end of 1971, but left British forces nevertheless with a capacity for strategic mobility which, in the Western world, only the Americans out-matched. When the Conservative Government came to power in June 1970, faced with the same economic facts as their predecessors, they could do no more than slightly to change the emphasis between Europe and East of Suez, without changing the basic plan for withdrawal. As far as the RAF was concerned this meant that, up to the end of 1971, Lightnings remained in Singapore in the air defence role, and Shackletons for maritime reconnaissance, together with supporting transport aircraft and helicopters. After 1971, the new Government decided that the RAF should leave a token force in the Far East consisting of up to four Nimrod long-range maritime reconnaissance aircraft and a squadron of Whirlwind helicopters, as the RAF's contribution to the Five Power (Malaysia, Singapore, Australia, New Zealand and UK) defence arrangements. In addition, it was agreed that frequent visits would be made by Vulcan bombers, Victor tankers and Buccaneer and Phantom ground attack aircraft to air bases throughout the Far East, and that RAF transport aircraft would provide a scheduled service (via Cyprus and the RAF staging post at Gan in the Indian ocean) to Singapore and Hong Kong. It was also confirmed that a garrison of two army brigades, supported by a RAF helicopter squadron, should remain in Hong Kong.

Lord Carrington, the Secretary of State for Defence in the new Government, decided that the major Far East reinforcement exercise 'Bersatu Padu' (Malay for 'complete unity') should go ahead as planned by his predecessor, between April and June 1970. The exercise visualised a situation in the year 1975 in which the imaginary state of Ganasia, located between Malaysia and Thailand, after infiltrating terrorists and saboteurs into Northern Malaysia, had embarked on overt military action. The main object of this exercise from the RAF's point of view was to demonstrate the United Kingdom's ability rapidly to deploy ground and air forces over 8,600 miles to support her treaty obligations to Malaysia, Singapore, New Zealand and Australia. The RAF strategic airlift was split into two parts, the first during ten days in April carried some 2,300 men of the Army Strategic Reserve, 200 fully laden vehicles, 170 fully laden trailers, 20 helicopters, 12 howitzers and about 90,000 lb of cargo. During the second stage of the airlift, between May 14 and June 3, RAF transport aircraft carried another 1,300 men to Singapore and a further 250,000 lb of freight.

No 54 (Phantom) Squadron from RAF Coningsby was required to fly ten aircraft out to Singapore to take part in the exercise. The original plan was that all aircraft would be refuelled in the air en route by Victor tankers of 57 and 214 Squadrons from RAF Marham, but would anyway land at Masirah, the RAF island airfield off the south coast of Muscat and Oman, to rest pilots and navigators at about the half way point in the long journey. After practising fifteen-hour trips by flying five times non-stop round the United Kingdom (with air-to-air re-fuelling) however, it was confirmed that oil consumption would permit a *non-stop* flight of some 7,500 miles to Singapore. Permission was given for four of the squadron's aircraft to attempt this world record flight.

The route would be the standard eastabout reinforcement route from the UK over France, down the west coast of Italy, across the Mediterranean to Cyprus, then north into Turkey, east into Iran, south over the island staging posts of Masirah and Gan, then again east to Singapore. Nine airborne refuellings would be required from tankers operating from Marham, Akrotiri (Cyprus), Masirah and Gan. Rolls-Royce and McDonnell Douglas put up the sponsorship money for the Royal Aero Club's official record. The official observer started his stop-watch as he saw on the London Airport radar the first pair of Phantoms pass over Hornchurch at noon Greenwich Mean Time on May 18, 1970. At the top of their climb the aircraft rendezvoused with two Victor tankers from Marham, and with a short refuelling test over the English Channel checked that all systems were working satisfactorily. One Victor tanker continued to fly with her Phantom 'chicks' over France and only turned for home after two more successful feeds. The two Phantom pilots were then able to relax with their aircraft being flown by auto pilots. The two navigators meanwhile assessed a slightly stronger tail wind than had been forecast, and it was agreed to bring forward by a few precious minutes the rendezvous (RV) time with the two tankers pre-positioned at RAF Akrotiri in Cyprus. This was arranged by passing an HF radio message to Akrotiri control. After this second rendezvous, one tanker accompanied the Phantoms on over the mountains of central Turkey where, after a fifth fuel transfer at dusk, the two would-be record breakers headed eastward towards the lights of Tehran. The loneliness of the night was relieved by a radio chat with a homeward bound RAF VC.10 and a radio message from Bahrain confirmed the weather at RAF Masirah was clear for landing if anything went wrong with refuels six or seven. North of Masirah, a third RV with a tanker was made on schedule and refuel number six was carried out high over the Arabian Sea.

Approaching the island of Gan, the Phantoms started to run through the turbulent tops of thunder storms which seriously reduced the range of radio transmissions. Nevertheless, a message was received from Gan that only one of the two Victor tankers was serviceable, with enough fuel for two feeds for *one* Phantom only. "Knowing the disappointment and frustration they must inevitably be feeling," wrote Squadron Leader Arkell-Hardwick afterwards, "we watched our companion turn away and drop down towards the RAF's remote coral island airfield. The eighth fuel transfer in the dark turned out to be the hardest of all," the Squadron Leader stated in his report. "Severe turbulence as experienced as we passed in and out of the tops of thunder storms. The link up seemed impossible, while St Elmo's fire [a bluish glow caused by electrical discharge from thunderclouds, a phenomenon familiar to sailors at their mast-heads for hundreds of years] added drama to the scene." Nevertheless, both eighth and ninth fuel transfers were successfully accomplished, and as the tanker turned to head back into the night: "dawn was breaking in the east. We were now starting the last 1,000 miles of our 7,500-mile flight, feeling a little tired. But the end was in sight. We celebrated with a drink of squash and our last sandwiches."

A Shackleton came out to meet them from Singapore and: "at 0214 GMT on May 20, we flew past Tengah control tower. We had made it, and the time — 14 hours and 14 minutes was a new world record."

While in Singapore, 54 Squadron took part in the tactical phase of the exercise in attacks on a variety of ground targets. Strike Command Vulcans from 44 Squadron, based at RAF Waddington, also re-deployed to Singapore to provide an even heavier weight of attack against the more distant enemy targets, and Canberra PR.7s re-deployed from 58 Squadron, Wyton, to provide the all important photographic reconnaissance capability by night as well as day. RAF Lightnings for air defence were from 74 Squadron which, in 1970, was still based at RAF Tengah on Singapore Island.

Highlights of the tactical phase of the exercise occurred when, after marine commandos carried in Wessex helicopters from the Commando carrier HMS *Bulwark* had secured the airfield at Penarek, on the East Coast of Malaysia, RAF and RNZAF Hercules together with RNZAF Bristol freighters, controlled by a mobile air movement squadron from

RAF Abingdon, started intensive operations. In just over four days, 2,800 men, 323 vehicles and 285,000lb of freight were flown into the previously unused airfield. Simultaneously, Wessex helicopters of 72 Squadron, which had been airlifted to Singapore from RAF Odiham by Belfast transport aircraft, carried men of the 9th Royal Malay Regiment into their 'front-line' positions in jungle covered foothills and kept them supplied there throughout June. Speaking on the same day about the exercise, Australian Defence Minister Malcolm Fraser in Singapore, and Singapore Defence Minister Lim Kim San in North East Malaysia, told the press that the United Kingdom had demonstrated its ability to reinforce the region with air and land forces, in a matter of days. In ten days, VC.10, Belfast, Hercules and Britannia aircraft of the RAF carried more than 2,200 men, over one and a half million pounds of freight, 350 vehicles and 20 helicopters totalling one and a third million miles in about 4,500 flying hours. The fact that the United States Air Force has a far greater air lift capacity for the reinforcement of NATO confirms the agreed priorities of Western defence, and in no way detracts from the RAF's ability to help Britain fulfil her obligations elsewhere.

Back in Britain, in Februry 1970, the Royal Air Force College, Cranwell started its second fifty years existence. Since the war, the role of the College had been constantly evolving. Until 1947, all officer cadets were trained as pilots. Later the scope widened to include the training of cadets for the Equipment and Secretarial Branches and for the RAF Regiment. Navigator training started in 1956, and in 1957 flying training changed to a piston-engined Provost and jet-engined Vampire T.11 sequence for pilots. This again, at the end of the 1950s, gave way to all-through jet training using the Jet Provost T.3. In the mid-1960s, the Technical College from Henlow in Bedfordshire, where officer cadets were trained for the RAF's Technical branch, merged with Cranwell and a two-and-a-half year course was evolved for officer cadets of the RAF's five principal branches.

In 1970, students were still coming to Cranwell from more than a dozen different countries: Australia, New Zealand, Ghana, Nigeria, Kenya, Pakistan, Malaysia, Singapore, Lebanon, Iran, Jordan, Saudi Arabia and Sudan, thus maintaining a tradition which started in the early 1930s when the first officers for the newly created Indian Air Force came to Cranwell for their training.

After 1970, to qualify for Cranwell, young men would be required to read for degrees at civilian universities. There had been a period during the 1960s when cadets could read for degrees while undergoing training at Cranwell, and whereas a number did obtain Diplomas in Technology and other degrees in this way, it was finally decided that the extent of academic study required to obtain a degree, could not be mixed satisfactorily with intensive officer and professional (particularly flying) training, and this scheme was abandoned in favour of the Graduate Entry Scheme whereby prospective RAF officers, before undergoing Service training at Cranwell, read for degrees at civilian universities, either under their own

153

arrangements, or sponsored by the RAF as university cadets.

That the fiftieth anniversary of No 1 School of Technical Training at Halton fell in the same year as the fiftieth anniversary of the RAF College was no mere coincidence. Both were founded by Trenchard to be complimentary to each other. Since 1920, more than 6,000 ex-apprentices had gained commissions in the RAF as pilots, navigators and engineers and in various other branches. More than forty-five achieved Air rank: one, Air Marshall 'Tubby' Dawson, gave his name to Dawson Field in Jordan which was in the news when a hijacked BOAC VC.10 was blown up there in September 1970; he completed his career as Managing Director of the Handley Page Aircraft Company. Another, Air Chief Marshal Sir Alfred Earle, became Deputy Chief of the Defence Staff under Lord Louis Mountbatten. It is a record of which both the School and the Royal Air Force can be proud, and ex-apprentices continue to play their part as the backbone of the Service. The following year, Flight Lieutenant the Prince of Wales spent four months at Cranwell and on Friday, August 20, 1971, received his wings from Air Chief Marshal Sir Denis Spotswood, Chief of the Air Staff, at a passing out parade attended by his father, Marshal of the Royal Air Force the Duke of Edinburgh. While at Cranwell, the Prince had become the first heir to the British throne to make a parachute descent.

Throughout 1970/71, increasing violence in Northern Ireland had continued to present the Army with its most immediate operational role. RAF Air Support Command had continued to provide the essential air mobility backing for the Army's security operations, including a detachment of Wessex helicopters. By the end of 1971, ground forces in Northern Ireland comprised sixteen major units in the infantry role including elements of the RAF Regiment. Air Support Command, however, during these two years, was involved in an astonishing variety of other operations. In early September 1970, for example, an Arab girl Commando, Leila Khaled, who had made an unsuccessful attempt to hijack an Israeli airliner en route from Amsterdam to London, was languishing in jail in a London suburban police station. After much diplomatic activity, it was agreed that she and several other Arab terrorists in jail in Germany would be exchanged for hostages from the hijacked BOAC VC.10, some of whom were still held in Middle East. Miss Khaled was flown in a RAF Wessex helicopter from RAF Northolt to RAF Lyneham. There, under a strong police escort, she was put on board a RAF Comet 4 of 216 Squadron. The aircraft first flew to Munich to pick up three more released Arab terrorists, then to Zurich to pick up another two (with a Swiss police escort). On October 1, 1970, all the released terrorists were handed over to the Egyptian authorities at Cairo airport. The Comet took off for Cyprus shortly before Cairo airport was closed prior to President Nasser's funeral, at which the United Kingdom was represented by Sir Alec Douglas Home, who had flown out in another VIP Comet from 216 Squadron.

In mid-September 1970, the Jordan Government had appealed for help in dealing with the large number of casualties resulting from their near civil war with Palestine guerillas. Nine RAF Hercules flew two sorties to Beirut and six to Amman carrying an Army field surgical team, part of a Field Ambulance Unit and a section of No 2 Field Hospital with staff for 50 beds. In late November, a cyclone struck the east coast of Pakistan, 200,000 lives were lost, thousands of homes damaged and half a million tons of crops destroyed. On November 20, a VC.10 from 10 Squadron positioned Hercules 'slip' crews along the route and then flew on to Singapore with 20,000 lb of rubber rafts and boats. Two Hercules followed, delivering 50,000 lb of rubber rafts, medical supplies, blankets and a party of Marines to the stricken area. Together with Hercules from Far East Air Force in Singapore, the Air Support Command Hercules ferried 350,000 lb of supplies into the Chittagong area. Before the end of 1970, a VC.10 of 10 Squadron had flown the Prince of Wales to represent the Queen at the Fiji Independence celebrations. Just short of Bahrain in the Persian Gulf on the first leg of the flight, an engine had to be shut down. Another VC.10 already out on the route was diverted to Bahrain and got the Prince to his appointment on time. Early in 1971, No 72 Squadron's Wessex helicopter detachment in Northern Ireland was increased from four to eight aircraft, while in August, thirty-five Hercules and eight Britannia sorties flew Army and RAF Regiment reinforcements into Northern Ireland. Meanwhile, the internal security task in the West Indies island of Anguilla, which started in 1969, came to an end. The RAF Andover aircraft and ground crew left Coolidge on March 18, 1971, and the rest of the ground party plus their equipment returned to UK by Hercules and VC.10. In June, both East Pakistan and India suffered further devastating floods. Despite the imminence of the most intensive part of Air Support Command's operations in connection with the planned withdrawal from East of Suez, six Hercules, five VC.10 and two Belfast aircraft flew over 390,000lb of supplies and passengers into Calcutta during June and July. Between August and December 1971, intensive flying by VC.10 and Hercules transport aircraft carried 38,00 passengers and 2,800 tons of freight from Singapore and the Persian Gulf, so completing withdrawal of the bulk of British Armed Forces from East of Suez (except Hong Kong) by December, 14 1971.

With the disbandment of 114 Squadron (the first to be equipped with the Armstrong Whitworth Argosy C.1 in 1962) at RAF Benson in October 1971, and withdrawal from the Gulf, Argosy operations in Air Support Command ceased, although some Argosies continued in use in Cyprus and Training Command. Compared with Hastings and Valettas, the Argosy's ten year service had been relatively short, but as a transport aircraft it will be remembered for its high standard of reliability, particularly during operations in the Middle and Far East. In the previous month, however, the helicopter element of Air Support Command received a welcome reinforcement when 33 Squadron re-formed at RAF Odiham in September, equipped with the Anglo-French Puma. They were joined later by 230 Squadron similarly equipped, and four of the Whirlwind helicopters previously belonging to 230 Squadron were transferred to 1563 Helicopter Flight in Cyprus in support of the United Nations Force located there.

In 1970, No 1 Parachute Training School had completed twenty years' association with the Air Support Command station at RAF Abingdon, and while at Abingdon, instructors on the staff of the school had formed a 'skydiving' team that in 1965 had been officially named the Royal Air Force free fall parachute display team — the Falcons. During the winter 1970 training period at RAF Sharjah, the team equalled the British record by forming an eight-man star with all hands linked while falling earthwards at 120 mph before opening their canopies. The team had put in a lot of experimental work designing and making a suitable helmet on which to mount a fully automatic cine camera. By 1971, this camera was working well enough for the team to make a film for the BBC entitled 'The Flying Falcons'.

In the sphere of maritime operations, a Hawker Siddeley Nimrod was called upon on January 21, 1970, to carry out its first operation (with a crew still under training on board). The aircraft concerned was on a training flight from 236 Operational Conversion Unit at St Mawgan in Cornwall, and was ordered to find, shadow and report on the movement of a small force of Russian ships, some 200 miles south-west of Lands End. The Russian ships, which included the helicopter cruiser *Moskva* and two Kashin-class surface-to-air missile ships, had been under surveillance by NATO forces since they had left the Mediterranean a few days earlier.

Developed from a Comet 4C with Rolls-Royce Spey (instead of Avon) engines, the Nimrod carries a crew of twelve composed of captain and co-pilot, two navigators, an engineer, an air electronics officer and six NCO air signallers. Its target detection system includes sonar devices, electronics, ionisation and magnetic-anomaly detectors and an air-to-surface radar powerful enough to pick up a petrol can floating several hundred feet below. The weapon system includes a digital computer which takes its inputs from the navigation and target detection systems, and then presents information to the navigators about their aircraft's position, track and speed, and similar information on the position and movement of identified targets.

During 1970, the first of five planned Nimrod squadrons (No 201) had formed at RAF Kinloss in Scotland, and by the end of 1971 the Nimrod force was virtually complete and additional aircraft had been ordered. In September 1970, Nimrods, alongside the Shackletons they were replacing, took part in the NATO exercise 'Northern Wedding' in the North Sea and Baltic approaches, in co-operation with air forces from Belgium, Canada, Denmark, Germany, Holland, Norway and the United States. Speaking at Hatfield in January 1970, the Vice Chief of Air Staff, Air Marshal Sir Peter Fletcher, had said: "Nimrod, the 'mighty hunter' of the Book of Genesis, is not a Comet in uniform. It is an absolutely brand-new aeroplane at the beginning of its career, but with a birthright of many years experience built in." As though to demonstrate the truth of these words, it was a Nimrod from 201 Squadron at Kinloss which, in the spring of 1971, in competition with maritime aircraft from Australia, New Zealand and Canada, won the Fincastle Trophy for the RAF, having obtained top marks in locating and attacking a submerged submarine both at night and in daylight. Other competition successes during 1971 were achieved by RAF fighter squadrons which won both the Huddleston and Burniaux Trophies (named after Air Chief Marshal Sir Edward Huddlestone and Lt. General F. Burniaux of the Royal Belgian Air Force respectively) in competition with Belgium, Dutch and American Squadrons in NATO's Central European defence region.

Outside Europe, as a result of communal disturbances in East Pakistan in 1971, about five million refugees had crossed the border into India by mid-June. On December 3, war broke out between India and Pakistan and between December 10 and 12, Hercules transport aircraft from RAF Lyneham in Wiltshire evacuated more than 900 British and friendly foreign nationals from Islamabad and Karachi in West Pakistan to RAF Masirah on the south-east coast of Arabia. From there, RAF VC.10s flew them on to Cyprus. On December 12, in an operation described by the Foreign and Commonwealth Office as a "miracle", three more RAF Hercules, led by Wing Commander Hannah, evacuated more than 400 people from the bomb-cratered runway at Dacca in East Pakistan to Calcutta and thence to Singapore. In recognition of his outstanding leadership, Wing Commander Hannah was awarded the Air Force Cross.

On the opposite side of the Gulf of Oman from West Pakistan, at the easterly corner of Arabia, the Sultan of Oman's air force, commanded by a seconded RAF Officer, was occupied in these years with operations against a communist-sponsored guerilla movement. Muscat and Oman covers an area about the size of the British Isles, between the 'empty quarter' of the Arabian desert and the Arabian sea. Its coast line stretches for 1,000 miles from Salalah in fertile Dhofar province in the west, via the capital of Muscat where the air force headquarters is located, to a north-easterly promontory which commands the strategically important Strait of Hormuz, entry to the Persian Gulf. Britain honours her treaty of friendship with the Sultan by providing one-third of the pilots for his air force from volunteers seconded from the RAF, and the remaining two-thirds from civilian pilots under contract. The territory over which they fly their BAC 167 Strikemasters and Beavers on close support, interdiction and reconnaissance missions, their Caribous and Skyvans carrying troops to battle or the sick to hospital, varies from the fertile fields and valleys of Dhofar in the south-west to the barren 9,000-ft high Jebel Akhdar mountains in the north. Where the terrain is impractical for fixed wing aircraft, Bell 205 (Iroquois) helicopters can carry thirteen armed men and Bell Jetrangers can carry out less weighty communications tasks. It is a rugged, challenging and manly life, enjoyed by the same sort of young men in this generation whose fathers revelled in RAF life on the North-West Frontier of India and in Iraq before the war, and the same close understanding exists between Army and Air Force who share the same joys and tribulations and live in the same Mess at Bait al Falag. The Sultan's air force seldom lacks volunteers from the RAF for an eighteen month tour of duty.

The desert island staging post operated by the RAF at Masirah, is just off the south coast of Muscat and Oman almost on the same degree of latitude as the Muslim holy city of Mecca further west, and Bombay, the gateway to India, further east. During these years it was playing a vital role in RAF deployment exercises to the Far East, acting as a re-fuelling base for Vulcan bomber and Victor tanker aircraft and receiving regular visits from UK-based Phantoms and Lightnings. Because it would assume increased importance after withdrawal from East of Suez after 1971, plans were in hand to improve communications and radar for air traffic control and amenities for the 300 or so British Servicemen and civilians based there.

In the Persian Gulf itself, 210 Shackleton Maritime Reconnaissance Squadron re-formed at Sharjah in the Trucial States on November 1, 1970. Its chief task was to patrol the coast line looking for Arab dhows carrying possible illegal immigrants. Any vessel with more than thirty passengers was photographed and reported to the local authorities who intercepted it with fast patrol boats from Abu Dhabi.

In February 1970, the Labour Government's last Statement on Defence had stated: "Britain's military role has been transformed over the last five years by the historic decision to withdraw our forces from their bases East of Suez and to concentrate them in Europe". By April 1, 1971, the RAF Indian Ocean staging post at Gan in the Maldive Islands, mid-way between Singapore and RAF Masirah on the south coast of Arabia, had been transferred from the control of Far East Air Force to be directly administered by Air Support Command who were its principal users. The final parade of the Queen's Colour for the Far East Air Force took place on September 18, 1971, at RAF Changi, situated at the eastern tip of Singapore island. Changi had served for many years as the RAF's main maritime reconnaissance and transport airfield in the Far East. It had been at the height of its activities during confrontation with Indonesia in the 1960s and in more normal times had been the terminal for RAF strategic routes and the base for Shackletons operating on anti-piracy patrols in the South China and Celebes Seas. The Commander Far East Air Force, Air Vice-Marshal Maynard, reviewed the parade and Guard of Honour from 63 Squadron RAF Regiment, before a distinguished audience including Dr Gow Keng Swee, the Singapore Minister of Defence, Air Commodore Robey, the Senior Air Staff Officer of the Royal Australian Air Force, and Air Chief Marshal Sir Brian Burnett, C-in-C Far East Command. Three days earlier, on September 15, RAF Tengah (on the north-west coast of the island) commemorated the hand-over of command of the Station to the Singapore Armed Forces in a similarly impressive parade. The RAF

Station Commander had concluded his speech with the words: "We leave tonight twice blessed. We have been part of both the old and the new Tengah." By this he aimed to remind his audience of the fact that the first RAF aircraft had landed at the newly constructed airfield of Tengah in August 1939. They were Blenheims of 11 and 39 Squadrons from Risalpur in India. Now Tengah houses Hunters of 140 Squadron of the Singapore Air Defence Command and although no longer an RAF Station, RAF Shackletons (later Nimrods) and helicopters, together with units of the Royal Australian and Royal New Zealand Air Forces, continue to be based there as part of the Five Power defence force. In 1928, eleven years before Tengah had been built, four RAF Supermarine Southampton flying boats had landed at Singapore after a long, slow flight from the United Kingdom. HQRAF Far East had been formed in Singapore in 1933 with one flying boat squadron and one torpedo bomber squadron, both based at RAF Seletar, as its total strength. Now after forty-three years the wheel had turned full circle, and the RAF presence in Singapore was back to two or three maritime reconnaissance aircraft and ten Whirlwind helicopters. But the years had wrought one outstanding change: The RAF's ability, demonstrated in Exercise 'Bersatu Padu' the previous year, to reinforce the Far East in a time of need in a matter of days.

By November 1, 1971, the Far East Air Force had been disbanded. By the end of 1971, withdrawal from the Persian Gulf (including the RAF Stations at Sharjah and Bahrain) had been completed, but RAF Masirah off the coast of Muscat and Oman was retained as an important staging post under control of Headquarters Near East Air Force in Cyprus.

Meanwhile, there had been developments of major importance both in the strategy and equipment of the RAF in Germany. Strategically, there had been a basic change in NATO policy away from the trip-wire philosophy of a massive nuclear retaliation to a large scale Russian attack, to a far more flexible non-nuclear response. British Forces in Germany were now required, in face of a massive conventional attack by Russian land and air forces, to win a few days grace for the politicians by the use of conventional weapons alone. But, as *The Economist* has pointed out: "NATO's greatest weakness on the central front is the inferiority in the air which hangs like a black cloud over all military thinking and planning in Northern Germany."

Already in 1970 action was in hand to rectify this situation. On June 1, No 4 Squadron, which claims the distinction of being the first military unit in the world to operate a fixed-wing V/STOL combat aircraft anywhere outside Britain, converted to Hawker Siddeley Harriers at RAF Wildenrath. Formerly a fighter-reconnaissance squadron based at RAF Gutersloh flying Hunter FR.10s, all pilots were enthusiastic about their new aircraft. One Flight Lieutenant who, after two years flying Hunters with 20 Squadron in Singapore, had converted to Harriers with 1(Hunter)Squadron at RAF West Raynham, had some intriguing comments to make about the conversion training. "The final stage of our training," he said, "was designed to familiarise us with the aircraft as much as possible before actually flying it (his training took place before the dual control Harrier T.2 had become available to assist conversion). This involved taxying around the airfield carrying out three acceleration runs to a speed of about 140 miles per hour down the runway. We reached this speed in a few seconds, and it was the first time we had experienced such fantastic acceleration. Regarding one's feelings during the first 'hover'," he continued, "they are hard to describe. There's not much time to look around and think about it! My thought was merely 'what on earth am I doing up here?' The sensation of sitting for the first time in a jet-fighter stationary in mid-air can only be compared with one's first solo flight, in fact for me it was even more memorable." Two more re-formed RAF Germany squadrons, 16 and 20, were well on their way to becoming fully operational on Harriers by the end of 1971.

From July 1, 1970, No 14 Squadron (previously equipped with Canberras) became the first in Germany to convert to the Phantom FGR.Mk2. Their role was conventional ground attack and reconnaissance and, if need be, nuclear strike. Four RAF Germany squadrons had been re-equipped with Phantoms by the end of 1971. It was also planned to deploy further Buccaneers to Germany during 1972, and these, carrying Martel missiles would concentrate in particular on the nuclear strike role. These new aircraft made an important contribution to the high morale of the RAF in Germany and, therefore, to NATO's 2nd Allied Tactical Air Force of which they were a part. Air Marshal Sir Harold Martin (a war-time pilot of the famous 617 Squadron) was now in command of 2ATAF, and he worked hand-in-glove with General Sir Peter Hunt, commanding NATO's Northern Army Group, to exploit this more favourable situation.

On the southern flank of NATO, in November of 1970, No 38 Group of Air Support Command had taken part in a major exercise code-named 'Follicle'. This involved the use of Hercules, Argosy and Andover aircraft from which 1,200 paratroopers of the Italian Commando Brigada from Livorno made 2,950 descents, using *British* parachutes. Use of the British parachutes was necessitated by the discovery during trials at the Aeroplane and Armament Experimental Establishment at Boscombe Down in Wiltshire, that the larger, faster opening Italian parachutes tended to hit the tail of the Hercules. Some of the exercise dropping zones were as far south as Sicily and Sardinia. Italian parachutists and RAF air and ground crews rated the exercise a great success, not only from a professional point of view, but also because of the good will created between men of the armed Services concerned.

During 1971, there was another batch of anniversaries to celebrate. No LXX Hercules Squadron (one of the few whose badge has Roman numerals) based at Akrotiri in Cyprus, celebrated fifty years of operational flying in the Middle East and Mediterranean. No 4 Flying Training School, at RAF Valley in Anglesey, was fifty years old on 'All Fools Day' 1971. First equipped with Avro 504Ks it initially trained pilots for

Plate 26 A Hawker Siddeley Harrier of 20 Squadron taxying out of its camouflaged 'hide' during an exercise in Germany. Reconnaissance aircraft were unable to discover their 'hides' from the air.

Plate 27 A Royal Air Force Hercules parachuting grain to starving Nepalese in a deep valley in the Himalayan foothills. Operating 'Khana Cascade' in 1975.

squadrons in the Middle East. In 1971, equipped with the Gnat 1 and Hunter 7, it was training pilots for Hunter, Harrier, Lightning, Buccaneer and Phantom front line squadrons. The Air Support Command Examining Unit based at RAF Abingdon celebrated its twenty-five years existence on July 9, 1971. Its purpose in life is to maintain the extremely high standards of safety and efficiency of RAF transport crews throughout the world. This involves snap-testing periodically for professional ability and operational efficiency all categories of aircrew — pilots, navigators, engineers, signallers and loadmasters, on up to ten different fixed-wing transport types and several different types of helicopter. The Aeroplane and Armament Experimental Establishment at Boscombe Down celebrated its 50th anniversary on March 19, with a flying display and static exhibition. Unhappily, Her Majesty the Queen was not well enough to attend but Princess Anne, deputising for her mother, unveiled the AAEE's new shield and took particular interest in the static display which included R.J. Mitchell's Supermarine S.6B of Schneider Trophy fame, and forerunner of the even more famous Supermarine Spitfire.

A note of sadness was struck during these two years by the deaths of five of the RAF's most famous leaders. First to go, on February 14, 1970 was Air Chief Marshal Lord Dowding who had been Commander-in-Chief of Fighter Command during the Battle of Britain. Gruff and unapproachable, except by those who knew him well, he had acquired the nick-name 'Stuffy' at the Army Staff College, Camberley, before the First World War and this remained with him for the rest of his life. He had commanded 16 Squadron RFC on the Western Front and in the spring of 1936 was appointed Commander-in-Chief of the newly formed Fighter Command. Due for retirement in June 1939, in fact he stayed on as C-in-C for four-and-a-half critical years, by the end of which the daylight air battle over Britain had been won. No-one today would dispute that Dowding led Fighter Command with great humanity and determination to victory in one of the decisive battles of the world.

In the Spring of 1970, Air Marshal Sir Richard Atcherley died. In the Schneider Trophy days of 1929, he had been holder of the world air speed record of 332 mph. 'Batchy' Atcherley and his twin brother David (who as an Air Marshal went missing on a solo flight from the Canal Zone to Cyprus in 1952) were two of the most colourful RAF characters. Apart from his pre-war air speed record, 'Batchy' was also well known pre-war for his exhibitions of crazy flying. He was first post-war Commandant of the RAF College, and helped form and initially commanded the Pakistan Air Force.

Air Chief Marshal Sir Arthur Longmore died in December 1970. He had been the first CO of No 1 RNAS Squadron in 1914, and on January 3, 1971, a Nimrod of its successor, 201 Squadron RAF, scattered his ashes over the Solent in accordance with his wishes. Before he retired from active service in 1942, Sir Arthur as AOC-in-C Middle East in the dark days of 1940 had prepared the air support for General Wavell's advance through Libya at the end of that year.

Marshal of the RAF Lord Portal, who died in the spring of 1971, had graduated from the Central Flying School, Upavon, on April 27, 1916. In 1917, he was awarded the military Cross for conspicuous gallantry while flying with 3 Squadron of the RFC based at St Omer. Six months later, commanding 16 Squadron, he was awarded the DSO. In the Second World War he was Commander-in-Chief of Bomber Command from April to October 1940, and as Air Chief Marshal Sir Charles Portal was appointed Chief of the Air Staff on October 25, 1940, a high office in which he dischharged his great and grave responsibilities for five long years of war. General Lord Ismay said of him that "Academically and scientifically he was probably the best education of the Chiefs of Staff, and there was no aspect of Royal Air Force work in which he was not thoroughly versed." His portrait in Garter robes, painted by Sir Oswald Birley, hangs today in the hall of his old College, Christchurch, Oxford.

Air Marshal Sir Robert Saundby, who died in the autumn of 1971, had been awarded the Military Cross for destroying a Zeppelin airship while serving in 41 Squadron of the RFC on the Western Front. He is chiefly remembered for his long period of service at Bomber Command HQ during the 1939-45 war, where he first served as Senior Air Staff Officer and later as Deputy Air Officer Commanding-in-Chief under 'Bomber' Harris.

Some other events of these two years which deserve a mention include the closing of the 'Gee chain' navigational aid system, which had played a vital role in the final years of the bomber offensive against Hitler's Germany, after twenty-eight years' service; the first entry to Cranwell of a course consisting entirely of university graduates who had read for their degrees at civilian universities, either sponsored and paid by the RAF as 'University Cadets' or on their own initiative; arrival of the first Buccaneer Squadron — No XV — in Germany in January 1971, and in the same month, delivery to Air Support Command of the first Anglo-French Puma helicopters; the arrival in Malta on October 4, 1971 of Nimrods to replace Shackletons; the decision to negotiate contracts for purchase of the Hawker Siddeley 1182 advanced jet trainer to replace Hunters and Gnats, and to buy more than 100 Scottish Aviation Bulldogs to replace the Chipmunk primary training aircraft. Finally, during 1971, the RAF's Skynet world-wide communications system using one spacecraft and nine earth stations, all controlled from the Telemetry and Command Station at RAF Oakhanger, conducted successful operational trials. The RAF, through HQ No 90 (Signals) Group, was conducting its first communications operations outside the earth's atmosphere.

Two bravery awards merit special mention: that of the Air Force Cross to Master Pilot Alexander Riddoch, and of the Air Force Medal to Sergeant Michael Richard Birley. Both men, on detachment to the Royal Brunei Regiment in North Borneo, were members of a crew of a Wessex helicopter sent to help the crew of an oil drilling barge on fire after a gas explosion off the coast of Sarawak. Master Pilot Riddoch flew 180 miles at low level in darkness and pouring rain. On arrival, the barge was still burning fiercely and corkscrewing in an eigh foot swell. There was danger of further explosions. Once over the barge Riddoch positioned his aircraft, avoiding a collapsed derrick and trailing wires, entirely on directions from his winchman, Sergeant Birley. A third crewman was then winched onto the deck of the barge. Birley, affected by fumes, smoke and heat, calmly directed his captain and exercised the utmost care and gentleness in getting a badly burned survivor into the aircraft cabin, where he gave immediate first aid. Later in the day, Birley flew four further sorties with different captains and carried out eight further winching operations on and off the barge. Well aware of the danger from a second explosion, Riddoch and Birley had displayed the highest standards of determination, professional skill, coolness, judgment and courage in the highest tradition of the Royal Air Force.

In bringing this review of the RAF's first two years of a new decade to an end, we must return to the quotation from the Irish writer James Joyce which gave this chapter its title: "History is a nightmare from which I am trying to awake." In his speech in the General Assembly of the United Nations in New York on September 24, 1970, Sir Alec Douglas Home, Secretary of State for Foreign and Commonwealth Affairs had said with reference to the Strategic Arms Limitation Talks (SALT):

"If the United States and the Soviet Union can reach agreement on limitations to their nuclear arsenals, that will be a long step forward. I say that even as a European on whom the missiles will still be concentrated. We hope for the success of the SALT negotiations. It will not free us from the recurring nightmare of global destruction: that possibility will remain as long as states have access to the ultimate weapon. But such an agreement could slow down the growth of the means of destruction ...."

One month later at th same venue, the new British Prime Minister the Rt Hon Edward Heath spoke at the commemorative session for the twenty-first anniversary of the United Nations. Referring to the growth of political violence he said: "Today, we must recognise a new threat to the peace of nations, indeed to the very fabric of society. We have seen in the last few years the growth of a cult of political violence ... It is a sombre thought, but it may be that in the 1970s civil war, rather than war between nations, will be the main danger which we face." The crucial division in Northern Ireland," he continued, "is not now between Protestant and Catholic, or between right and left, it is between those who believe that constructive change is the only sound basis for peace, justice and progress, and those who reach at the first opportunity for the gun and the bomb."

It seems probable that in future the choice that faces civilisation will no longer be between peace and declared war, but between orderly progress and undeclared violence, sabotage and subversion. More than ever in the 1970s and 1980s, the job of the Royal Air Force and her sister Services will be to deter violence whenever possible, and to contain violence whereever it breaks through the tragically thin veneer of our Twentieth Century society.

Mind Over Matter

'No lifetime in Man's forty thousand years has seen such astonishing accomplishments, or such a majesty of mind over matter'
FLIGHT INTERNATIONAL (December 13, 1973)

The year 1973 marked several anniversaries of outstanding significance not only to the RAF, but to aviation in general. First and foremost, the seventieth anniversary of the start of powered flight, for it was on December 17, 1903 that the American brothers Orville and Wilbur Wright achieved at Kitty Hawk in North Cartolina the first "controlled, sustained, powered flight by a heavier-than-air machine." The year 1973 was also the fiftieth anniversary of Senor Juan de la Cierva's first flight (on January 9, 1923) in his C.4 Autogyro.

For the RAF, 1973 also marked fifty years of dedicated service on the part of Princess Mary's Royal Air Force Nursing Service. During her lifetime Her Royal Highness, Princess Mary (later the Princess Royal) had been closely associated with the development of the Service and had given her name to the oldest RAF hospital at Halton, Bucks, and also to the newest at RAF Akrotiri, Cyprus. By 1973, the RAF hospital group comprised seven hospitals extending from the centre of England to Cyprus, and members of Princess Mary's could be found serving on exchange duties in America, Australia, at the Anzuk military hospital in Singapore and on an aero medical duties flying patients from places as far apart as Paris and Peru.

The twenty-fifth anniversary of the RAF Provost Branch was celebrated Margaret at Debden (the RAF Police Depot). In December of the previous year, the twenty-fifth anniversary of the RAF Secretarial Branch had been commemorated by presentation during morning service of a Treasury — a cupboard for storing Church plate — to the RAF Church of St. Clement Danes in the Strand. 1972 was also the sixtieth anniversary of the RAF's Central Flying School (CFS), where flying instructors for all three Services are trained, and the forty-fifth anniversary of the formation of the Examining Wing at CFS, responsible for spot checking of qualified flying instructors and their students, and thus for maintaining the high standard of flying training for which the RAF is known throughout the world.

At the end of August 1972, a Vulcan bomber of 9 Squadron had taken off from its base in Cyprus for a commemorative flight to Norway, marking the thirtieth anniversary of the formation of the RAF Pathfinder Force, whose courageous leadership and special target marking techniques had revolutionised the accuracy of Bomber Command's mass attacks in the last two years of war, and also to commemorate the sinking of the German battleship *Tirpitz* in Tromso Fjord. In its crew room at Akrotiri, the squadron had a permanent reminder of its own part in the successful attack on the *Tirpitz* in the form of a bulkhead from her Petty Officers' Mess, presented by the Royal Norwegian Air Force.

After all the anniversary celebrations of those two years, it was irony indeed that an event should occur, in the autumn of 1973, that was to throw the whole future of aviation into the balance. In October, as a result in particular of America's support of the Israelis in the fourth Arab-Israeli war, Arab oil supplies to America, Britain and the whole of Europe were drastically reduced, thus dramatically bringing forward the start of a world energy shortage that few Governments had had the vision to foresee, and none the courage to forecast.

While the British press was full of the problems of private motorists searching for petrol, the RAF was far more concerned with whether the 5,000 kilometres length of the central European pipeline system, which supports all NATO's forces in central Europe, including the RAF's squadrons in Germany, could be kept full. United States navy ships using Singapore for refuelling, for example, found themselves without supplies of oil. All British Services made an immediate ten per cent cut in the use of fuel, although certain front-line units such as the RAF's air defence forces, nuclear bombers and others involved in Northern Ireland were on a priority list which allowed them all the fuel they required to remain fully operational. But it was the reduction of training flights that had possibly serious implications. Provided the reduction was short-term, the resulting backlog could probably be overcome by more intensive flying when the longer days and better weather of summer arrived. A prolonged curtailment of flying training hours, however, could result in a serious shortage of new pilots for front-line squadrons.

The oil crisis of 1975 signalled the end of an era, an era of cheap and plentiful fuel. The implications for the world of aviation in particular were extremely serious. For manned aircraft, during this century at least, no alternative means of propulsion to the oil-burning pure jet, prop-jet or piston engine is likely to be available. From a military standpoint, the Arab-Israeli war of October 1973, had changed the balance of power in the Middle East, and from the point of view of economics, the balance of power in the world. But what particular lessons for the RAF had come out of this war?

Perhaps the first lesson learned was that of numbers: the numbers and variety of modern weapons available in the 1970s to countries like Egypt and Israel, hitherto regarded as third-rate military powers. Israel's total population was after all less than one third that of the population of Greater London. Yet, as pointed out in the *Sunday Times* (December 30, 1973), in the great tank battle fought in the Sinai Desert on the second Sunday of the war: "more armour was engaged than the 1,600 British, German and Italian tanks which fought the Battle of Alamein."

The second lesson, but in no sense second in order of importance, was the potential of the anti-aircraft radar-guided and heat-seeking missiles, operated by even comparatively simple soldiers, against aircraft inadequately equipped with Electronic Counter Measures (ECM), or employing the wrong tactics in trying to knock them out. The Israeli Air Force learnt this lesson the hard way, through the loss of nearly one third of her front-line strength — probably more than one hundred aircraft — to surface-to-air missiles alone. Nevertheless, even during the early stages of the war, the Israeli Air Force appears to have put out of action many of the anti-aircraft missile batteries on the Syrian front, and was then equally successful in knocking out both Syrian and Egyptian tanks. It seems probable that, in the later stages of the war, stand-off guided missiles flown in from America added still further to the success of the Israeli Air Force attacks against armour and anti-aircraft missile sites. Some reports have suggested that, although IAF losses were heavy, compared with the high number of sorties flown the loss rate was less than in the Six-Day War of 1967, and certainly in air battles, Egyptian and Syrian Air Force losses were far heavier.

For the RAF and NATO, there are perhaps some hopeful conclusions to be drawn from the large-scale air and ground battles of this fourth Arab/Israeli war. Firstly, they showed that armour is vulnerable to accurately guided missiles whether fired from high performance aircraft, helicopters (which trials have shown can achieve a kill-rate in appropriate circumstances of 20 to 1 against tanks) and the shoulders of infantrymen. This suggests that British and NATO Services armed with *sufficient* guided missiles could go a long way towards offsetting the enormous preponderance of Warsaw Pact armour in Europe, a defensive counter-balance which, only a few years ago, it was believed could only be achieved by the use of tactical nuclear weapons.

Secondly, the RAF has more than a quarter of a century's experience of ECM which goes back to the Second World War, when specially equipped aircraft in Bomber Command carried out spoof raids and jamming in support of all major air operations over Germany and occupied Europe. Today, backed by an advanced electronics industry and research at the Royal Radar Establishment, Canberra T.17s of 560 Squadron specialise in the ECM role, and keep the RAF up to date in this field. This squadron is unique in that one quarter of its men come from the Fleet Air Arm, and every fourth Commanding Officer is a pilot from the Royal Navy. No matter what the colour of their uniform, members of the squadron work and fly as a highly specialised, close-knit team.

Finally, it is worth remembering that there are possible alternative ways of destroying anti-aircraft missile units in the tactical area, such as conventional artillery fire and commando raids. This would inevitably be less true, however, of the defence-in-depth situation in the European theatre, where anti-aircraft missile batteries would seldom be within range of conventional artillery, and where possibilities of camouflage and mobility are much greater than they were in Egypt, the Sinai desert and on the Golan Heights.

Throughout October 1973, No 56 (Lightning Fighter) Squadron in Cyprus (whose First World War members included two winners of the Victoria Cross — Albert Ball and James McCudden) were inevitably involved in the high intensity of Russian transport aircraft flights across the Mediterranean to re-supply Egyptian and Syrian forces. There were many scrambles to identify and escort the Russian aircraft out of Cyprus air space, and friendly hand waves were exchanged between Russian and British pilots in that strange camaraderie of the air that exists between men possessing similar professional skills.

The RAF became even more directly involved in the aftermath of the Middle East war when, at 4 am on the morning of October 26, a telephone call from London to Headquarters Near East Air Force in Cyprus, ordered an air lift to be mounted to fly several hundred Finnish, Swedish and Austrian United Nations troops from Cyprus to Egypt. The main problem was a requirement to carry a large number of vehicles including Swedish armoured personnel carriers, which would not fit into a Hercules. A Belfast, two VC.10s and two more Hercules were flown out from UK to reinforce 70 (Hercules) Squadron already alerted at RAF Akrotiri. The UN advance party started loading shortly after dusk on the evening of the day of the telephone call from London. One of the Scandinavian parties arrived at Akrotiri Air Movements having lost their liaison officer on the way. As they spoke no English, briefing at Akrotiri was hilarious and conducted in sign language, obviously successful, as the aircraft left on time.

There was little information on conditions at Cairo International Airport, other than a rather terse message from the RAF air attaché saying that all was *expected* to be well, and *if* he could gain access to the airfield he would be there to meet the RAF aircraft. Crews were warned that control and reporting procedures would have to be modified as all radar and navigational aids were believed to be shut down. Having heard about this, the OC S70 (Hercules) Squadron at Akrotiri (motto 'Usquam' ie 'anywhere') being a navigator, decided to fly in the first aircraft using his doppler inertial navigation equipment. On landing at Cairo, he confirmed that navigational aids and radar were non-existent. Air traffic control was working, however, and runway lights were on. Later the runway was shared with a number of Soviet Air Force transport aircraft, which added to the excitement!

Phase One of the operation was completed in forty-one hours on October 29. Phase Two would have started immediately, but the next contingent, consisting of troops from the Irish Republic, was delayed. The Irish Parliament had to foregather and give authority and as it was a long weekend in Southern Ireland, including Monday, no decision was immediately forthcoming: but on October 31, permission was received and they were flown in eight sorties to Cairo, completing the move in nineteen hours.

Prior to flying to Egypt the first contingents of the 4,000-strong UN Force required to defend the fragile peace in the Middle East, the RAF in 1972 and 1973 was involved in a wide variety of other operations. Apart from Northern Ireland, however, only one of them can be described as being of a warlike nature. This was the continued requirement for air support of the Sultan of Oman's armed forces against rebels in Dhofar, the South-West province of Oman, where in addition to providing close air support, men of the RAF Regiment were involved in defence of the airfield at Salalah against rebel attacks on the ground.

In September 1972, the Royal Naval air station at Lossiemouth on the Moray Firth in Scotland was transferred to the RAF, both as a base for the build-up of the RAF Jaguar force and for 8 Squadron, which had reformed earlier in the year at RAF Kinloss with Shackleton Mk2 aircraft equipped for the Airborne Early Warning role. In June of the same year, the Canberra bomber (the first jet engined bomber to enter service with the RAF) was withdrawn from service after twenty-one years, when 16 Squadron at RAF Laarbruch in Germany gave up its Canberra Mk 8 'intruder' bombers and re-equipped with Buccaneers.

Under the heading of missions of mercy, there were, amongst others, further flights to Saigon to carry relief supplies for refugees from the tragically continuing civil war in Vietnam, to Nicaragua after an earthquake, and a medical evacuation flight for seriously injured passengers of a civil air crash in Addis Ababa. Two flights were in a rather different category. The first was when a RAF Hercules dropped by parachute an intrepid team of Army and Royal Marine bomb disposal experts in mid-Atlantic, alongside Queen Eizabeth II, to search for a suspected bomb on board the luxury liner!

The second, on May 31, 1972, was when a 10 Squadron VC.10 flew the body of the late Duke of Windsor from Paris to RAF Benson in Oxfordshire, en route for St. George's Chapel, Windsor. Thus ended a long association between the Duke and the RAF, for his early enthusiasm for air travel, as Prince of Wales in the 1920s, had led to the addition of a Bristol Fighter to 24 Squadron at RAF Northolt for his use. He was given dual instruction by a Squadron Leader Don in 1929, and shortly after his accession to the throne as King Edward VIII, Flight Lieutenant 'Mouse' Fielden (now Air Vice-Marshal Sir Edward Fielden, retd) was appointed, in July 1936, as first Captain of the King's Flight.

During January and February 1973, aircraft and crews from the five tactical transport (Hercules) squadrons based at Lyneham, Wilts, operated a shuttle service between Khartoum and Juba, a scrubland community on the banks of the White Nile some three hundred miles north of the equator. Urgent aid had been called for by the Sudanese Government to help in the resettlement of more than 700,000 refugees who had fled from their homes during civil war the previous year, and all too many of whom were in desperate need of food, medical supplies and shelter.

Hard on the heels of the Sudanese operation, the same five squadrons were involved in an even more demanding famine relief operation code named 'Khana (Urdu for food) Cascade,' in the dramatic scenery of the high Himalayas. During 1971 and 1972, there had been an almost total crop failure in the mountain-ringed valleys of Nepal from where, for over a century and a half, Gurkha soldiers had been recruited and served Britain, always with unswerving loyalty and often with supreme courage. Many Nepalese families were, by February 1973, in imminent danger of starvation, and the RAF welcomed both the opportunity to discharge a debt of honour, and the challenge involved in low flying in deep valleys and amongst mountain peaks which include the highest in the world. Only by air could the essential 2,000 tons of food be got to where it was required before the monsoon broke. First it required fourteen Hercules sorties to position RAF servicing men and equipment and men from Army Air Dispatch Squadrons at two air strips 100 and 200 miles respectively on opposite sides of Khatmandu. Although some supplies were parachuted, sackloads of grain had to be dropped in remote valleys from only fifty feet above the ground, to prevent their bursting open on impact. This meant tight turns round mountain peaks, flaps and under-carriage lowered to ensure a steep descent down precipitous mountain sides into deep valleys where the Dropping Zone might only be sighted at the last moment. In such country there were of course no radio aids to navigation. "It was back to basics," as one of the co-pilots was recorded as saying, and called for "the best kind of team work." Three of the Hercules captains were later awarded Queen's Commendations For Valuable Service in the Air for their "exceptional courage and devotion to duty".

Nepal was not the only part of the world in 1973 where successive crop failures were threatening starvation. In West Africa, Mali, one of the countries of the Sahelian Desert which used to be one of the main grain-producing nations in Africa, had suffered a seven-year failure of the annual rains. Again it was RAF Hercules from Lyneham which, during August, carried nearly 2,500 tons of grain from the port of Dakar in Senegal to various remote townships in Mali, including Timbuktu.

Finally, during the last three months of 1973, Britannia transport aircraft from 99 Squadron at RAF Brize Norton in Oxfordshire, were positioned at Karachi in Pakistan to fly a daily shuttle service to Dacca in Bangladesh, carrying refugees in both directions. There were some 150,000 refugees to be flown from Pakistan to Bangladesh, and another 60,000 to be moved in the opposite direction. The UN referred to it as the "biggest ever human airlift," and the RAF crews found themselves working on it alongside Russian and Afghan civilian aircraft crews.

On September 1, 1972, the final step in the rationalisation of the RAF's Command structure in the United Kingdom had taken place, when Strike Command absorbed Air Support Command (previously Transport

Command) meaning that, henceforward, all operational aircraft in the UK would be under a single command, with all other RAF units in UK either in Training Command or in Maintenance Command (itself renamed Support Command on September 1, 1973). The multi-role Strike Command was soon put to the test, because between September 14 and 28, the Command participated, with about 150 aircraft, in NATO's biggest ever exercise, 'Strong Express', involving 64,000 troops, 700 aircraft and some 300 ships from twelve participating nations. During the exercise, fighters of the UK interceptor alert force were kept busy identifying and escorting Soviet aircraft intent on watching the exercise, when they intruded into the UK air defence region.

In November and December, five crews from Hercules squadrons at Lyneham gained invaluable experience of flying in extreme conditions when they participated with the US Navy in 'Operation Deep Freeze,' flying supplies from Christchurch, New Zealand to McMurdo Sound in the Antarctic (close to where the explorer Captain Scott had met his death) in support of the National Science Foundation's Antarctic Research Programme. The runway in McMurdo Sound consisted of sea-ice cleared of snow. The ice would support a loaded Hercules provided it did not get thinner than sixty inches, but as one RAF pilot commented: "Landing a Hercules weighing 120,000 lb on six feet of ice, knowing there was 1,500 feet of sea beneath, was a strange experience. The runway could actually be seen to dip at touch-down!"

In the following year, the Harrier concept of operations from 'hides' around a derelict airfield, was successfully practised in Exercise 'Sky Mist'. It was when returning in his Harrier from a sortie in the Cairngorm Mountains on this exercise that, cresting a ridge at low level, Squadron Leader Pugh felt several birds from a large flock strike his aircraft. The engine started vibrating, its note changed and the aircraft decelerated rapidly. The engine failed to 'relight' and still decelerating rapidly, Pugh selected a point on the ground ahead at which he would have to eject and informed his leader accordingly. Speed was falling off rapidly from 270 knots to 200 knots, but just as he was about to fire the ejection seat, he heard the engine pick up. Although the aircraft was sinking rapidly towards a ridge, the engine responded to a tentative throttle movement and Pugh immediately elected to sit tight. Clearing the ridge by about a hundred feet, he then diverted to RAF Kinloss and made a safe landing. For saving a valuable aircraft in a critical situation, Squadron Leader Pugh was awarded the Air Force Cross.

In the autumn of 1972, many nostalgic memories had been stirred by the opening by the Queen on November 15, of the RAF Museum at RAF Hendon, scene of so many pre-war RAF flying displays. Exhibits range from a Bleriot XI to a Lightning, but the museum also depicts the role played by some of the men and women who have helped to create the spirit and traditions of the youngest of the three Services. Thinking of these men and women brings us back into the 1970s, and in particular, to the wide ranging responsibilities of Training Command for the future standards of skill and professionalism of every man and woman in the RAF. Since June 1, 1968, this one Command had been required to do the jobs that, previously, were done by Flying Training and Technical Training Commands separately. This meant that their responsibilities now ranged from training of RAF technical apprentices through training of adult airmen and airwomen, training of offices for a dozen specialist ground branches, and all forms of aircrew training including the supervision of University Air Squadrons and training of flying instructors.

The Flying Training function alone, in 1972 and 1973, accounted for nearly a third of all flying hours in the RAF world-wide, and it was costing an average of £300,000 to put one pilot into a front-line squadron. By the time he has completed sixteen years service, something like another £1½ million would have been invested in his experience. Because, quarter of a century earlier, no agreement had been reached between the RAF and civil aviation on common standards, there was no automatic way in which RAF pilots leaving the Service at thirty-eight — at the peak of their experience — could be accepted into British Airways (previously BOAC and BEA) with appropriate recognition of such experience. Too many were, therefore, being lost to aviation altogether. It has been calculated that if twenty RAF pilots are lost to British Airways for this reason each year for the next ten years, the Country will have failed to make the most of a national investment in pilot training and experience of some £380 million! This whole subject became tragically topical as a result of Britain's worst air disaster in June 1972, when a BEA Trident crashed killing all 118 people on board. In a profession demanding high standards of skill and discipline, as the flying profession does, there is always great concern and sympathy amongst all flyers, whether Service or civilian, when accidents happen as, from time to time, they inevitably will. All learn lessons from them and make improvements to their training procedures, when it is considered that changes may help to avert a similar accident in future.

Meanwhile, in RAF Training Command during 1973, the Scottish Aviation Bulldog started to replace the DH Chipmunk primary training aircraft; the Jetstream (last brain-child of the ill-fated Handley Page Aircraft Company and now also being built by Scottish Aviation) was due to take the place of the Vickers Varsity for advanced flying training for pilots destined for transport and maritime reconnaissance squadrons and was already being used for training instructors. The Westland Gazelle helicopter was starting to take the place of Sioux and Whirlwinds for advanced training on helicopters. A decision had also been taken to buy the Hawker Siddeley Hawk (first designated HS.1182) as a replacement for the Gnat advanced trainer, for pilots selected for squadrons equipped with high performance aircraft such as Lightnings, Buccaneers, Phantoms, Harriers and Jaguars: but the Hawk was not expected to be in service before 1976.

Now we must return again to people, and first to one of those young women 'whose talent it is to serve'. In September 1972, a twenty-five year old woman graduate engineer received the Sash of Merit from Air Chief Marshal Sir Christopher Foxley-Norris, the Reviewing Officer, at the passing out parade at the RAF College, Cranwell. At RAF Wildenrath in Germany she gained another distinction — that of being the first woman engineer officer to be employed on the second line servicing of Harriers: the RAF of the 1970s believes in equal opportunities for women.

Before the end of 1973, Air Chief Marshal Sir Andrew Humphrey, Air Officer Commanding in Chief of Strike Command, gave evidence to the Defence and External Affairs Sub-Committee of the House of Commons Expenditure Committee. What he told them, in a nutshell, was that whereas he was well pleased with the quality of Servicemen and women, he had three particular problems. First, to convert a force designed originally for a nuclear response to a massive attack in Europe into a force more appropriate for the NATO policy requiring a non-nuclear flexible response. This in particular called for more air defence fighters and up-dating radar coverage. Second was to maintain training standards in a country with a crowded airspace and despite escalating costs. Third was the need to perfect the command and control structure.

Early in 1974, the Air Chief Marshal would take up his new appointment as Chief of Air Staff, and subject to adequate political and financial support — and this was an important proviso — he would then be in a good position to bring about the improvements he considered necessary. His wide flying and staff experience in war and peace suited him well to the challenging tasks ahead. He had been a Spitfire pilot during the Battle of Britain and continued to fly fighters or fighter bombers for the rest of the war in UK, the Middle and Far East. After the war, he served in Field Marshal Auchinleck's staff in India, and later took part in an aerial survey of British Territories in Africa, flying Lancasters. While instructing at the RAF Flying College in the 1950s, he established a new Cape Town to London record (1953) and carried out the first RAF jet flight to the North Pole '1954), both in the Canberra 'Aries IV'. He is one of a very small number of RAF offices to hold three Air Force Crosses. After commanding RAF Akrotiri in Cyprus from 1959 to 1961, he attended a course at the Imperial Defence College (now the Royal College for Defence Studies), served as Director of Joint Plans in the Ministry of Defence from 1962 to 1965, and became the last Air Officer Commanding Air forces Middle East before the withdrawal from Aden. He became a Knight Commander of the Order of the Bath in 1968, and as Air Member for Personnel from 1968-70, introduced the graduate entry scheme in place of the Cadet entry scheme to the RAF College, Cranwell. On January 5, 1971, he was appointed Air Officer Commander in Chief of RAF Strike Command.

Maintaining The Stand

'The West must under no circumstances allow the weakening of its stand against totalitarian nations' ANDREI SAKHAROV, *Nobel Prize Winner and architect of the Russian H-bomb.*

On February 28, 1974, a Labour Government was returned to power. On March 21, the new Secretary of State for Defence, the Rt Hon Mr Roy Mason, announced in Parliament that the Government had "initiated a review of current defence commitments and capabilities against the resources that, given the economic prospects of the country, we could afford to devote to defence."

It was not until December 3, 1974, that Mr Mason was in a position to outline to Parliament the order of magnitude of the proposed cuts in defence spending, and the probable effect of such cuts on the three Services. The Government aim, he explained, was to achieve total savings over the next ten years of £4,700 million, all at 1974 prices. He emphasised that conclusions reached were provisional and firm decisions could only be arrived at after consultation with NATO allies and other Governments affected by the proposals.

Air Chief Marshal Sir Andrew Humphrey, who had taken up his appointment as Chief of the Air Staff on April 1, 1974, explained the likely effect of the cuts on the RAF in the following general terms. It was a fundamental feature of the defence review that our national defence effort would be concentrated in future, even more than at present, on our crucial commitment to NATO. To this end the RAF combat strength committed to NATO would be maintained and in some respects increased. Thus the Government was proposing to bring to an end or reduce the number of our remaining overseas commitments. There would also be substantial reductions in specialist reinforcement forces and consequently in the airlift which they required. He went on to explain that, whereas there would be some increase in air defence and offensive support forces, there would be a major reduction of the transport force by a half together with some reduction in the Nimrod and helicopter forces outside Europe.

The RAF Regiment would eventually be reduced in size but the programme for the Rapier surface-to-air missile would go ahead. There would also be reductions in training, support and communications aircraft. Staffs at Headquarters, including the Ministry of Defence, would be reduced. Twelve RAF Stations would be closed, and the plan here would be to concentrate on the larger and better equipped stations and close those which offered less scope for future development.

The measures as a whole would be spread over the next four to five years and by April 1, 1979, RAF manpower would have been reduced by some 18,000. To view this figure in perspective it should be noted that during the five years concerned, nearly 60,000 men could be expected to flow through the Service. This meant that the greater part of the manpower reductions could be achieved through normal exits and by adjusting intakes. But reliance on these means alone would jeopardise the manpower structure of the Service in the long term. Regrettably, therefore, about 4,000 men (including some 800 officers) would be redundant. For those, the Government was pledged to provide fair redundancy terms and adequate time for planning future employment. But the majority of men serving in 1974 would be unaffected by redundancy. The Chief of Air Staff emphasised that for them, and for those who intended to serve in future, a thoroughly challenging and worthwhile career would continue to be available.

The RAF, he explained, was in the midst of a major re-equipment programme which would extend over the next decade, and introduce a range of new combat aircraft and weapons.

The Hawker Siddeley Hawk would become the RAF's advanced training aircraft. The Hawker Siddeley Nimrod's capabilities would be enhanced. The Shackleton would be replaced in the Airborne Early Warning role, and the Victor tanker force would be further modernised. Meanwhile, development and production of the Tornado Multi-Role Combat Aircraft would proceed and the aircraft would form a major part of the RAF's future front line strength.

How then would these defence cuts affect some of the RAF's operational roles? Firstly, there would be no reduction in the twelve Harrier aircraft and four Wessex helicopters with which the RAF supported the battalion group which was the British contribution to the Allied Command Europe (ACE) Mobile Force. This specialist reinforcement force would continue to be available to the Supreme Allied Commander Europe (SACEUR) for deployment throughout the NATO European command.

Then there was the United Kingdom Mobile Force available for deployment to the Central and Northern Regions of Allied Command Europe. In 1974, the RAF contribution to this Force consisted of three squadrons of Phantom offensive support and reconnaissance aircraft (due to be replaced by Jaguars), one squadron of Andover short-range transport aircraft and three squadrons of support helicopters, all in support of three air-portable brigades with divisional troops and logistic support. By 1979, this Force would be reduced to an air-portable reinforced brigade group, with a limited parachute capability and the same RAF support less the Andover squadron.

The defence review indicated that the RAF Indian Ocean staging post on the island of Gan would be given up by April 1976, but that an airfield being built by the Americans on the Island of Diego Garcia would provide an alternative staging post in the Indian Ocean if required. The RAF would continue to provide air support for the Sultan of Oman's forces in their fight against an externally supported rebellion, because of Britain's interest in the stability of the Arabian Peninsular. In the Far East, the RAF would continue to deploy helicopters in support of the Hong Kong garrison, but the Wessex helicopters based in Singapore in support of the Five Power Defence Arrangements would be withdrawn and detachments of Nimrod aircraft would be discontinued.

To case the accommodation problems that arose in Cyprus as a result of the emergency in July and August 1974, by the end of the year, the Lightning and Hercules squadrons based at RAF Akrotiri and the Vulcan strike aircraft permanently stationed there in support of th Central Treaty Organisation (CENTO) had been withdrawn and replaced by smaller numbers of aircraft on detachment from the United Kingdom. Although the United Kingdom would continue its membership of CENTO, no forces would in future be 'declared' to the Organisation and, by 1979, therefore, it was proposed to withdraw from Malta the CENTO-assigned Nimrods and Canberras.

The reason it was regarded as vital not to reduce the RAF's contribution to NATO was that, by 1974, the Soviet Union was known to have achieved nuclear parity with the United States. Furthermore, in Europe the NATO Alliance was faced with the Warsaw Pact's marked superiority in manpower and conventional weapons. In Central Europe, for example, the Warsaw Pact had twice as many aircraft and army divisions as NATO, two and a half times as many tanks and twice as many field guns. On NATO's northern flank, facing Norway and Denmark, the balance in favour of the Warsaw pact was even greater.

By 1974, all front-line squadrons of the Royal Air Force were contained in three regional Commands: Strike Command (which contained all front-line squadrons in the UK), RAF Germany and Near East Air Force (NEAF) with Headquarters still in Cyprus. To fulfil the all-important commitment to NATO, all operational aircraft in Germany, most of those in Strike Command and a part of the Near East Air Force Nimrod and Canberra force in Malta, were assigned to or earmarked for either the Supreme Allied Commander Europe (SACEUR) or the Supreme Allied Commander Atlantic (SACLANT). It was planned for the future that NEAF squadrons would be disbanded or redeployed to the United Kingdom and re-allocated to priority NATO tasks. Remaining tasks for the Cyprus base would in future be met by aircraft detached from their home bases in the United Kingdom.

In 1974, there was still a wide variety of aircraft committed to the RAF's traditional roles. In the nuclear strike and conventional attack roles there were Vulcan B.2s in Strike Command and NEAF; Buccaneers specially designed for low-level operations in both Strike Command and RAF Germany; and Phantom FGR.2s in RAF Germany which, when replaced by Jaguars, would transfer to the air defence role. For the offensive support role, there were Jaguars in Strike Command and V/STOL Harriers in RAF Germany and Strike Command. For reconnaissance there were Vulcan Strategic Reconnaissance 2s in Strike Command; Canberras in Strike Command and NEAF; and Phantom FGR.2s in Strike Command and RAF Germany. For the air defence role there were Phantom FG.1s and FGr.2s in Strike Command; Lightnings in Strike Command, RAF Germany and NEAF; Bloodhound surface-to-air missiles in RAF Germany and NEAF; and Shackletons for airborne early warning in Strike Command. For maritime reconnaissance and anti-submarine warfare there were Nimrods in Strike Command and NEAF: this force would be reduced by a quarter. Low-level air defence squadrons of the RAF Regiment, equipped with Rapier or Tiger Cat surface-to-air missiles or anti-aircraft guns, were deployed in Strike Command and RAF Germany; field squadrons of the RAF Regiment for local ground defence of airfields were deployed in RAF Germany, NEAF and Strike Command.

During the year, the RAF Regiment had units serving in Northern Ireland, Hong Kong, Oman and Belize in British Honduras. The RAF's Strategic Transport squadrons were still equipped with VC.10s, Comets, Belfasts and Britannias, and the Tactical Transport squadrons were equipped with Hercules (which also had a strategic capability) and Andovers. By early 1970 it was planned to disband the Comet, Britannia and Andover squadrons, a total of 39 aircraft, and to reduce the number of VC.10 and Hercules aircraft in operation from 66 to 47. The Belfast Squadron of ten aircraft would remain, but the helicopter tactical transport force would be reduced by about one quarter by cutting the number of Whirlwinds in Cyprus, by disbanding the Wessex squadron in Singapore, and by abandoning plans to purchase medium-lift helicopters for support of the Army.

It was ironical that in the year in which the Government decided to reduce the RAF's transport force by half, that same force had been called upon to undertake the biggest emergency airlift, between Cyprus and the United Kingdom, since the Berlin airlift. The trouble had started when the Greek-officered Cyprus National Guard had deposed President Makarios by attacking his palace in Nicosia on July 15. On July, 16 the RAF received an urgent message from the Archbishop indicating that his hideout in Paphos, in the western corner of the island, was being shelled by Greek Cypriot gunboats. A RAF helicopter, in spite of the shell-fire, succeeded in picking up the Archbishop and in flying him to the safety of RAF Akrotiri. The same night he was flown by the RAF to Malta from where he later continued his journey by RAF Comet to London, and thence to the United Nations in New York.

Meanwhile, Turkey was becoming increasingly concerned for the welfare of the Turkish minority in Cyprus because of the pro-Enosis record of Mr Nicos Sampson, the new Cypriot President. On Saturday, July 20, 1974, Turkish forces invaded Cyprus at dawn. About 6,000 troops and 40 tanks were landed on the beaches around Kyrenia on the north of the island. Greek Cypriot forces in and around Kyrenia were attacked by F-100s with rockets and bombs and air attacks continued throughout the day. Turkish paratroops landed between Kyrenia and Nicosia and further troops were landed on a hurriedly prepared landing strip in more than fifty transport aircraft sorties. Greece continued to mobilise throughout Sunday, July 21 and to build up forces on the Greek-Turkish border. She intimated that war with Turkey would be declared within 48 hours if Turkish forces were not withdrawn from Cyprus, but she later withdrew this threat.

Back in the United Kingdom, on the afternoon of Friday, July 19, Headquarters 46 Group, the Strike Command strategic transport Group at RAF Upavon on Salisbury Plain, had received a series of warning orders indicating that a major airlift to Cyprus was imminent. Staffs concerned worked on the planning throughout the night. By 2040 hours GMT on Saturday, July 20, the first aircraft, a Britannia, was airborne. The initial outgoing flights carried slip crews to be based at RAF Akrotiri, additional men for servicing transport aircraft, seven Mobile Air Movement Teams (MAMS), men to take the place of local civilian labour no longer available in the British Sovereign Base Areas, and additional fighting units from the Royal Marine Commandos, the Army and the RAF Regiment.

On the afternoon of Saturday, July 20, thousands of tourists and refugees of more than forty different nationalities started to flood into the Sovereign Base Areas, and arrangements had to be made to fly them back to the United Kingdom.

Thus the first phase of the airlift ran from July 20 to August 5, during which Cyprus was reinforced and evacuees (mainly holiday makers) were flown out to the United Kingdom. From August 6 to 10, a ceasefire was declared and a number of the reinforcing units were flown back to the UK. When the Geneva peace talks broke down, however, reinforcements were again flown out to Cyprus, including some of the units that had just been flown home. During this period all RAF and Army dependents living outside the Sovereign Base Areas were flown to the United Kingdom. This was the peak period of the airlift. For two-and-a-half days 4,000 passengers were flown daily to the UK, and it has been estimated that during this period there were 33 aircraft with 1,000 passengers airborne at any one time. The final phase of the airlift occurred from August 18 to 28, when emergency food supplies and equipment were flown out to Cyprus for the Greek and Turkish refugees camped within the Sovereign Base Areas, and also to support the increased number of British troops on the island. By the time the airlift was over, more than 22,000 people had been flown out of Cyprus in some 360 sorties by RAF Hercules, Britannia, VC.10, Belfast and Comet aircraft.

Another remarkable achievement during the Cyprus emergency was the RAF's quick response to a call for help from the commander of the United Nations peace-keeping force. Major General Prem Chand had only 200 troops and no anti-tank weapons with which to hold a 500-yard wide neutral zone round the perimeter of Nicosia airport. He made an urgent request for RAF support against a possible Turkish tank attack. On the night of Wednesday, July 24, twelve Phantom FGR.2s, armed with rockets, from 6 and 41 Squadrons at RAF Coningsby, took off at two hours notice. Flying through the night, they were refuelled in the air by Victor tankers from RAF Marham which then landed at Malta. By first light on Thursday, July 25, the Phantoms were on a ten minute standby at RAF Akrotiri, and one of their pilots took up his position as a Forward Air Controller on the roof of a hangar at Nicosia airport, from where he would be in a good position to direct them onto a tank target if the need arose.

By Friday, July 26, the RAF in Cyprus had been further reinforced by four Puma troop-carrying helicopters which had been flown out in two Belfast aircraft. This made possible the airlift of 300 men of the Coldstream Guards and the 16/5 Lancers and their Ferret armoured cars and Wombat anti-tank guns into the battered remains of Nicosia airport, to reinforce the United Nations troops already there.

Although the Cyprus operation was by far the largest to involve the RAF during 1974, there were a variety of other small-scale operational commitments in other parts of the world. Starting in January, three Canberra PR.9 aircraft from 39 Squadron, RAF Wyton, carried out a seven-week air survey in the Caribbean. The object was to update maps and charts of two areas. One task involved photographing island areas including Antigua, the other task involved photographing more than 4,000 square miles of reefs and islands off Belize in British Honduras. Later in the year, RAF photographic reconnaissance aircraft carried out aerial surveys in Norway, Oman, Fiji, the Yemen Arab Republic and Kenya.

A 47 Squadron Hercules was involved in an urgent transport operation in the Caribbean in the autumn. Arriving in Belize on a routine supply mission to the British garrison there, they found themselves taking part in an emergency relief programme for thousands of people rendered homeless by hurricane Fifi. They airlifted men of the 1st Battalion The Light Infantry, Royal Engineers, medical teams and assault boats and vehicles to San Pedro Sula in the middle of the disaster area. Then at the request of the British Ambassador, the Hercules carried food supplies from the capital city to the disaster area on the north coast.

On the African continent, Hercules and Belfast aircraft airlifted a number of trucks to Ethiopia, Niger, Chad and the Sahelian region of West Africa. These were required urgently to help in distribution of accumulated relief supplies in the famine relief operations in these different parts of Africa. In Australia, in December, two RAF transport aircraft took part in relief operations following the destruction of Darwin by cyclone Tracy.

It was during this year that a new defence commitment arose in respect of the rapidly increasing number of offshore oil and gas rigs in the North sea. Ships of the Russian navy had been taking a close interest in these installations, and in an age of terrorism, it was obvious that they also presented possible targets for terrorist activities. Although the civilian police were responsible for the safety of oil and gas rigs in the first instance, the RAF and Royal Navy had to be prepared to come to the aid of the civil power. RAF Nimrod and Vulcan aircraft, during 1974, undertook reconnaissance and surveillance of Russian ships in the vicinity of British oil and gas rig installations, and it was stated in Parliament that RAF aircraft would if necessary be modified to suit them better for this specialised offshore surveillance work. Similarly, Nimrod and Vulcan aircraft monitored the movements of Russian naval ships in the Mediterranean, North Atlantic and other waters around the United Kingdom. Meanwhile, RAF Lightning and Phantom fighters, supported by Victor tankers and Shackleton airborne early warning aircraft, continued to intercept and shadow Russian aircraft entering the United Kingdom Air Defence Region to the north and north-west of the UK.

The Airborne Early Warning (AEW) role of 8 Squadron was still only two years old in the RAF in 1974. When the decision was taken to phase out fixed-wing aircraft carriers from the Royal Navy, the RAF was called upon to provide warning of low-level air attack upon the Fleet. At the same time it was appreciated that, to overcome the problem of low-level air attack against the United Kingdom itself, it was necessary to put the early warning radar in the air to increase the range at which it would be able to 'see' low flying aircraft. With the Shackleton redundant in the maritime reconnaissance role it was the obvious aircraft for the job; with its large crew and long endurance it would be able to remain on patrol for at least eight hours.

The radar scanner is mounted in a large radome at the front of the bomb bay. Accurate navigation over the sea is made simpler because of new Loran and Decca Doppler equipment. The crew consists of two pilots, an air engineer, two navigators, and four airborne early warning (AEW) Operators. The AEW Shackleton normally patrols on a line from 30 to 40 miles long, at an altitude between 1,000 and 5,000 feet. While on patrol, the Shackleton is under control of a Defence Radar Station. As soon as a target is detected, its position and direction of flight are passed to the Radar Station. If the target remains unidentified, a fighter aircraft may be allocated so that the AEW Shackleton can control the fighter to intercept and identify the target. In addition to its AEW role, the Shackleton is equipped for air-sea rescue.

On the other side of the North Sea, RAF Germany was active throughout 1974 scrambling Lightning fighters to intercept and identify unknown aircraft crossing the Border — in either direction — between the German Democratic Republic and the Federal Republic of Germany. In the sphere of passive defence, the Supreme Allied Commander Europe (SACEUR) had issued instructions to the effect that all Allied Command Europe airfields should construct concrete bomb-proof shelters to protect individual aircraft against air attack. The four RAF airfields concerned were RAF Bruggen, Wildenrath, Laarbruch and Gutersloh. By autumn 1974, work had started at RAF Bruggen and the whole programme was expected to take about two years to complete. Each aircraft shelter would be capable of housing one aircraft together with ground support such as changing rooms, operations and briefing rooms. Aircraft would be able to start up and scramble from within the shelter, and on return would be winched back into the hangarette.

In the field of active defence, by the beginning of November 1974, the second RAF Regiment Rapier squadron — No 58 — was operational at RAF Laarbruch, a Buccaneer and Phantom base. The first Rapier squadron — No 63 — had become operational at RAF Gutersloh in August. Rapier is a remarkable weapon and probably one of the world's most advanced low-level surface-to-air missile systems. The RAF Regiment had taken part in a series of trials, including hot weather trials in Australia when the RAAF provided targets by flying past in Mirage aircraft at 150 feet and Mach 1.2. The Rapier squadrons were forming at RAF North Luffenham, Leicestershire, where they spent a month collecting their men and equipment. They then moved to the Royal School of Artillery on Salisbury Plain for a three-and-a-half month course, and finished up with two weeks at Benbecula, the missile range in the Hebrides where live missiles were fired at low-level high-speed targets. On the RAF Germany Stations concerned, twenty-four to thirty-six Bofors guns were being replaced by about eight Rapier fire units, each of which had one launcher carrying four missiles. One of the advantages of Rapier is that a typical airfield can be defended by 80-90 men using the missile, compared with more than 400 needed to operate sufficient guns to achieve the same result.

With the Rapier, the operator does not have to guide the missile but simply tracks the target. A computer signals the right moment for firing the missile within seven seconds of picking up the target, and then guides it along the optical sight line to the target at a speed of more than Mach 2. The operator controls the optical system manually by means of a joystick, and the missile can pull 20g to follow a high-speed aircraft manoeuvring violently. Trials had shown that for a typical low-level target, Rapier achieved a better than 50% kill probability. Initially a daylight and fair weather weapon, additional radar was to be provided to give it a night and all-weather capability. At RAF Bruggen, No 4 Wing RAF Regiment had been formed to supervise all Rapier training and to exercise operational control of the RAF Rapier squadrons in Germany.

Nearer home, in Northern Ireland, throughout 1974 squadrons of the RAF Regiment had continued to provide close defence for the airfield at RAF Aldergrove and the radar unit at Bishops Court. At the same time, RAF helicopters continued to provide essential support for the Army in their anti-terrorist operations.

In addition to operational activities, RAF squadrons in Strike Command and RAF Germany were involved in a variety of highly realistic exercises during the year. One such was Exercise 'Big Tee' held in Norfolk. In this exercise, 1 Harrier Squadron was allocated to the support of 19 Airportable Brigade who were threatened by the advance of a heavy armoured column. Due to the high standard of reliability of the Harrier and to the fact that it could be dispersed safely close to the battle area, 1 Squadron, with only twelve aircraft, was able to fly 100 sorties a day for three days. Pilots flew five successive sorties of about thirty minutes duration each, remaining in the cockpit during refuelling and rearming. Based upon lessons learned from the 1973 Arab-Israeli war, it was felt that the exercise confirmed the ability of intensive ground attack from the air to hold up the advance of enemy armour. As a demonstration of their unique flexibility, the Harriers flew from ten different landing strips during the exercise.

During the NATO Exercise 'Crack Force', some 2,000 sorties were flown by American, Italian, Danish, Canadian and British aircraft. Phantoms and Lightnings of RAF Strike Command flew in the air defence role assisted by Airborne Early Warning Shackletons and refuelled by Victor tankers. RAF Germany flew Phantoms and Buccaneers as targets for other NATO air defence forces, and UK-based Hunters, Canberras and Vulcans flew as targets for other countries as well as for the UK air defence fighters. For No 63 Rapier Squadron RAF Regiment based at RAF Gutersloh, this was the first opportunity to participate in a major NATO exercise.

In early September, the RAF played an important part in Exercise 'Bold Guard', whose principal object was to practise the reinforcement of Schleswig-Holstein and Denmark. 42,000 men participated, most came from West Germany but Danish, American and British Forces also played their part. For the RAF it was the first opportunity for 54 (Jaguar) Squadron, which had only arrived at their UK base, RAF Coltishall, four weeks before, to take part in a realistic exercise in support of NATO ground forces. From their Danish base at Karup, 54 Squadron was able to provide the high-speed low-level close-support and armed reconnaissance for ground forces for which the Jaguar had been designed. At the same time Puma helicopters from 33 and 230 Squadrons from RAF Odiham were carrying troops and supplies into the battle area and evacuating casualties; while thirty-seven Hercules from RAF Lyneham flew into the combat zone at 250 feet, pulling up at the last moment to 1,200 feet to drop two separate groups of paratroops. The general conclusion from Exercise 'Bold Guard' was that it provided an impressive demonstration of the ability of the RAF, and of the United Kingdom Joint Airborne Task Force, to reinforce a NATO flank swiftly and effectively.

Later in the same month, the RAF was involved in a larger scale NATO exercise code named 'Northern Merger'. The exercise area included the North Sea, Norwegian Sea, the English Channel and adjacent land areas, and involved three NATO Commanders, the Supreme Allied Commander Atlantic (SACLANT), Commander-in-Chief Channel (CINCHAN) and

Supreme Allied Commander Europe (SACEUR). Taking part were nearly 200 ships, 750 aircraft and 40,000 men on the ground, from eight different NATO nations. The day before the exercise started, air and sea reconnaissance reports disclosed that the number of Russian spy ships off the British Isles had doubled! Throughout the exercise, a number of Russian Tu-95 long-range reconnaissance aircraft entered the UK Air Defence Region and were intercepted and identified by Lightnings of 23 (Red Eagle) Squadron, based at RAF Leuchars in Scotland.

RAF maritime reconnaissance and submarine attack Nimrods operated in conjunction with maritime reconnaissance aircraft from other countries — Neptunes, Arguses, Orions and Atlantics. Buccaneers of 12 Squadron operated on detachment to RAF Lossiemouth in support of NATO naval forces in the North Sea and the Norwegian Sea. Phantoms and Lightnings operated in the fighter interception role supported by Victor tankers of 55, 57 and 214 Squadrons, and by Shackleton Airborne Early Warning aircraft of 8 Squadron. Strategic and tactical reconnaissance was carried out by Vulcans of 27 Squadron and Canberras of 39 Squadron.

So much for some of the more important exercises of 1974, now for some of the RAF's achievements in international competitions. From May 25 to June 7, the Allied Forces Central Europe tactical weapons meet took place at the Canadian Air Base at Baden Soellingen in Southern Germany. The 2nd Allied Tactical Air Force team was made up of Dutch, German, Belgian and British aircraft and crews and they were competing against the 4th Allied Tactical Air Force team made up of American, Canadian and German aircraft and crews. The 2nd ATAF won the tactical phase of the competition — involving bombing and strafing — and also the standard phase which included navigation, rocketing, bombing and strafing.

The 2nd ATAF also won the attack section and was the overall winner with the highest total of points. The RAF Phantom crews from 14, 17 and 31 Squadrons, from RAF Bruggen, achieved the highest score among the seven *national* teams in the competition.

During November, a team of four RAF Vulcans achieved a double success in the United States Air Force Strategic Air Command's competition 'Giant Voice' at Barksdale, Louisiana. The Mathis trophy for the best combined results in bombing and navigation was won by a Vulcan from 230 Operational Conversion Unit from RAF Scampton. This crew also came fourth in the bombing trophy. A Vulcan from 101 Squadron based at RAF Waddington, Lincs won the navigation trophy. This second success in the competition completed a hat-trick for the RAF following the news that a Nimrod from RAF Kinloss, in Scotland, had won the Fincastle Trophy in New Zealand, competing in an anti-submarine competition, with crews from New Zealand, Australia and Canada.

The results in the American bombing competition were the best ever achieved by the RAF in this competition, and it was the first time the RAF had won two major trophies. The RAF's achievement can be better appreciated when it is noted that they were competing against some fifty-two American hand-picked crews, flying eight-engined B-52 Stratofortresses and swing-wing F-111s, from Strategic and Tactical Air Command bases throughout America.

On June 21, the BBC broadcast live from RAF Wittering a forty-five minute documentary programme, designed to give viewers an insight into some of the capabilities of the RAF of the 1970s. The programme included Vulcans, Nimrods, Harriers and Buccaneers, the Red Arrows aerobatic team from Central Flying School, Jet Provost training aircraft and a Bulldog flown by an undergraduate member of London University Air Squadron. A commentary was provided by Raymond Baxter assisted by Group Captain Davenport.

One of the most outstanding items in the programme was provided by two Phantoms of 2 Squadron from RAF Laarbruch in Germany. They were required to fly a low-level reconnaissance sortie from Laarbruch to Wittering, keeping to precise timing at their targets and on arrival at Wittering. They flew first from Laarbruch to Cologne, where they photographed the cathedral, then after crossing the North Sea they photographed the BBC Studios at Pebble Mill at precisely 8.20 pm. After arriving at Wittering exactly on time, as witnessed by more than 10 million viewers on their TV screens, they landed and off-loaded their films for processing. Before the end of the programme, the developed films were shown to viewers. BBC cameras had caught the Phantoms flying past Pebble Mill with a clock superimposed upon the TV screen to demonstrate the accuracy of their timing.

Meanwhile, threatening defence cuts during 1974 did not create a favourable climate for recruiting. Officer recruiting targets, however, were somewhat lower than in previous years, and in spite of fewer applicants, the requirement for the flying branch and for most ground branches was met. Similarly, most airmen recruiting targets were met except in some of the less popular trades.

Publication of a White Paper at the end of May, detailing new pay rates for the Services, was something of a morale raiser in a difficult year. Basic pay rates were increased by about ten per cent for the lowest paid, reducing to about five per cent for Air Commodores, and all increases were back-dated to April 1. In addition, the 'X' factor, which is designed to compensate for the peculiar problems of Service life, was increased from five to ten per cent for men, and from one to five per cent for women.

Flying pay up to and including the rank of Squadron Leader was increased by seven per cent, and there were similar improvements in parachute pay and parachute jumping instructors' pay. For those serving in Northern Ireland there was an additional payment of £3.50 per week up to and including the rank of Air Commodore. Perhaps of most significance historically, the White Paper emphasised that in 1975 equal pay for Servicemen and women would be introduced, and as a step in this direction, the five per cent difference in basic rates was halved with effect frm April 1, 1974.

Now we must take a look at some of the new aircraft entering service or under development in 1974. Pilots for the first Anglo-French SEPCAT Jaguar squadron started their operational conversion training at RAF Lossiemouth in Scotland in January, and the first Jaguar squadron, No 54, formed there on July 1. All pilots were enthusiastic about the Jaguar both because of its good handling qualities and because of its outstanding serviceability even in the early months of its RAF service. By the middle of August, 54 Squadron had moved to its operational base at RAF Coltishall in Norfolk. Four weeks later the squadron had deployed to Karup in Denmark to take part in the NATO Exercise 'Bold Guard'.

On October 1, No 6 (Phantom) Squadron, the oldest continuously serving squadron in the RAF, handed over its number plate and Standards to the new 6 (Jaguar) Squadron. The ceremony took place at RAF Coningsby where 6 Squadron's Phantom FGR.2 aircraft were due to be handed over to 29 Squadron, when they would change their role from ground attack to air defence, and thus replace 29 Squadron Lightnings at RAF Wattisham. On November 6, 1974, the RAF's second Jaguar Squadron, No 6, joined 54 Squadron at RAF Coltishall.

In May, the first of twenty-nine Victor K.2 tanker aircraft arrived at No 232 Operational Conversion Unit at RAF Marham. The Victor K.2 tanker had a greater fuel capacity than the K.1, and its improved performance meant that it would be able to lift a bigger fuel load from airfields such as RAF Masirah off the coast of Oman, where the temperatures are high and the runway length limited. Tanker operations had increased in importance for several reasons. The number of penetrations of United Kingdom airspace by Russian aircraft appeared to be on the increase. To ensure the best chance of interception and identification, and economy in the use of RAF fighter aircraft, it was essential to provide refuelling in flight for Phantoms and Lightnings. Now that most RAF combat squadrons were based in the UK or Germany, the ability to reinforce rapidly overseas areas of interest depended upon refuelling in flight. The reinforcement of the United Nations force in Cyprus with Phantom ground attack aircraft, at short notice, during July was a good example. Finally, the RAF commitment to provide air defence and air support for Royal Navy ships at sea involved a further requirement for air-to-air refuelling.

In September, Squadron Leader Symons, RAF project officer at the Ministry of Defence for the Hawker Siddeley Hawk, flew the aircraft for the first time at the manufacturer's airfield at Dunsfold, and he commented on its brisk performance and first class handling qualities. The Hawk was due to start entering RAF service in the autumn of 1976. It would replace the Gnat and Hunter, and would be used to train pilots for front-line combat aircraft such as the Panavia Tornado Multi-Role Combat Aircraft and the Jaguar.

On August 14, at Manching in Southern Germany, the Anglo/German/Italian Multi-Role Combat Aircraft flew for the first time. Some five weeks later, Mr Paul Millet, the British Aircraft

Corporation test pilot who had carried out the maiden flight, gave a demonstration flight at Manching before an audience of high Government officials, senior air force officers and the press. Mr Brynmor John, the Under-Secretary of State for the RAF commented: "Here is tangible evidence of what European countries can do to pool their resources in the interests of their common defence..." In the 1980s, the Tornado was expected to provide about half the combat strength of the RAF. It would replace both the Vulcan and the Buccaneer in the nuclear strike and conventional attack roles. It would also have a tactical reconnaissance capability, and an interceptor version of the aircraft would eventually replace the Phantom in the air defence role. On October 30, Mr Millet flew the first British-assembled MRCA from BAC's airfield at Warton, Lancashire.

In the field of new weapons, by the end of 1974 most RAF Buccaneer squadrons had been equipped with the Anglo/French Martel air-to-surface missile system. Both the television-guided and the radar-homing versions of the missile were available. The range of Martel made it possible for Buccaneers to attack targets from outside the area of local defences.

In the training sphere, towards the end of 1974, pilot training was reorganised in the interests of economy, and a new pattern of pilot training was introduced which reduced the flying hours without reducing the standard attained. One outcome of these economies was the closing of RAF Oakington, near Cambridge, in December. By the end of the year, the re-equipment of University Air Squadrons with the Bulldog training aircraft, replacing the Chipmunk, was nearing completion.

Due to the shortage of fuel in the early months of 1974, the Red Arrows aerobatic team could not start their training until May. Nevertheless, they had made sufficient progress by the third week in June to participate in the RAF Wittering demonstration of air power for BBC TV.

Before bringing this chapter to a close it is worth recording some of the anniversaries that were celebrated during 1974, and some of the awards that were made.

In October, the Royal Auxiliary Air Force celebrated its 50th anniversary. On October 25, there was a civic reception in London's Guildhall attended by the Queen and the Queen Mother. On Sunday, October 27, there was a commemoration service in Westminster Abbey, and on Monday, October 28, the Air Force Board gave a dinner at Headquarters Strike Command, High Wycombe, at which the Duke of Edinburgh was the guest of honour.

The Auxiliary Air Force (the prefix Royal was granted in 1949) was formed in October 1924, and by the outbreak of the 1939/45 war had grown to twenty squadrons. Auxiliary pilots were credited with the first two German aircraft shot down over the United Kingdom in the war, and in the Battle of Britain, the fourteen Auxiliary squadrons involved claimed 700 enemy aircraft destroyed. The complexity of modern air operations, however, meant that full-time professionals were required in the flying and most other roles. By 1974, therefore, the Royal Auxiliary Air Force was confined to three Maritime Headquarters Units: No 1 (County of Hertford) Unit at Northwood, No 2 (City of Edinburgh) Unit at Pitreavie Castle in Scotland, and No 3 (County of Devon) Unit at Mount Batten (Plymouth). Here there was still an important task for the part-time volunteer. The units were responsible for monitoring the movement of potentially hostile submarines and surface vessels. Training was given in intelligence, communications and control of RAF aircraft and Royal Navy ships.

On Sunday, May 12, twenty-five years after the lifting of the Berlin blockade, the Royal Air Force, with their French and American allies, took part in a wreath laying ceremony at the Air Lift Memorial at Tempelhof airport. The RAF contribution included the band of Royal Air Force Germany and a guard of honour of airmen from Gatow, still the RAF base in Berlin, which had been one of the terminal airfields during the airlift.

May 13 was the twenty-fifth anniversary of the first (prototype) Canberra flight. On May 22, the anniversary was celebrated by a Canberra 'meet' at RAF Cottesmore in Leicestershire. Thirty-three Canberras of a dozen different Marks were present. In the evening there was a reunion dinner of many of the personalities associated with the Canberra success story. Test pilot Roland Beamont, who had been the first to fly the Canberra, was Guest of Honour. Other guests included Marshal of the RAF Sir Dermot Boyle, who had established a Canberra record from London to Valetta, Air Chief Marshal Sir Lewis Hodges (London to Colombo, record still standing) Air Marshal Sir John Whitely (London to Nicosia) and Air Vice-Marshal I.G. Broom (Ottawa to London, record still standing).

On January 31, King Hussein of Jordan visited RAF Coningsby to attend the Diamond Jubilee celebrations of 6 Squadron. In his speech, King Hussein referred to the close association the Squadron had maintained with Jordan over many years which had resulted in his grandfather, King Abdullah, presenting his personal Standard to the squadron in 1950.

In a very different field, on December 15, the RAF Gliding and Soaring Association celebrated its twenty-fifth anniversary. They had played an important part in the development of the sport in the United Kingdom, and by 1974 there were fourteen RAF GSA clubs in the UK with affiliated clubs in Germany and Cyprus.

Finally, not forgetting the important contribution made by women to the efficiency of the RAF, February 1, 1974, marked the twenty-fifth anniversary of the Womens Royal Air Force as a fully integrated element of the RAF and as one of the regular forces of the Crown.

It is appropriate to bring this chapter to an end by mentioning some of the awards that were made during 1974 for outstanding service, outstanding skill and often outstanding courage. In May, the Air League Founders Medal awarded for the most meritorious achievement in British aviation during the previous year, was presented to the Red Arrows RAF aerobatic team. The award recognised the success of the Red Arrows in upholding the prestige of the RAF at home and abroad and providing a stimulus to recruitment. In their nine years of continuous service, the Red Arrows had given many hundreds of displays in Europe, the Mediterranean and North America. The medal was received by Squadron Leader Ian Dick, the team leader. In thanking the Air League for the award, he pointed out that he represented 47 officers and 150 groundcrew "who have been and are the aerobatic team..."

The London Gazette of March 26, notified the award of the Queen's Commendation for Valuable Service in the Air to the navigator of a Buccaneer, who talked his temporarily blinded pilot to safety after their aircraft had been struck by lightning.

The lightning had caused an explosion in the nose of the Buccaneer of XV Squadron as it was climbing, during a night exercise, from its base at RAF Laarbruch, in Germany. The pilot was temporarily blinded, suffering severe pains in the head and arms, and neither of the two-man crew at first realised what had happened. Flight Lieutenant Colin Tavner, the navigator, checked that there were no obvious signs of severe damage, sent a distress call and using the few flight instruments repeated in the rear cockpit, talked his blinded pilot into a controlled climb to a safer altitude. The pilot gradually recovered his night vision and managed to assume normal control of the aircraft. The citation said that Flight Lieutenant Tavner's reactions to a "frightening and potentially disastrous situation" were in keeping with the finest traditions of the Royal Air Force and an outstanding example to other aircrew.

It was notified in the spring that Flight Lieutenant Braithwaite and Master Air Electronics Officer More, both from 'B' Flight of 202 Squadron, RAF Leconfield, were to receive, in Washington, the eighth annual award of the (American) Avco/Aviation Writers' Association for helicopter heroism. Both men had already been awarded the Air Force Cross for their part in the rescue of sixteen men from the 2,000-ton ship *Amberley* foundering in a storm off the Norfolk coast.

Flight Lieutenant Braithwaite had to fly out to the ship blind because heavy snow had jammed the aircraft's windscreen wipers. On arrival, the ship was seen to be listing about 60 degrees and rolling and pitching violently. The first six seamen were winched up from the heaving deck in almost impossible conditions and in spite of overloading the helicopter. Flt. Lt. Braithwaite realised that only by himself accepting an overload would it be possible for the remaining ten men to be rescued by two other helicopters that were on their way. Master Air Electronics Officer More, the winchman, in addition to winching up the six seamen in extremely difficult conditions, volunteered to remain behind on the ship so that another seaman could be rescued. "Unbounded courage and compassion joined."

We Seek the Sky

'We seek the sky itself' HORACE

The Royal Air Force has come a long way and its air crew have flown almost unimaginable millions of miles in the thirty-odd years of dramatic, crowded life packed between the two covers of this book. Yet much that many will feel is important has had to be ruthlessly pruned out to limit the account to digestible proportions.

In each chapter I have tried to high-light one or two events which appear to have had the greatest impact on RAF development in the years concerned. If now I try to pick out a single thread that binds the whole together, it is perhaps that those who continue to be drawn to the RAF way of life in the 1970s are drawn for the same reasons as in previous generations, because they "seek the sky itself", and the even greater challenges that flying offers today than ever before. True, that never again will young pilots catch the scent of peach blossom as they drop down from the cool sky in open cockpits into the hot air of spring in the vale of Peshawar at the foot of the Khyber Pass: yet today in a pressurised fighter they can reach twice the height of Everest in a flight before breakfast, and climb in a Phantom from brakes-off on the runway to 40,000 ft in less time than it takes for astronauts to reach that altitude from light-up on a launch pad. Refuelling in the air, they can fly from England to Singapore in a few minutes over nine hours, whereas in 1927 it took four Supermarine Southampton flying boats thirty-five days to complete the same journey in fourteen stages.

Now that so much emphasis has been placed on the low level "under-the-radar" approach to a target, the new generation of pilot is experiencing the same thrills of flight at low level — at five times the speed — as the pre-war army co-operation pilot. Not long ago I flew with a crew of a Handley Page Victor (whose average age was half my own) on a high-low sortie over Scotland and the north of England. We had flown north at high level over the forest of Argyll, Inveraray and the Firth of Lorne, until the Island of Mull was showing on radar, like a miniature of the whole of Britain. A change of course brought us eastwards over Ross and Cromarty where we started to descend at about 4,000 ft per minute. At 500 ft over the grey waters of the Moray firth, we were soon rapidly approaching the coast of Aberdeenshire. Twenty miles away, the coastline showed up sharply on radar and within minutes the old walls of the herring port of Fraserburgh came clearly into view on our starboard bow. The navigator ordered: "Up two hundred feet," and our progress over the gently undulating land became suddenly like a cavalry charge in which "Flashed all their sabres bare. Flashed as they turn'd in air ..."

The junction of the railway from Peterhead and Fraserburgh next came up on radar. We were accurately on track and at the gallop we leapt first the River Don and then the Dee. Every two or three minutes, captain and co-pilot reported visual sightings to confirm what the navigator had already seen on radar. Quick and concentrated teamwork between all crew members was now vital to the safety and success of our low-level high-speed flight.

We were approaching the high moors of Kincardine. "Up to 1,800 feet," called the navigator. The captain signalled with his fingers to the co-pilot for increased power and the latter pushed forward the throttles until the appropriate engine power was showing on the instruments. Up came the aircraft's nose and the deserted moorland rushed by below. The motto of this squadron's home base — "We rise to our obstacles," had been chosen for this sort of flying in the First World War. I can remember thinking: "The more things change, the more they remain the same."

"Mount Battock, spot height 2,500 feet at 2 o'clock one mile," the navigator announced. "Confirmed," the captain replied.

Soon the two Forth bridges appeared on radar and through the flight deck window we could see a train crawling across one like a caterpillar on a twig. We hurtled on over East Lothian, Berwick, the winding Tweed and the Cheviot Hills. Next we were over the River Tyne and then the Tees, and the countryside was now more lush than the dark peat moors of Scotland. Over the North Riding of Yorkshire we photographed our check point at the end of the low-level route and started to climb on our final course for home.

Once caught by flying fever it never leaves you. Looking back one realised, to summarise the words of one of Sir John Hacketts' Cambridge lectures, that: "I should not have been content doing anything for a living in which it was never important to me what time the sun rose. Dawn, dusk, moon rise and moon set, what the wind does .... the form of the clouds .... the weather and the stars — these are matters of compelling importance in the lives of sailors, soldiers, airmen; and so, too, at all times and above all, are people."

It is to be closely associated with flying, with aeroplanes and with people, that equally attracts the best men and women to the RAF's many specialist trades and officer branches on the ground. But in these days when it requires so many more people on the ground, in operations rooms, air traffic control towers, at the work benches and office desks, in order to get a single aircraft into the air, let it never be forgotten that the only justification for their existence — regardless of their rank or professional specialisation — is to make the job of the man in the air that much easier, that much more efficient and that much more certain of success.

In order to remind myself of one shining example of the recognition of the above basic fact of air force life, and to reassure myself about the future of manned flight, I visited the RAF Institute of Aviation Medicine at Farnborough. Here, information on the performance of the human brain, heart, skin and so on, from experiments in the pressure chambers, in the climatic and radiant heat laboratories, in the centrifuge and vibration apparati, are passed to a central computer recorder; "and the conclusion that we come to," my guide — a flying doctor — summed up by saying, "is that, in the future of flight, in air and space, man's ability to think (still vastly superior to any electronic or mechanical device) will continue to be used, but reliable mechanical aids must be available to help overcome his limitations. By relieving the human work load involved in controlling high speed flight in detail, with a degree of automation, man will be left free to make the big decisions, not merely as monitor, but as captain of his craft."

There remains only one thing more to say. As has been shown throughout this book, the aeroplane is an instrument that can be used for good or ill, to destroy life or to save and succour suffering humanity throughout the world. Provided we continue as a nation to get our priorities right and have the courage of our convictions, by contributing *adequately* to NATO, there is a good chance that we can continue to deter the use of nuclear weapons for the next thirty years as we have succeeded in doing during the last thirty years. It is a strange paradox, but a fact of life that must be faced, that we can only hope to be successful in this high endeavour if we can convince other nuclear Powers that, as a last resort, we would be prepared to use nuclear weapons in our own defence.

Summary of Operations and Emergencies 1946 to 1974

Chap.	*Year*	*Operation or Emergency*
1	**1946/47**	1. Repatriation of prisoners of war and air transport of replacements for men demobilised from overseas Commands: 9,000 passengers per month.
		2. Air transport of food and medical supplies to sick and starving throughout the Far East.
		3. Air Support for Allied Forces against Indonesian insurgents.
		4. Air Support for Indian Brigade against pirates and robbers in islands of South China Sea east of Singapore.
		5. Air Support for army and police in Palestine to maintain order and prevent illegal immigration.
		6. Occupation of Germany and Austria and disarming of Luftwaffe.
		7. Partition of India and withdrawal of British forces.
2	**1948/49**	8. Berlin Air-lift June 1948 to May 1949.
		9. Start of operations against terrorists in Malaya, June 1948 (operation 'Fire Dog' continues for 12 years).
		10. Evacuation of British civilians from Burma.
		11. Provision of flying boat support to HMS *Amethyst* damaged by communist Chinese gun-fire in Yangtze river.
		12. Air Support for evacuation of Palestine — 1948.
		13. Air Support for minor operations in Aden Protectorate and Eritrea.

3	**1950/51**	14. Korean war from June 1950 to July 1953.
		15. Malayan operations continue.
		16. Internal Security operations in Canal Zone — Egypt (until 1956).
		17. Abadan oil crisis.
4	**1952/53**	18. Operations continue in Malaya and Korea.
		19. British Atom Bomb test in Indian ocean.
		20. Operations against Mau Mau terrorists in Kenya (until 1956).
		21. Rescue and reconnaissance in UK east coast floods (1953).
		22. Persian Gulf: Buraimi dispute.
		23. Earthquake relief in Cyprus and Ionian Islands (1953).
5	**1954/55**	24. Continuation of operations in Malaya, Kenya and Suez Canal Zone.
		25. Operations against EOKA terrorists in Cyprus (until 1959).
6	**1956/57**	26. Suez crisis and major operations by British, French and Israeli armed forces, until United Nations Organisation intervenes. British Prime Minister Sir Anthony Eden resigns. Place taken by Harold Macmillan.
		27. Civil unrest in Bahrain.
		28. Internal Security Operations in Muscat and Oman. Aden and Southern Arabia.
7	**1958/59**	29. Jordan/Lebanon emergencies (in 1958).
		30. Civil unrest at RAF Gan, Maldive islands, Indian ocean. RAF Regiment detachment sent from Singapore.
8	**1960/61**	31. Kuwait reinforcement operation against threat from Iraq.
		32. Air Transport of Ghana Brigade to Belgian Congo and re-supply (1960/61), in support of United Nations Force.
		33. Air-lift of food and medical team and supplies after hurricane in British Honduras.

194

34. Supplies of tents, blankets and medical materials flown to Agadir, Morocco after earthquake disaster.
35. Air transport in connection with unrest in Zanzibar and Laos.
36. Air-lift of food for Kenya after famine and floods.
37. Air-lift to help maintain stability in Cameroons.

9 1962/63

38. Crisis in Cuba. RAF Bomber Command nuclear force alerted.
39. Confrontation with Indonesia and evacuation of British nationals (until August 1966).
40. Air evacuation of British families from Assam after Chinese invasion across north-east frontier of India, followed by reinforcement of Indian Air Defence Force with RAF Javelin squadron.
41. No 20 Hunter Squadron sent to Thailand against threat from Laos.
42. Reinforcements flown to British Guiana to help quell riots.
43. Air patrol in Bahamas against Cuban ex-patriots.
44. British contribution to United Nations force in Cyprus.

10 1964/65

45. Air transport of Army reinforcements to help quell unrest and mutinies in Zanzibar, Tanganyika, Uganda and Kenya.
46. Air Support to ground forces operating against tribal terrorism in Kenya.
47. Reaction to Russian interference in Berlin air corridor.
48. Air transport of reinforcements to Mauritius to help quell rioting.
49. RAF fighter squadron flies to Zambia together with air transportable fighter control system, after unilateral decloration of independence (UDI) by Rhodesia. Maritime reconnaissance of Beira Channel by RAF Shackletons to prevent oil reaching Rhodesia.

11	1966/67	50. RAF assistance in Laos flood relief.

11   1966/67

50. RAF assistance in Laos flood relief.
51. Indonesian confrontation ends in August 1966.
52. Anti-terrorist operations in Aden and air defence of Aden Federation frontiers.
53. Interception of Russian reconnaissance bombers by Lightnings over North Sea.
54. Air attacks on oil tanker *Torey Canyon* aground off Scilly Isles, to burn escaping oil, and reconnaissance of oil slicks.
55. Air-lift for evacuation of Aden for British families and forces.

12   1968/69

56. Air evacuation of British servicemen and families from Libya.
57. Air support of internal security forces in Hong Kong.
58. Air-lift of troops to Mauritius to maintain law and order.
59. Continued patrolling of Mozambique Channel by RAF Shackletons.
60. Maritime reconnaissance Shackletons support Trucial Oman Scouts in Persian Gulf.
61. Detachment of Royal Irish Rangers flown by RAF to Bermuda to help quell rioting.
62. RAF Argosies, Hercules and Britannias of Air Support Command carrying reinforcements to Northern Ireland: RAF Regiment also participate in Northern Ireland security duties.
63. RAF fighters attached to Gibraltar to help maintain confidence.
64. Detachment of civilian police and parachute regiment flown by RAF to Anguilla in West Indies to restore law and order. RAF assistance in flood disaster in Algeria and Tunisia.

13   1970/71

65. Nimrod's first operational flight — shadowing Russian warships.
66. Far East reinforcement Exercise 'Bersatu Padu'.
67. RAF Comet flies six released Arab terrorists to Cairo.

68. Field hospital and surgical team flown to Jordan to succour civil war casualties.

69. Rubber rafts, medical supplies and Royal Marines flown to East Pakistan for cyclone relief.

70. RAF helicopter reinforcements sent to Northern Ireland.

71. Six Hercules, five VC.10s, two Belfasts carry supplies and passengers to Calcutta for flood relief work.

72. 38,000 passengers and 2,800 tons of freight air-lifted from Singapore and Persian Gulf on British withdrawal from East of Suez.

73. 900 British and friendly foreign nationals evacuated by air from Pakistan during Indo-Pakistan war.

74. 400 people evacuated from bomb-cratered runway at Dacca in East Pakistan (Bangladesh).

75. Air support for Sultan of Oman's operation against guerrillas continues.

14   1972/74

76. Withdrawal of squadrons from Malta to Sicily and Cyprus, and return later in year.

77. 2,000 tons of grain, maize and rice dropped by Hercules aircraft to Himalayan villages in Nepal.

78. 730 troops, 55 vehicles, 450,000 lb freight of United Nations Force in Cyprus flown to Cairo.

79. RAF Regiment involved in ground defence of RAF Salalah, Muscat and Oman, against guerrilla attacks.

80. Supplies flown to Saigon for Vietnam civil war refugees.

81. Medical and other relief supplies flown to Nicaragua after earthquake.

82. Hercules shuttle service flown between Khartoum and Juba (in southern Sudan) to aid 700,000 refugees of civil war.

83. Hercules carry 2,500 tons of grain from Dakar (Senegal) to Mali, West Africa to feed starving people after seven years, failure of annual rain.

84. Britannia shuttle service between Karachi (Pakistan) and Dacca (Bangladesh) transferring a total of 210,000 refugees in both directions.

15   1974

85. Cyprus Airlift.
86. Reinforcement of United Nations Force in Cyprus by Phantom squadrons.
87. Pakistan/Bangladesh airlift continues.
88. African drought relief.
89. Air surveys in Caribbean, British Honduras, Norway, Oman, the Yemen Arab Republic and Kenya.
90. Airlift of Britons from Darwin following destruction by cyclone Tracy.
91. Surveillance of Russian ships in the vicinity of North Sea oil rigs.
92. Periodic interception of Russian reconnaissance aircraft entering the UK Defence Region.

RAF Search and Rescue 1963 to 1974

Persons Rescued

by Helicopter

by Land Rescue Team

by Marine Craft

RAF Defence Expenditure 1946 to 1974

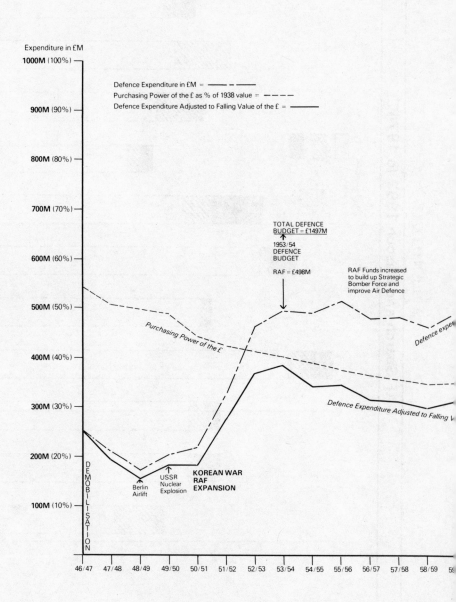

Expenditure in £M

1000M (100%)

Defence Expenditure in £M = — · — · —
Purchasing Power of the £ as % of 1938 value = — — — —
Defence Expenditure Adjusted to Falling Value of the £ = ——————

900M (90%)

800M (80%)

700M (70%)

TOTAL DEFENCE
BUDGET = £1497M
1953/54
DEFENCE
BUDGET

600M (60%)

RAF = £498M

RAF Funds increased
to build up Strategic
Bomber Force and
improve Air Defence

500M (50%)

Purchasing Power of the £

Defence exper

400M (40%)

300M (30%)

Defence Expenditure Adjusted to Falling V

200M (20%)

DEMOBILISATION

USSR
Nuclear
Explosion

KOREAN WAR
RAF
EXPANSION

Berlin
Airlift

100M (10%)

46/47 47/48 48/49 49/50 50/51 51/52 52/53 53/54 54/55 55/56 56/57 57/58 58/59 59

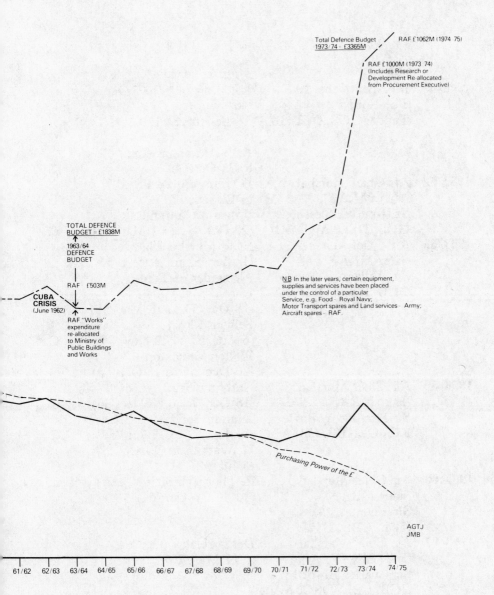

Total Defence Budget
1973/74 - £3365M

RAF £1062M (1974/75)

RAF £1000M (1973/74)
(Includes Research or
Development Re-allocated
from Procurement Executive)

TOTAL DEFENCE
BUDGET = £1838M

1963/64
DEFENCE
BUDGET

RAF £503M

CUBA
CRISIS
(June 1962)

RAF "Works"
expenditure
re-allocated
to Ministry of
Public Buildings
and Works

N.B. In the later years, certain equipment,
supplies and services have been placed
under the control of a particular
Service, e.g. Food - Royal Navy;
Motor Transport spares and Land services - Army;
Aircraft spares - RAF.

Purchasing Power of the £

AGTJ
JMB

61/62   62/63   63/64   64/65   65/66   66/67   67/68   68/69   69/70   70/71   71/72   72/73   73/74   74/75

APPENDIX IV

Chiefs of Air Staff and Ministers of Defence 1946 to 1974

Date	CAS	Minister	Party
1946/49	Marshal of the RAF The Lord Tedder GCB, DCL, LLD.	J. J. Lawson★ (to 7 Oct. '46)	C
		F. Bellenger★ (to 16 Oct. '46)	C
		A.V. Alexander (Jan. '47 to 28 Oct. '49)	L
1950/52	Air Chief Marshal (later MRAF) Sir John C. Slessor GCB, DSO, MC. ADC.	E. Shinwell (28 Feb. '70 to 12 Sept. '51)	L
		Winston Churchill (28 Oct. '51 to 1 Mar '52)	C
1953/55	Air Chief Marshal (later MRAF) Sir William F. Dickson GCB, KBE, DSO, AFC.	Field Marshal Earl (1 Mar '52 to 19 Aug '54) Alexander of Tunis	C
		Harold MacMillan (18 Oct '54 to 18 Mar '55)	C
		Selwyn Lloyd (6 Apr '55 to 22 Nov '55)	C
		Walter Monckton (20 Dec '55 to 16 Oct '56)	C
1956/59	Air Chief Marshal (later MRAF) Sir Dermot A. Boyle KCVO, KBE, CB, AFC.	Anthony Head (18 Oct '56 to 23 Dec '56)	C
		Duncan Sandys (13 Jan '57 to 18 Jun '59)	C
		H. Watkinson (14 Oct '59 to Jul '62)	C
1960/63	Air Chief Marshal (later MRAF) Sir Thomas Pike KCB, CBE, DFC.	P. Thorneycroft (Jul '62 to Oct '64)	C
1963/67	Air Chief Marshal (later MRAF) Sir Charles Elworthy GCB, CBE, DSO, MVO, DFC, AFC, MA	Denis Healey (Oct '64 to 27 Mar '70)	L

1967/71	Air Chief Marshal (later MRAF) Sir John Grandy GCB, KBE, DSO.	Lord Carrington (Jun '70 to Feb '74)	C
1971/74	Air Chief Marshal (later MRAF) Sir Denis Spotswood GCB, CBE, DSO, DFC, ADC.	Ian Gilmour (Feb '74 to Mar '74)	C
1974/	Air Chief Marshal Sir Andrew Humphrey GCB, OBE, DFC, AFC, ADC.	Roy Mason (Mar '74 to —)	L

*Secretary of State for War. Title of Minister of Defence started with Mr. A.V. Alexander.

C = Conservative   L = Labour

APPENDIX V

Awards of George Cross and George Medal

Since 1946, up to the end of 1973/4, there have been four awards of the George Cross to men serving in the Royal Air Force, and thirteen awards of the George Medal. The stories of some of these awards have been related in the appropriate chapter of this book. A selection from citations for those not mentioned in the book are summarised below.

GEORGE CROSS
Squadron Leader Hubert Dinwoodie, O.B.E., M.C. (72819). Royal Air Force Volunteer Reserve. No. 5140 (Bomb Disposal) Squadron.

GEORGE MEDAL
1805558 Corporal Roland Norman Garred, B.E.M., Royal Air Force Volunteer Reserve. No. 5140 (Bomb Disposal) Squadron.

On August 20, 1946, German high explosive aircraft bombs were being loaded into vessels at Lubeck for disposal at sea, and two train loads of bombs, weighing approximately 1,100 tons, were drawn into the quay side. Loading into barges was in progress, when a 50 kilogram bomb, fitted with a "tel" fuse, was accidentally dropped a distance of about four feet by the German loading party. The bomb, which was one of a batch of twelve similar bombs being handled at the time, exploded, killing six persons and injuring twelve. There was grave danger that one or more of the eleven bombs immediately involved would also detonate and that bombs of a similar construction would function and thus blow up the trains. As a result grave apprehension was felt for the safety of the port. There was nothing to guide a bomb disposal party as to the cause of the detonation of what should have been a harmless bomb. Squadron Leader Dinwoodie was sent at once to Lubeck, to report on the situation and, if possible, to clear the dangerous missiles. He found, on starting his hazardous work, that the eleven bombs were of an experimental type, fitted with a special shock-sensitive electrically operated fuse. Corporal Garred was detailed to assist Squadron Leader Dinwoodie to deal with these bombs and to take action to safeguard the munitions trains. Despite the very considerable risk involved, Squadron Leader Dinwoodie and Corporal Garred proceeded to defuse one of the bombs in an attempt to discover the cause of the explosion. They found that the accident was due to defective German

204

workmanship or design and that, in several of the bombs, the fusing device had already moved, rendering the bombs dangerous. All the work on the shock-sensitive electrically-operated fuses, already damaged in the previous explosion, took place in an atmosphere of tension caused by lack of knowledge about the cause of the accident and uncertainty as to whether the action of defusing the bombs would not, in itself, cause a detonation. Also, in view of the length of time these bombs had been in storage, the state of the main filling was not above suspicion and sensitive exudation products might have formed round the main tube. Had this been the case, the removal of the tube could, by itself, have caused detonation. With extreme care, Squadron Leader Dinwoodie, assisted by Corporal Garred, rendered the eleven bombs safe. From the information obtained by them, it was possible to minimise the danger and clear the trains. The docks at Lubeck are situated in the centre of the town, therefore the explosion of the contents of the trains would inevitably have wrecked the whole area and caused many casualties. Throughout the operation, Squadron Leader Dinwoodie was a fearless leader who displayed cold blooded heroism and initiative in extremely critical circumstances. He was ably assisted by Corporal Garred who showed courage and devotion to duty of a very high order. Although both were aware that they were in great personal danger, they completed a task which probably averted a serious disaster to the port of Lubeck.

GEORGE CROSS

521319 Sergeant John Archibald Beckett, Royal Air Force, Royal Air Force Station, Ein Shemer, Air Headquarters, Levant.

On the night of March 28, 1947, during refuelling operations on a Lancaster aircraft of No. 38 Squadron, a violent fire broke out suddenly in the pumping compartment of the refuelling vehicle of which Sergeant Beckett was the driver. The flames enveloped Sergeant Beckett and set alight the front of the Lancaster's fuselage. Another airman beat out the flames on Sergeant Beckett but not before the latter had sustained very severe burns on the hands and face. At this moment, there was grave danger that the main tank of the refuelling vehicle, containing over two thousand gallons of fuel, would explode, in which case it is practically certain that most, if not all, of the twenty or more aircraft in the park would have been destroyed. In spite of his serious injuries and the pain he was suffering, Sergeant Beckett got into the driver's seat of the blazing vehicle and drove it a distance of about four hundred yards to a point outside the aircraft park, where it could do no further damage. After this he collapsed and was taken in the ambulance to the Station Sick Quarters dangerously ill. He died on April 12, 1947. The fires in the Lancaster aircraft and in the vehicles were eventually brought under control, and extinguished with no further damage to persons or property. There is no doubt that, by his prompt and gallant action, Sergeant Beckett saved a number of valuable aircraft from almost certain destruction and his comrades, who were working in the vicinity, from the risk of serious injury.

GEORGE CROSS (posthumous)

3500148 Aircraftman 1st Class Ivor John Gillett (deceased), Royal Air Force, Far East Flying Boat Wing, Seletar.

Aircraftman Gillett, a Fitter Armourer, was a member of the ground crew on board a Sunderland Flying Boat which blew up at its moorings at RAF Flying Boat Base, Seletar, on March 26, 1950. Rescue surface craft were quickly on the scene but the aircraft and a bomb-scow alongside sank rapidly and survivors from the explosion were hurled into the water. A life-belt was thrown to Aircraftsman Gillett from a rescue launch. He was seen however to throw the life-belt to a seriously injured corporal who was in danger of drowning near him. In the confusion the rescuers had not been able to reach the corporal. Gillett was a great friend of his and knew he was not a strong swimmer. The life-belt kept the corporal afloat until he was rescued unconscious from the water several minutes later. In the meantime Aircraftman Gillett disappeared; his body was washed ashore two days later. It was discovered that his body had suffered superficial injuries and that death was due to the combined effects of blast and drowning. By his action in deliberately saving the life of his injured friend, whilst injured and in great danger himself, Aircraftman Gillett displayed magnificent courage. His extreme unselfishness in his last living moments, which resulted in the sacrifice of his life to save another, was seen in this act of great heroism which was in accordance with the highest traditions of the Royal Air Force.

GEORGE CROSS (Posthumous)

Flight Lieutenant John Alan Quinton, D.F.C., (deceased) (115714). Royal Air Force. No.228 Operational Conversion Unit, Fighter Command.

On August 13, 1951, Flight Lieutenant Quinton was a Navigator under instruction in a Wellington aircraft which was involved in a mid-air collision. The sole survivor from the crash was an Air Training Corps cadet who was a passenger in the aircraft, and he has established the fact that his life was saved by a supreme act of gallantry displayed by Flight Lieutenant Quinton who in consequence sacrificed his own life. Both Flight Lieutenant Quinton and the cadet were in the rear compartment of the aircraft when the collision occurred. The force of the impact caused the aircraft to break up and as it was plunging towards the earth out of control Flight Lieutenant Quinton picked up the only parachute within reach and clipped it on to the cadet's harness. He pointed out the rip cord and a gaping hole in the aircraft, thereby indicating that the cadet should jump. At that moment a further portion of the aircraft was torn away and the cadet was flung through the side of the aircraft clutching his rip cord, which he subsequently pulled and landed safely. Flight Lieutenant Quinton acted with superhuman speed, displaying the most commendable courage and self-sacrifice as he well knew that in giving up the only parachute within reach he was forfeiting any chance of saving his own life. Such an act of heroism and humanity ranks with the very highest traditions of the Royal Air Force, besides establishing him as a very gallant and courageous officer who, by his action, displayed the most conspicuous heroism.

GEORGE MEDALS
Warrant Officer M. Davies. London Gazette 2.7.46

W/O Davies was engaged in the demolition of unserviceable detonators, when a premature explosion occurred. W/O Davies sustained injuries including a large wound in the side and injuries to both eyes, while his body was hit in many places by flying fragments. The officer with whom he was working was mortally wounded. Although dazed and bleeding profusely, W/O Davies drove a 15 cwt vehicle 4 miles over open country to summon help for the officer in the belief that he was still alive. By the time help arrived, the Warrant Officer was in a state of collapse, but insisted on returning to the scene of the explosion to satisfy himself that all possible assistance was given to the officer. Only then did he allow his own injuries to be treated.

Warrant Officer R.C. Jones. London Gazette 2.7.46

W/O Jones was wireless operator in an aircraft which crashed on a mountainside in the Isle of Man. On recovering consciousness, he found he had been thrown clear of the aircraft. In spite of a badly injured leg, he crawled round the wrecked aircraft and found both pilot and navigator alive but pinioned by wreckage. Two other crew members were dead. Unable to stand or extricate his comrades, he crawled up the hill in the dark to try to establish his whereabouts. Seeing no lights, he crawled back to the aircraft and lost consciousness. On coming to, he heard both comrades moaning and told them he was going for help. Unable to make a splint for his leg, he started to crawl over rough ground, through gorse and marsh. Fainting repeatedly, he carried on as soon as he recovered. Seeing a lighted window, he fired a Very light with no result. His hands were torn and broken bones were protruding from his leg. In great pain, he at last reached a house from which a woman sent for the police who organised aid for his comrades. Jones himself was found to have a double fracture in his right leg, a fractured skull and injuries to his ribs.

Flying Officer V. McNabney. London Gazette 9.12.47

Flying Officer McNabney was a member of a mountain rescue team which went to a steep hillside where a glider had crashed. The position of the glider was such that F/O McNabney had to be lowered to it from above by rope. The rope was then used to haul the unconscious glider pilot — in darkness — up to the main party, while McNabney climbed alongside him to protect him from bruising and to hold him clear of a waterfall. After 30 ft of the climb, McNabney slipped and fell back to a ledge where he lay unconscious for 30 minutes, meanwhile the glider pilot died. McNabney was stranded on the ledge, washed by the waterfall, until rescued next morning.

Flight Lieutenant S.I. Cunningham. London Gazette 16.2.48

This officer was a passenger in a Sunderland flying boat which crash landed on the sea as a result of an engine fire. Breaking his way out of the damaged aircraft, he sustained injuries to his hands, legs and face. Although he could not swim, supported by his life jacket, he paddled to the assistance of the pilot who was in the water close to the blazing aircraft. Disregarding his own injuries, he dragged the pilot clear of the flames and supported him in the water until a rescue launch arrived.

Pilot R. Colbourne. London Gazette 15.7.49

Colbourne was pilot of a Mosquito which crashed when carrying high explosive ammunition. The aircraft caught fire but Colbourne extricated himself and beat out the flames coming from his own clothing. Not finding his navigator, Colbourne crawled back into the blazing wreckage, with ammunition exploding around him which then caused an explosion in the fuel tanks. Although badly burned, he succeeded in extricating and caring for his navigator.

Squadron Leader R.E. Wooley M.R.C.S.,L.R.C.P. London Gazette 28.3.50

This RAF medical officer was called to the scene of a flying boat accident that had occurred in a violent storm off Singapore. The pilot was trapped in his cockpit, and ignoring the state of the sea and the imminent danger of fire from escaping petrol whose fumes were almost overpowering, Sqdn. Ldr. Wooley freed the pilot after giving first aid and amputating his trapped leg.

Flight Lieutenant L.C. Newton and Leading Aircraftman R. W. Riseborough. London Gazette 19.2.52

Early in 1952, a Buckmaster aircraft crashed outside the boundary of RAF Benson aerodrome. The aircraft immediately broke up and caught fire. F/L Newton and LAC Riseborough entered the wreckage in spite of intense heat and damage from spreading flames to rescue two members of the crew. These two members were, unfortunately, found to be dead when extricated from the wreckage. Both Newton and Riseborough suffered severe burns to hands as a result of these gallant efforts, and displayed great courage and tenacity of purpose.

Warrant Officer Tasker Keith RAF (on loan to The Arab Legion Air Force, Amman. Jordon) London Gazette 28.10.52

On May 21, 1952, an Auster Aircraft crashed at Ras-El-Negeb. On impact, it caught fire and was completely wrecked. The door beside the pilot was jammed and that on the other side could only be opened slightly, thus making exit extremely difficult. The pilot and passenger (W/O Keith) were both dazed and suffering from burns and injuries as a result of the crash. In spite of his condition W/O Keith, with great presence of mind and disregard for his own safety managed to extricate the pilot and instructed him to run from the wreckage. This was blazing furiously and an explosion from the petrol tanks appeared imminent. The pilot only managed to get a short distance from the aircraft before he collapsed. Again, with complete disregard for his own safety, W/O Keith returned and carried him to safety despite his own injuries. Shortly afterwards the tank exploded scattering blazing petrol over a wide area. W/O Keith's repeated efforts undoubtedly saved the pilot from serious, if not fatal injury. His courage and determination were of a very high order.

RAF University Air Squadrons

Air Squadron	Universities/Colleges Affiliated for Ordinary Membership
1. Aberdeen	Aberdeen Robert Gordon's Institute of Technology
2. Birmingham	Birmingham Aston Keele
3. Bristol	Bristol Bath
4. Cambridge	Cambridge
5. East Lowlands	Edinburgh Heriot-Watt St. Andrews Dundee Stirling
6. East Midlands	Nottingham Trent Polytechnic Loughborough Leicester
7. Glasgow and Strathclyde	Glasgow Strathclyde
8. Liverpool	Liverpool Lancaster Liverpool Polytechnic
9. London	London City
10. Manchester	Manchester Salford
11. Northumbrian	Newcastle Durham Sunderland Polytechnic Newcastle Polytechnic

12.	Oxford	Oxford
13.	Aueen's (Belfast)	Queen's
		New University of Ulster
14.	Southampton	Southampton
		Portsmouth Polytechnic
15.	Wales	Wales—Aberystwyth
		Bangor
		Swansea
		Cardiff
		Lampeter
		Uwist
16.	Yorkshire	Hull
		Leeds
		York
		Sheffield
		Bradford

Note: RAF University Cadets at Polytechnics and Colleges of Technology not listed above will be allocated to University Air Squadrons by HQ UAS, RAF College, Cranwell, in consultation with MoD as necessary.

RAF Officer Branches Mid-1970s

General Duties (Flying) Branch
Pilots, navigators, air electronic officers, air engineers, air loadmasters. (Note: non-commissioned aircrew include the majority of air engineers and air loadmasters, also all air signallers and a decreasing number of pilots and navigators).

General Duties (Ground) Branch
Air Traffic Control (Specialisation). Control from the ground, by means of radio and radar, of the movement of all RAF aircraft on and in the vicinity of RAF airfields and passing through controlled airspace. Fighter Control (Specialisation). Control of air defence fighters, with assistance of automatic data processing, radio and radar.

RAF Regiment
Responsible for ground and anti-aircraft defence of RAF installations and also for all RAF fire fighting services.

Photographic Interpretation Branch
Interpretation of air photographs for intelligence and survey purposes.

Engineer Branch
Engineering management with specialisations in the Mechanical, Electrical, and Photographic fields.

Supply Branch
Recently integrated with the Engineer Branch. Responsible for planning and executing the logistic support (supply and movement) of the RAF.

Secretarial Branch
The RAF's administrators, accountants and personnel managers.

Education Branch
Provision for further education facilities for all men and women in the RAF and of educational elements of flying, technical and administrative training.

Physical Education Branch
Supervision of physical training throughout the RAF, including the training of parachutists.

Catering Branch
Control and supervision of catering in airmens/airwomens messes, RAF hospitals, hotels on the strategic routes and airborne meals.

Marine Branch
Responsible for operating RAF Marine Craft Units for sea rescue, target towing and related duties.

Provost Branch
Responsible for RAF police and security.

The names of remaining Branches:- Medical, Dental, Chaplains and Masters of Music are self-explanatory. All Branches are open to women except RAF Regiment, Marine and Chaplains. In the General Duties (Flying) Branch, women are accepted only in the air loadmaster category, for employment in strategic transport squadrons.

RAF Command Structure 1974

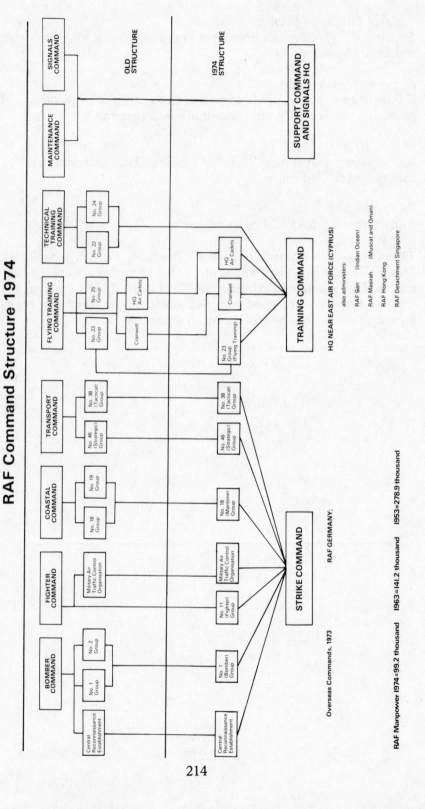

OLD STRUCTURE

1974 STRUCTURE

Overseas Commands, 1973

RAF GERMANY:

HQ NEAR EAST AIR FORCE (CYPRUS)

also administers:

RAF Gan   (Indian Ocean)

RAF Masirah   (Muscat and Oman)

RAF Hong Kong

RAF Detachment Singapore

RAF Manpower 1974 = 99.2 thousand   1963 = 141.2 thousand   1953 = 278.9 thousand

Career Diagram for a Typical Trade Group

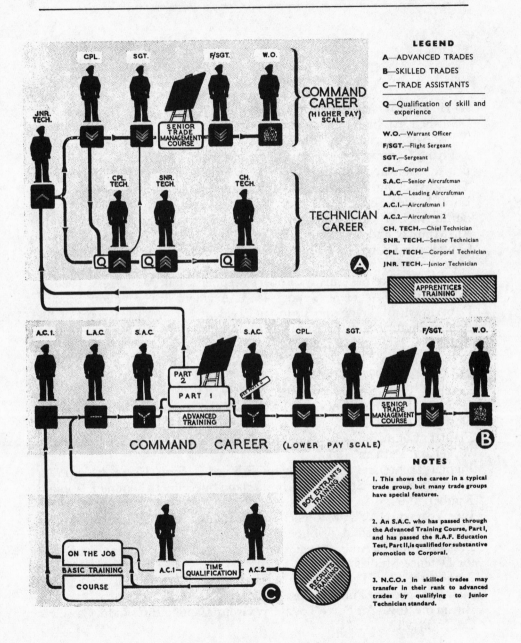

LEGEND

A—ADVANCED TRADES
B—SKILLED TRADES
C—TRADE ASSISTANTS

Q—Qualification of skill and experience

W.O.—Warrant Officer
F/SGT.—Flight Sergeant
SGT.—Sergeant
CPL.—Corporal
S.A.C.—Senior Aircraftman
L.A.C.—Leading Aircraftman
A.C.1.—Aircraftman 1
A.C.2.—Aircraftman 2
CH. TECH.—Chief Technician
SNR. TECH.—Senior Technician
CPL. TECH.—Corporal Technician
JNR. TECH.—Junior Technician

NOTES

1. This shows the career in a typical trade group, but many trade groups have special features.

2. An S.A.C. who has passed through the Advanced Training Course, Part I, and has passed the R.A.F. Education Test, Part II, is qualified for substantive promotion to Corporal.

3. N.C.O.s in skilled trades may transfer in their rank to advanced trades by qualifying to Junior Technician standard.

Bibliography

A History of Air Support Command 1967-1972, by G.E. Bowles. Published by Air Support Command. 1972.

A Pride of Unicorns by John Pudney. Oldbourne Book Co. Ltd. 1960.

A Flying Command by Tom Dagger. Putnam, 1961.

British Arms and Strategy 1970-1980, by Neville Brown. Published by The Royal United Services Institute for Defence Studies, 1969.

Royal United Services Institute for Defence Studies, 1969.

Berlin Air Lift. An Account of the British Contribution. Prepared by the Air Ministry and the Central Office of Information. HMSO, 1949.

Captains and Kings by Alan Branson and Neville Birch. Pitman and Sons, 1972.

Cyprus. A Place of Arms by Robert Stephens. Pall Mall Press, 1966.

Civil Aircraft Accident Report 4/73. Accident Investigation Branch, Department of Trade and Industry. Trident 1, G-ARPI. Report of the Public Enquiry into the causes and circumstances of the accident near Staines on 18 June, 1972. HMSO.

Crisis in European Defence by G.L. and A.L. Williams. Charles Knight and Co. Ltd. 1974.

Defence White Papers. Published by HMSO.

Defence. Britain's Policy in the '70s. An Economist 'Brief Book' by Gordon Lee, 1971.

Fighter Command. A Study of Air Defence 1914-1960, by Peter Wykeham. Putnam, 1960.

Fighter Tactics and Air Strategy by Edward H. Sims. Cassel & Co. 1972.

Flying Boats. The Story of the Sunderland by Kenneth Poolman. William Kimber, 1962.

Five Years of NATO. A Report on the Atlantic Alliance. Reprinted from the New York Herald Tribune, 1954.

Lessons from the Arab/Israeli war. Report of a Seminar held at The RUSI for Defence Studies. January, 1974.

Lion in the Sky. The Story of Seletar and the RAF in Singapore by N. Shorrick. Federal Publications, 1968.

Life in the Royal Air Force Today, by Group Captain E.C. Kidd. Cassell & Co. Ltd. 1957.

Military and Pooitical Consequences of Atomic Energy by P.M.S. Blackett. Turnstile Press, 1948.

Mission Completed by Air Chief Marshall Sir Basil Embry. Methuen & Co. Ltd. 1957.

Mosquito by Martin Sharp and Michael J. F. Bowyer. Faber & Faber Ltd. 1967.

NATO. Facts About the North Atlantic Treaty Organisation. NATO Information Services, 1962.

NATO. The First Five Years by Lord Ismay. NATO Information Services, 1954.

NATO Handbook. NATO Information Service. 1974.

Notes on Running an Operational RAF Station by Group Captain K.R.C. Slater. Gale & Poulden Ltd. 1961.

Oil — Strategic Importance and Future Supplies. Report of a Seminar held at The Royal United Service Institute for Defence Studies, March, 1973.

One of the Few by Group Captain J. A. Kent. William Kimber, 1971.

Partners in Blue. The Story of Womens' Service with the RAF by Katherine B. Beauman. Hutchinson, 1971.

RAF Briefing Book. Issued by the Directorate of Public Relations (RAF), MoD.

RAF News. Edited by W. Locke. Published by RAF News.

Report on The Chief of the Air Staff's Conference "Ariel". Issued by the Air Ministry, July, 1949.

Report on the Atom by Gordon Dean. Eyre & Spottiswoode, 1954.

SHAPE and Allied Command Europe. In the Service of Peace and Security. SHAPE Public Information Division, 1973.

Strictly Private. Their own stories by three serving officers: Norman King, Richard Lawson and Dick Peirse. First published as All The Queen's Men by Educational Explorers of Reading. This edition brought up to date and prepared for the Ministry of Defence by the Central Office of Information, 1972. HMSO.

The Broken Wing. A Study in the British Exercise of Air Power by David Divine. Hutchinson & Co. Ltd., 1966.

The Central Organisation of Defence by Michael Howard. RUSI for Defence Studies, 1970.

The Effects of Nuclear Weapons. Edited by Samuel Glasstone. Prepared by United States Department of Defence. Published by U.S. Atomic Energy Commission. 1962.

The Great Deterrent by Marshal of the RAF Sir John Slessor. Cassell & Co. Ltd., 1957.

The Legacy of Trenchard by Wing Commander H.R. Allan. Cassell & Co. Ltd., 1972.

The Man in the Hot Seat by Doddy Hay. Collins, 1969.

The Murder of TSR2 by Stephen Hastings MC.MP., Macdonald & Co. 1966.

The Role of the Armed Forces in Peacekeeping in the 1970s. Report of a Seminar held at the RUSI for Defence Studies, April, 1973.

The Royal Air Force. The First Fifty Years by Charles Sims. Adam & Charles Black, 1968.

The Security of the Cape Oil Route. Report of a Study Group for the Study of Conflict. Institute for the Study of Conflict, March, 1974.

Trenchard by A. Boyle. Collins, 1972.

To Know the Sky. The Life of Air Chief Marshal Sir Roderick Hill by Prudence Hill. William Kimber, 1962.

Index

221

229